Slow Boat to the Bahamas

by Linus Wilson

Swimming Pigs in the Bahamas

Oxriver
Publishing

Lafayette, Louisiana, U.S.A.

a division of

Vermilion
Advisory
Services

ISBN-10: 0692-58539-7

ISBN-13: 978-0-692-58539-9

Dedication

To my daughter, Sophie Wilson, so that she may better know her father, and to my wife, Janna Wilson, M.D., because I have yet to name a boat after her.

TABLE OF CONTENTS

1. THE CURSE OF EYJAFJALLAJÖKULL

Eyjafjallajökull made me do it. Eyjafjallajökull is not some obscure name for the devil from the apocryphal gospel of Skippy. Eyjafjallajökull is an Icelandic volcano that scrambled air travel in 2010. I was corrupted by Eyjafjallajökull better than Beelzebub himself could have done. Eyjafjallajökull introduced me to sailing, indirectly. Since then my finances have suffered, my once promising career has stalled, I am less public minded, and I am absent from home more. Eyjafjallajökull induced me to travel to the Bahamas by the slowest means of travel known to man, the sailboat.

Nevertheless, the sailboat is fast compared to waiters in Paris. I had spent the last two big vacations in Paris struggling to become more cultured. When Eyjafjallajökull spewed its wrath onto the ionosphere, we were thinking of going there for a third year. Our European vacation plans seemed risky with air travel to the old world interrupted by the eruption of a volcano that no-one could pronounce. With our plans to soak up European culture in a fortnight covered in ashes, we refocused our attention on soaking up the sun. It was our last big vacation as a childless couple. My wife was pregnant with our daughter. Any future vacations were going to revolve around cartoon mice. This one had better be good.

The Caribbean sounded exotic to my American ears. Nevertheless, where does one go in the Caribbean? There are so many different islands and countries. Who can keep track! I knew Cuba has an evil bearded dictator, mojitos, and good cigars. Despite these inducements it was the travel ban that kept me away. Puerto Rico may become the 51st state so that was too dull. Ronald Reagan conquered Grenada in the 1980s. Yep, it must be another American colony— boring. I heard everything awful happens in Haiti. And then there were dozens of countries and hundreds of islands that I had never heard of. A simple solution was to pick the island at the start of the alphabet. We picked Antigua. (Technically, the country and island of Anguilla comes before Antigua in the alphabet, but I never said I majored in Caribbean geography.)

Linus Wilson

The airport was exotically small, and the jeep we rented was romantically old. On our way to our second honeymoon suite, we got lost through dirt trails overrun by a herd of goats. We wound past cricket stadiums funded by the second largest Ponzi scheme in history. (The former Knight of Antigua and Barbuda, Alan Stanford, at the time of writing was serving a 110 year prison sentence in the U.S.) Chickens frequently interrupted our progress until we found ourselves at a six room "hotel" surrounded by tropical plants with a little beach facing onto Falmouth Harbor.

An Antiguan traffic jam. A herd of goats is blocking the road.

The trouble with paradise is, well, it can be kind of boring. Actually, as you may have gathered, I was running a little faster than island time. Boredom drove me to boating. There was little else to do. In addition, our room's air conditioner stopped because there was a blackout on our block for some inexplicable reason. I could not charge my laptop and the heat was oppressive. Thus, the water provided the best relief from the July swelter at 17 degrees north latitude.

Slow Boat to the Bahamas

The hotel had a Sunfish dinghy and kayaks for guests. I struggled with the 120 pound Sunfish dinghy, I could not drag it to the water. I only attracted the ire of the fire ants on the beach. Then, I opted for the lighter kayaks. There were some interesting rocks on the other side of the harbor; so I paddled out slowly.

I was kind of shocked by the sailboats at anchor in the harbor that morning. There were people on them. One unshaven man with hair askew sat out in the cockpit of a big catamaran with a cup of coffee. I had never considered the possibility that people might sleep or live on a sailboat, but that man appeared to be doing just that. After staring him for the five minutes that it took me to go 100 yards, he finally retreated to the cabin for privacy from prying eyes of the bumpkin on the yellow kayak. After my wife woke up, I told her of my little adventure, and my inability to move the Sunfish. I begged her to help me launch the strange contraption. "Oh, I used to sail a Sunfish all the time. Our neighbor in Wisconsin had one, and he let us use it," replied my wife. In eight years of marriage she had never mentioned her misspent youth gliding along the inland lakes. What other dark secrets was she hiding! I bet the "neighbor" had better hair than I. Of course, I had never been on a sailboat before.

The 5'3" pregnant lady had no trouble getting the boat into the water, and we piled into the boat. We flew around the harbor at ten times the speed of the kayak. In no time, we were at the mouth of the harbor and on the verge of entering the Atlantic Ocean. I was then struck with the sudden urge to sail to Africa. "Let's sail out the harbor and look around," I said. My wife dismissed my suggestion without comment and tacked back towards the hotel. It was a good thing too, because the northeast trades would have most certainly pushed us to Panama and not my intended destination of Africa.

After some begging, she gave me the thing that she seemed to steer with that she called "the tiller." This worked out fine until we had to turn. We eventually came on a collision course with one of the anchored boats. I tried pushing the tiller, which had us headed the opposite way that I wanted to go. Next, I pulled it the other way, which put us on a collision course for the anchored boat. Finally, I pulled it harder over and the metal thing attached to the sail started coming at me. I did the only rational thing that one can do when your boat takes a swipe at you. I jumped overboard. My wife ducked. I hauled myself aboard, and the laughing Sunfish skipper glided us back to the beach.

Janna is touring at an abandoned sugar plantation in Antigua. She was six months pregnant at the time.

Cooped up in a sweaty bungalow with my pregnant wife, cravings drove me to the only American style supermarket on the island. My craving for chocolate cake induced my wife to drive me to the condo jungle of Jolly Harbor. Antigua has rock vistas looking out to the sea, a quaint city in St. Johns, jungles, rolling countryside, and marvelous historic anchorages in Falmouth and English Harbors. Nevertheless, you can escape all that beauty in Jolly Harbor. For those who want their fix of Floridian heaven and trade winds, Jolly Harbor is the place.

Slow Boat to the Bahamas

After touring the set of the straight-to-DVD-movie, *Honey, I Shrunk the Grocery Store*, my wife and I strolled around the docks of the large, modern marina. Big, shiny new boats lined the docks. Unlike the more lived-in boats on the south side of the island, Jolly Harbor's docks screamed, "I have plenty of money to own a new boat that I am too old to use."

We stumbled upon a boat brokerage. I pored over the listings of boats by their length in feet. Suspiciously, the listings were not in the local currency, but in U.S. dollars. I had sticker shock. Where were all the zeros? Not bad, we could dump the house, liquidate the retirement accounts, and buy a boat for a few hundred grand. Natural child birth is free, right? I asked my wife, "Do you think we should pay twice as much for the catamarans, or should we settle for a larger monohull?" She said we did not need a catamaran. That was all the confirmation I needed. We were getting a boat that day!

We walked into the brokerage. "We are new to sailing, but we are interested in getting a sailboat," I blurted out. The kind woman must have either taken pity on me or the lady with child. "You might want to take some sailing lessons first," she suggested. She pointed out there were many educational sequences with United States or American in the title. I gathered that meant we might be able to take classes after we left paradise. "Yes, but I want to take lessons now!" I interjected. "The Antigua Yacht Club might be able to arrange some classes for you," she suggested.

Imagine walking into a Chevy dealership, saying you want to buy a Malibu, and the salesman suggesting that you go back to trade school before getting out your checkbook. Little did the kind broker know that suggesting to my wife and me that we should get more education was like giving vodka to a drunk. We could not resist. No couple is more overoptimistic about the value of formal education than we are. My wife was soon on the phone to the yacht club. We had a lesson at 4 PM!

There are many great mysteries of the world. At that moment, no greater mystery gripped my imagination than what was inside those sailboats that allowed poorly shaven men to live in them. I was foiled in my attempts to tour large sailboats at the brokerage, but on the way to our lesson we strolled past a huge boat yard. The yard had high, locked, chain-link fences and a forest of huge sail boats on blocks. If I stood on the shoulders of my wife, I might be able to scale the fence. Sadly, she strolled on before I could broach the cunning plan. We were running late after all.

The Antigua Yacht Club was just like other perceived bastions of elitism, the ancient colleges in England, which I had spent too much time in. It was a little dark, dank, and dirty. It had pool tables and a bar. I liked it immediately. Our sailing instructor was tall, young, and very confident. He pointed out the big pillar reaching for the sky in the middle of the dinghy we would train on. "That is da mast." Then, he pointed at the metal bar coming from the mast attached to the back sail. "This is da boom." What a fantastic langauge they spoke in Antigua! Everyone on the island speaks English, unless they are tourists like us.

"First, we have some classroom trainin', and, den, we get on da boat." He drew us a clock with the wind at 12 o'clock. "Between 10 and 2 o'clock is da no go zone. The boat no go that close to the wind. There you got to tack the boat so it faces below 10 and above 2. If da bow of da boat goes between 5 and 7 o'clock you gonna gybe and dat is dangerous," he said.

"Ok, so we should never gybe to be safe," I said.

"No, you just got to be careful 'cause da boom can swing around fast when you gybe. It may hit you on da head or knock you off da boat." If I had hands on experience, I might be able to understand more of what he was talking about. "When are we getting on the boat?" I thought.

All three of us got towed out in the 12-foot plastic sailing dinghy by an inflatable boat with an outboard attached. My wife and I would get a turn pushing the tiller this way and that while the sails were limp. English Harbor has high hills on almost all sides that protect it from the wind and make it a great anchorage. For that reason, and the guns mounted on those hills, the English Navy used to keep its sailing ships there. Lord Nelson battled malaria for a few years in this harbor before going on to eternal fame—that is his death—in the Battle of Trafalgar.

The instructor would pull on some rope leading to the front sail periodically, but most of the time we drifted. We had moved up in the world, we were on a sailboat with two sails not just one like the

Sunfish. If I became really good at sailing, I might have a clue what he was doing with those ropes.

"Does are not 'ropes' dey are jib *sheets*. Boats don't have ropes, dey either have halyards, fur raisen the sails, sheets for controlling de jib and main, and lines for everding else," he explained.

"You are moving the gybe sheets," I said.

"No, da *jib* is da front sail. *Gybe* is when da boom swings around when you are sailing downwind. Da words are spelled differently," he corrected.

As with all our other subsequent lessons, eventually he got tired of drifting and the lesson would end with another instructor towing us back into the dock. When I suggested moving out of the harbor into the Atlantic to get some wind, he just shook his head.

The power outage at our hotel lasted the rest of the stay. We were moved to an apartment with a landlord who gave us a ripe mangos as a gift. He took us to his outdoor bar and was disappointed to hear that we were both abstaining from alcohol for the pregnancy. Perhaps sailing is a substitute for strong drink? He told us of how our country invaded his boyhood island of Grenada two decades earlier. We found the American invasion of Antigua was ongoing when we moved to our last hotel next to the Sandals resort. We beat a hasty retreat from the island the next day.

2. NO WIND = GREAT SAILING

Some pastimes only make sense in a certain locale. One will only crave Philly cheese steaks in Philadelphia. Actually, I never craved Philly cheese steaks when I lived there. Anyway, what happens in Antigua stays in Antigua. Isn't that the slogan?

We waited a long time before we started sailing back in the U.S.A. My wife could not call the New Orleans sailing school until after the plane taxied to the gate. No one answered. It was Sunday. Because my wife and I did not want to take things too fast, we waited nearly two weeks before our first lesson in New Orleans. Our employers refused to let us off at noon so that we could drive to sailing lessons a hundred-plus miles away. My wife had to be in town for her patients every other weekend. Thus, we took the first lesson in New Orleans thirteen whole days after arriving in the U.S. We clearly had taken to heart a laid back island attitude towards life.

Weekend sailing lessons had one black, furry complication. Interstate 10 is really something that should not be experienced for more than three hours per day. That meant a round trip from NOLA to LALA, New Orleans, Louisiana to Lafayette, Louisiana, was out of the question. For this reason, we always got a hotel on Saturday night. We were limited to the deluxe accommodations that allowed dogs in the rooms. We could not abandon our four-pound toy poodle for two days straight. He might sleep 20 hours a day instead of 19 hours a day if we were gone. Our dog Daly, despite his insubstantial size, had an oversized idea of his importance as a guard dog. Very few non-expecting, visitors to NOLA stick to sobriety. When the obligatory drunken revelers on our hall stumbled into their rooms at 2 AM, Daly wanted everyone on the floor to know it and went into a mad barking fit. If we sailed in the Great Salt Lake country, we would have at least gotten some uninterrupted sleep.

Sleep deprivation made us susceptible to the weather disease. It started with the secretary who scheduled lessons; she would cancel lessons if the forecast was too rainy, too windy, or had too high a chance of lightning. Lightning almost always is on the forecast in the afternoon in Louisiana during the summer. Our instructor would always show us the satellite chart before going out. Was that spot of orange or red likely to roll in before we tied up? Our most used apps were the weather forecasts. The wind and wave forecasts were the most discussed. I never devised the formula decisively. Forecasts for calm, 5-10 knot winds, or 10-15 knot winds meant the lesson was on. 15 plus knots of wind meant the lesson was off. Rain cancelled the lesson. Inevitable thunder storms cancelled the lesson. What is the update of the wind projections from a half hour ago? Are the waves going to be one to two feet or one foot? I had to get half hour updates for the lesson five days away! The most common intraday text to my wife was about the Saturday/Sunday forecast on Lake Pontchartrain, the sailing playground of New Orleans.

Wind was not a key ingredient in our sailing lessons in both Antigua and New Orleans. Typically, it was hot and humid and without wind on the days we sailed. 90+ degrees Fahrenheit with 60+ percent humidity was the norm. The school looked out upon a beach volleyball center. The sand acted like an oven in the midday sun as we waited for the instructor to open up the air conditioned office.

The school's name sake came in to give us a pep talk on the first day. To borrow a phrase from a former Texas senator in reference to the 41st president in my opinion, the sailing school owner started on 1st base, was tagged out trying to steal second, and acted like he hit a home run. He told us about all the big yachts he had sailed on. Yes, he loved to call them "yachts." The sailing school owner had sailed on a lot of big mass produced boats with extraordinarily large crews. This clearly made him important and interesting. I wondered where I would find my able bodied crew of four for my brand new 50 foot production yacht. Perhaps that would be taught in the second lesson. After we were sufficiently awed with his presence, he said something relevant, "Remember, don't freak out on the water. The boat is going to heel. It won't fall over or capsize. You are not going too fast. The boat is only going less than six miles per hour." The sum of his wisdom having imparted to us, we were given over to a part-time instructor.

After the owner on the first day, we only had one instructor. He was an old maritime lawyer, former coastie—U.S. Coast Guard officer—, and all around old salt. Despite his love of sailboats, he did not own one. On Wall Street it is said, "The most money is to be made from managing others people money." He had a sailor's version. "The best way to sail is on other people's boats," he said. If only that latter phrase was in the textbook, my wife and I, who missed one and zero questions, respectively, on the written exam at the end of the course, might have learned it.

Linus Wilson

He extolled the virtues of crewing on other people's boats at races. I wondered if our newborn would make good crew for the Wednesday night beer can races. My wife always expressed a desire afterward to crew the races. She was never off on Wednesdays to attend them. The Sunday races for which she was in town subsequently she would always refuse to volunteer to race despite my offer of babysitting. I guess racing was something she wanted to do in theory more than practice.

I got a pretty macho vibe about the club racing scene and was skeptical if either my wife or I would fit in even if we had a transporter from Star Trek that would beam us to NOLA on a Wednesday night. There is limited machismo at cross country practice and even less at weekend 5K races. Club sports among university nerds in the U.K. was about all the tough guy team sports that would have me.

I could always tout my boating experience as a rower. After six weeks of intense training, my rookie crew's only race ended in disaster as I broke my oar, and the race turned into a rout. In rowing, as with many other things, my wife's rowing career was far more successful. Unlike our instructor who told stories of his sailing in diapers, sailboat racing would be a brand new sport for a pair of thirtysomethings who did not like to have the boat to heel too much.

Several years after our 101 lessons in New Orleans, I tried to beg myself on a Wednesday night race. On the superfast J-boat with a crew of 25, I nearly managed to fall overboard on a light wind day. Most of the other crew had never been on a sailboat. I was trying to act as rail meat, shifting myself from one side of the boat to another based on the more experience crew member's instructions. On an adjusted score basis the boat finished last in the field of 30. I'm still waiting for the invitation to crew for the next race.

Ninety percent of our on-the-water training consisted of figure eight man overboard drills. In this drill, you don't want to gybe. Thus, you turn around by always heading into the wind, tacking. One student is at the helm. One student tended the jib sheets, which control the front sail. Another, points at the flotation device, which is the man overboard. No, it is not a good idea to throw one of the students overboard unless he is very annoying. Then, the third or fourth student tries to grasp the float with her hands or a boat hook.

The curriculum emphasizes man overboard drills because it is an excuse for tacking into the wind. This is just an excuse to practice sailing close hauled and tacking. It has little to do with lifesaving. This is the most impractical safety drill devised by man. In practice, most non-racers will be lucky to have one other able sailor on board. The odds that the second sailor noticed that the first fell overboard is also slim. There will be no pointer or person to retrieve the drowning sailor. Moreover, doing a figure eight on a sailboat takes between 100 yards and 2 miles. Either way the man overboard will be almost impossible to find if there are any waves. Anyone with a lick of sense would turn on the engine and do a 360 degree turn to get back to the sailor as quickly as possible before she is lost in the waves or succumbs to hypothermia, which happens very quickly in all but the most tropical locations. Actually, the most difficult part is never practiced—getting someone aboard. If you don't have a boarding ladder or swim step, this person is almost guaranteed to drown if the water temperature is below 70 degrees. Yes, you may be able to string a line on the boom and through a winch and under the hypothermic sailor's arms, but the odds of this working in time is less than 50-50.

3. SERIAL KILLERS AND CRAB POTS: BOAT SHOPPING IN CAJUN COUNTRY

Owning a boat is widely considered equivalent to dread illness in its ability to siphon large chunks of one's time and finances. With our sailing 101 course behind us, it was time for my wife and me to buy a boat or give up on sailing. The charter market in New Orleans left a lot to be desired at that moment. You could charter a 22 foot daysailer with no cabin for $250 for four hours after paying a skipper $100 more for a check out cruise. That was the same boat we trained on. It was fast and maneuverable, but too much so for my taste.

Our last 101 lesson was with a squall approaching and the cold air blowing in. My seven month pregnant wife and I sat five feet off the water on a boat with 18" of freeboard, while another student steered with a mad scientist gleam in his eye which was shared by the instructor. I suggested that I would like to learn how to reef the boat when it was my turn to steer. The instructor ignored me and launched into another story of his racing days as a boy in the Bay State, which involved a wild gybe and a capsized boat. Finally, annoyed by my constant luffing of the sails, interjections about the virtues of reefing, and noticing that my non-existent biceps could barely budge the tiller of the over-canvassed boat, he relented and we pulled in a reef right before dropping all sail. Luffing is sailing too close to the wind and causing the front of the sail to collapse and lose power. I could never imagine having my soon to be newborn daughter on a charter of that boat.

Seeing the high prices of brokerage boats, I quickly turned to Craigslist's boats for sale by owner. I did not really have a budget in mind, I just wanted something cheap that was ready to sail. My wife bought me a book called *My First Sailboat*. It extolled the virtues and the money saving qualities of trailerable sail boats. Who wants marina fees when you can store you boat in your back yard! Unfortunately, I forgot that we lacked enough yard to park a boat in the front or back.

I visited a trailerable boat close to my house. The 23 foot O'Day was listed at about $5,000. Frankly, their house was a Cajun paradise of off road vehicles, big heavy equipment, and the horns of deer conquests of yore. I found it on a huge trailer in a huge airplane hangar. The pleasant owner and his wife showed me up an old step ladder and I plunged into the round tub while pestering them with questions.

I asked, "What do you tow this boat with?" The owner replied, "The truck in the driveway." He pointed to brand new Chevy Silverado 3500 extended cab that appeared that it could tow my house. "Do you think my car could tow the O'Day?" He shook his head, after I pointed to my sub-compact hatchback. "You'll need a truck. The trailer is not included in the price. $2,500 for the trailer."

"It is a nice trailer," I responded. "How long does it take to rig the boat after trailering?"

"About half a day," the kind man responded.

I asked the owners if they sailed the boat on Vermilion Bay, which was the closest access to the Gulf of Mexico from the owners' house. The owners' eyes widened. The man said, "We tried it a few times. Vermilion Bay gets rough. It can get pretty scary in this boat." The wife interjected, "We like Lake Arthur, it is only a few miles wide, but its closer and smoother sailing. The boat is a nice place to camp out in a secluded spot for the weekend." Lake Arthur was famous for its unsolved string of murders of eight young women at that time. "Perhaps my wife is too old to be a target of the serial killer," I thought. Smooth sailing and serial killers, that was something I never considered.

Clearly, it was time to explore other options. My wife and I liked the idea of spending more time in New Orleans so we turned our attention to boats listed on Lake Pontchartrain. A Cal 25 was listed for $2,000. With that price, I thought it had to be the boat for us! The owner met my increasingly pregnant wife and me at a swamp on the north shore of the lake. The Cal 25 was mud-bound next to a small finger slip with water plants floating on the surface and four inch dragonflies buzzing around. The owner talked about the TV set and microwave included in the price. "My wife and I just luv to watch that TV. It is great for DVDs," he said. If the 120 volt appliances from Walgreens were not nautical enough, the boat's walls were decorated in blue wallpaper that preserved the mold from the odd dry spell that occurs even in Louisana's swamp lands.

In retrospect, the boat had probably been stripped of every piece of useful gear which had been transferred to the owner's new bigger boat. The owner bragged, "I have only put $50 into this boat since I bought her. You won't have to worry about maintenance costs at all." What he should have said was, "I deferred all the maintenance costs for you to pay through the nose, newbie."

I asked if we could take it for a sail. The owner said that it was a little windy, and he prefers to go out in the morning before the wind picks up. After we reiterated our interest in a sail, it became a matter of pride for the big Cajun. The faded Evinrude 15 horse power long shaft choked to life after a few mighty tugs from the bearded giant and we puttered down the bayou into the great estuary.

Lake Ponchartrain at that inlet was about 25 miles north to south, and that means a south wind has a lot off fetch on the north shore where we were. The lake is shallow in most places under 15 feet, and thus turns up a lot of chop when the wind freshens. On a good sized boat or even this boat properly maintained and rigged, the conditions could have made for a fun sail. Here, the lines were near breaking point in several places and the winches were undersized or conspicuously missing. Thus, the 6'6" owner used his brute force to fling up the main sail, while we pondered what it felt like to be a sock during a spin cycle. We attempted to beat into the wind, but, lacking essentials like sheets long enough to be trimmed, the old boat was knocked around from side to side.

The sails only made us at the mercy of the building gusts and pushed us closer to the lee shore. The owner dropped the jib and I dropped the main while my wife tended the tiller. The owner took the helm and the outboard went clunk. More strenuous lifting by the big man ensued and he wrested the long shaft into the cockpit. A crab pot had wrapped the propeller. Lake Pontchartrain is littered with crab pots. (I have never wrapped the prop with one because I observed early on if I steer clear of them I will almost hit the thing I am trying to avoid. Ignoring the crab pot until the last second ensures it will pass far to the boat's port or starboard. When one is facing the front of the boat, the port is the left side of the boat, and the starboard is the right side of the boat.) After 5 minutes more of drifting towards the swamp reeds, he finally untangled the trap and plopped the prop back in the lake. More pulling, cursing, checking and pulling eventually willed the old outboard into life.

We motored up the bayou and back to the Cal 25's resting place in the mud. The owner ignoring the near drowning experience, said with his best used car salesman smile, "She's all yours for $2,000. You'll even get two weeks of free slip fees." I begged that he give us a moment. My very pregnant wife took me aside in the car and excitedly said, "That was fun! I like it. Should we get it?" My heart filled with love and pride for the mother to be.

4. SAILING PURIST

We saw an ad for 30 foot Hinterhoeller sailboat from 1969 and checked it out in Slidell. It was everything the other boats were not. It was full of dark wood not the plastic of the other boats we had looked at. It had an inboard engine, which we thought was fancier than the outboards of the previous ones. It had a water tank, a head, a holding tank, a sink, and a two burner pressurized alcohol stove. It was heavier than the trailerable boats we had seen. I could envision how our baby could be secure in the cabin while we sailed in the cockpit.

Our first sailboat sitting in the mud after the survey.

The owner and his two buddies agreed to take Janna and I for a test sail. We must have bobbed around for four hours in the calms. He said he raced for Canada and once was a sailing instructor. I thought his deep concentration while tacking in a narrow canal towards the slip meant he really loved sailing. He only turned on the engine, a few feet from the slip. Once in the slip we offered to buy it for the

Linus Wilson

princely sum of $4,600 or 90 percent of his asking price which he accepted. I also stipulated that he sail the boat across Lake Pontchartrain from Slidell to South Shore Harbor in New Orleans if the surveyors' inspection went well.

The surveyor and son thought it looked cluttered, but OK. I learned a lot from their digging about where things were. The surveyor was careful to stress that he could not vouch for the engine.

I promised to pay the owner once he brought the boat across the Lake. On the appointed day with light winds, it took the owner and one of his buddies 10 hours to sail the 18 miles across the lake. They sailed the boat into the slip in South Shore. We got the documents notarized, I paid the owner his money and the boat was ours.

Janna and I took the boat out the next weekend. We motored out the long canal by the executive airport. We bobbed around for a while, hanking on jibs and genoas and raising the main. Then, we went back into the slip. Some sailboats clip on their front sail with clips called hanks. Hanking is clipping the foresails hanks onto the forestay, the front wire rope that holds up the mast. The genoa is a foresail whose back corner, the clew, goes further back than the mast. A genoa is bigger foresail than a jib. A jib sail has a triangle that is not big enough to go beyond the mast. Janna helmed as I stood at the bow. She turned into the concrete slip at 3 knots, looked for the breaks, and found none. It was a good thing the concrete was there. Otherwise, we would have kept going. Crunch!

There were holes in the bow where the twisted bow rail had taken pieces of the deck with it. We had crashed our beautiful boat on the first sail. I moaned and writhed on the deck. We had at least two, three inch gaping holes. I remembered that the owner had mentioned that he bought his life jacket at a place called "West Marine." I called them.

"Uh, we crashed our boat into the dock," I said. "Do you have anything for filling in the holes?"

"Was the dock moving?" There was laughing in the background. "Sir, we don't work on boats," the store clerk said.

"I just want to plug the holes in my boat so it does not rain in while I'm gone," I said.

"We do have some epoxy that can seal up holes," the clerk offered. "We close in 20 minutes."

Janna and I raced over and got some epoxy. Before we had my daughter Sophie, we started supporting West Marine. The more expensive dependent was West Marine.

I filled the holes very sloppily. "Shouldn't you be more careful," Janna asked.

"It says you can sand it later," I offered. 15 minutes later it had set up and my sand paper could barely scratch the white globs on the deck. At least the holes were filled.

We crashed the boat into the dock right before Sophie was born. Janice Flint is saying hello to her new granddaughter, Sophie Wilson, who is held by her mother, Janna.

Janna's Mom and Dad visited our new baby Sophie. To avoid the breast feeding fest and save his granddaughter's young life from the death trap that we bought, my father-in-law Tom volunteered to look at the boat. Tom spent a couple weeks on the boat making friends with the other retired guys on the dock and correcting the deficiencies on the survey report. He replaced the battery, added a battery switch and a new battery, put in a water pump for the sink and replaced all the freshwater hose.

Sophie started joining us sailing when she was six weeks old. I bought a seat belt from an auto parts store and screwed it into the quarter berth on the starboard side. The quarter berth is a bed area in the back of the boat. We took out the cushion, and a car seat was secured with the seat belt. Sophie could be strapped into the car seat while we were sailing. Her Mom would look in on her while holding onto the tiller.

I had found a place that would paint our boat's faded green hull bright blue, but it was six miles away by water. In December, I convinced Tom to sail to Orleans Marina with me. Janna had resisted the six mile cruise, but Tom was game. Janna's crash at the dock had scared me too much to steer in a marina alone, and the boat turned immediately 90 degrees whenever the tiller was not tended. Thus, I could not raise sail without help at the helm. Soon after we started our journey, Tom noticed that the engine was overheating and the propeller shaft was vibrating like crazy. I had no idea how he could divine such things. "We have to sail in," Tom said. "The engine will overheat."

The impeller for the cooling water pump was cracked up and the water pump was leaking. We paid the yard to replace both. We got the bow pulpit replaced and the damaged and epoxied deck fiberglassed. At some point when we were racking up charges in the 5 digit range, I pushed the yard owner on what the charges were for the "cutlass bearing" and asked "why does the engine need a water pump?" (The cutlass bearing is where the shaft of the propeller enters the boat.)

He said in frustration, "If you own a boat you really should know a little more about engines."

I said smugly, "I don't need an engine. My boat has sails." Janna and her Dad insisted on getting the engine fixed.

We had the yard put on the name Penelope on the boat. Penelope was Odysseus' faithful and clever wife while he was lost at sea.

In the summer of 2011, less than a year after purchasing Penelope, Janna reluctantly agreed to visit Mandeville, over the July 4, holiday weekend. Mandeville was a town 24 miles away from our slip on the north shore of Lake Pontchartrain. "The cruising guides say Mandeville is great. We can sail there on Saturday and return on Sunday. We'll have Monday to drive home. Plus, it is impossible to get lost. You just follow the Causeway Bridge." The causeway bridge runs from the New Orleans suburb of Metairie on the south shore to Mandeville on the north shore.

Slow Boat to the Bahamas

The sail up went well with light south winds pushing us north. We each had to spend long turns at the tiller because Penelope with its fin keel would lose course if our grip slackened. We docked in a marina in Bayou Castine and went out to dinner. Before we left Janna asked, "Don't you think we should fill the gas tank? It is a little under half full."

"Nah, it will be fine we have plenty of gas to motor the whole way. Plus we will sail until we have to worry about it getting dark," I said.

While I had checked to see the weather to see that the winds were 5 to 10 knots, I did not look at the wind direction which was also south. We tacked Penelope in the light airs for a couple hours making about three miles. We had a late start and I decided to throw in the towel and start motoring. I went forward to take the jib off the forestay, while Janna held the course steady. I must have lazily secured it to the spinnaker loop on the mast. I steered while Janna fed Sophie and changed her diaper. Part of the sky turned from navy blue to inky black. I switched on the VHF that Tom had installed and tuned to the weather band. "Severe thunderstorm warning is in effect for Lake Pontchartrain. A line of thunderstorms located six miles south of Mandeville has gusts up to 35 miles per hour. Lightning, winds exceeding 25 miles per hour, and high waves that can overturn boats can be experienced near this storm. All mariners should exercise caution and seek safe harbor immediately," the computerized voice warned.

"Hey, Janna did you hear that?" I called down to the cabin.

"Severe thunderstorms are right ahead of us. Can you help me take down the main?" I asked. Janna clicked Sophie (who had tired of her mid-afternoon snack) back in her boat seat. Sophie's eyes shut and her head tipped to the side as she dozed. Janna climbed on deck.

"Should we turn around?" I asked.

"Yes, but we still have to turn into the wind to drop the main," Janna said as she turned into the blackness and what seemed to be a stiffening 10 to 15 knot breeze coming from the southwest. We had been flirting with the exclusion zones on the Causeway Bridge which extend out a mile. The three hours of tacking since our 11 AM departure had got us just under four miles away from Mandeville.

I dropped the flapping main as the waves started to bob Penelope up and down more violently. When I finished, the waves were much more violent building from one foot 30 minutes ago to three-to-four feet and breaking.

Janna steered a course south to New Orleans under power alone.

Without any sail up, we were knocked left and right and back and forth. We had no choice but to drop the main. Penelope's main sail only had one set off reef points and we did not even know how to secure it properly since there was no 1st reef clew block. The boat was set up to be boom furled. It would be nearly two more years before we found the crank that would twist the boom and furl it.

We were lucky we got to spend so much time sailing with the previous owner. (Nevertheless, our sailing in a calm with the prior owner did hide a broken cooling system.) On old brokerage boats, we would find that owners were often absent or too old to sail. The brokers had no interest in learning about the boat's systems or educating the buyers because they though the commissions were not worth their time. Sailing a brokerage boat only happened after the offer was accepted and deposit and sea trial were arranged. Fifteen minutes of sea time was all you got to observe the sailing systems at work, and, with the owner absent, probably no one on the boat had sailed the boat prior to the sea trial.

As we were banging into the seas, the Atomic 4 gasoline engine stopped. Janna tried restart the engine. We had 1/3 a tank of gas. It made no sense.

"What do we do?" Janna asked clearly frightened.

"Turn downwind while we have momentum. Wait for a smaller wave. I'll raise the jib," I said. Janna turned our bow with our two knot momentum and the motion was sickening to us greenhorns. I ran forward. I was used to going forward onto the pitching bow by this point. It was a struggle to stay low and hold on tight occasionally bracing with two hands and pausing. The 100 percent jib was pinned down on the deck by the spinnaker pole. I went to retrieve the jib halyard at the mast but it was up at the top of the mast dangling three feet from the top. There was a metal rope with a halyard. It was the spare or spinnaker halyard. Old boats sometimes had wire rope instead of halyards because low stretch ropes used on modern boats' halyards were not available. The metal rope was spiced to rope at the end which was cleated off at the mast. I removed it from the cleat and latched it to the head of the jib and raised it.

We picked up speed and headed for Mandeville. The waves died down and the storm passed. Janna tried the engine just as we entered the town's breakwater. It started up and we docked under power. I hiked forever to get gas to fill the tank. When I came back, Janna said she would not leave the next day. A mechanic had to check out the engine. She was too shaken to go the next day, and I took a cab back to the car.

We left the boat at Northshore Marine. I would return after the holiday alone in my car. Tom thought the engine needed a "tune up," but their mechanic suggested we might have just stirred up dirt in the tank. Engines often die in rough seas when debris in the fuel tank gets dislodged and sucked into the fuel system. This often happens when the tank is only partially full. This was the most likely cause of the engine stall. He asked, "When was the last time that you changed the fuel filter?"

"I don't think the boat has a fuel filter," I said. That was the wrong answer. We did not find and change the fuel filter element until two years later. We only belatedly changed the filter element when the tank filled with water, and we paid $500 to have a mechanic drain the fuel system of water. He needed us to get new filter elements to completely remove water from the fuel system.

I ran the engine for over an hour without it dying on the mechanic's time. We ordered a replacement coil and let the mechanic install it. I made a place for the coil which would be less prone to overheat. The engine getting hot and overheating the coil could have caused the dying also. After that, I was always fussing over Penelope's spark plugs and had about dozen spares because they were only $2 each.

The Mandeville yard retrieved the halyard. Janna refused to sail Penelope back with Sophie so we flew in Tom to crew with me and we crossed Lake Pontchartrain quickly under sail with a fair breeze. I was furious about this initially. I felt Janna had abandoned me and stranded our boat. Without an autopilot, Penelope was too difficult to sail by myself. Janna was petrified of sailing such a long distance until the engine was checked out, and the boat was made ready for higher winds. Moreover, it was hard to choose a good weather day if we were limited to Janna's days off call.

Tom Flint sailing Penenlope back from Mandeville, Louisiana to New Orleans.

I would pay a sailmaker to put in 2nd and 3rd reef points in Penelope that summer as well as install blocks at the mast to tighten the reef point clews. On deck, I installed the three reefing lines led to the clew points on the mast with blocks at the end of the boom and the bottom of the mast. These blocks would lead the reefing lines back to the cockpit and allowed someone to reef the sail in the cockpit. Reefing down before dropping also made the main sail much more manageable. It also meant that the default went from raising the full main to raising the third reef. That more conservative starting point made Penelope less of a wild stallion to sail, and more a comfortable cruising boat. For all the deck hardware, I followed Don Casey's advice in *The Sailboat Maintenance Manual* of hollowing out the balsa core and filling it with epoxy before drilling in screws.

The humiliation of having to have my father-in-law rescue the boat from Mandeville convinced me to buy an autopilot, which Janna initially resisted. I would install that gear myself. Tom, by this point, had tired of boat repair, but he did give me a manual on sailboat electronics. Do it yourself was the way forward.

As far as cruising was concerned, if the wind could not move Penelope four knots, the engine would. The almost constant chance of thunderstorms on Lake Pontchartrain meant that if you sailed for long enough you were almost certain to sail through a squall. When the sea gave me a weather window, I would take it by power or sail. If I did not, I would scare Janna away from all cruises and incur more expensive repairs. I believed Janna would be more resistant to cruising if I sailed into a squall than if I motored into port ahead of it. Janna may dislike motoring, but she disliked squalls more. I also resolved to make my trips in the morning when the chances of squalls were lower.

5. AN OPTIMIST ADRIFT

Listening to sailing podcasts and audiobooks of cruising sailors, I kept on running into the strange use of the word—"dinghy." The dinghy or "tender" in this context was the means by which sailors got from their boat at anchor to shore. It is a smaller boat that can be more easily rowed, fitted with an outboard, and beached on a tropical island with white sandy beaches. Thus, it was clear our cruising paradise, the good ship Penelope, lacked a key piece of equipment, a dinghy.

More importantly, since I was still scared to death about being at the helm while docking the big boat, a dinghy gave me practice at maneuvering in tight quarters. Our sailing certifications, 101, 103, 104, and 105 gave me absolutely no experience driving the boat into a slip. This was the one essential skill needed if you want to go out sailing on boat which permanently was in the water. Moreover, there was no training that practiced motoring the inboard cruising boat, which had

Linus Wilson

zero ability to move backwards, in and out of the slip. Our boat had what was called "prop walk." This meant that when reverse was used, the boat would eventually slow and drift sideways in an unpredictable direction.

When we did our 103 and 104 course during the summer, our first skipper on our Spanish Virgin Island vacation, who shall be known as Captain Ahab, said I could be "dinghy captain." He had no confidence in me in other matters, but he would entrust the rubber dink to my command when the motor was not on it, and he was not in it. This must be something I could handle.

I told my wife how we needed a dinghy so we could visit remote islands at anchor. She said, "We never anchor, and there are no good islands to visit around New Orleans." She was right, but why should reality get in the way of my first command. "Do you think we should get a rigid dinghy or an inflatable dinghy?" I pressed. "A rigid dinghy is easier to row and can be fitted with a sail which is useful and fun according to Lin and Larry Pardey."

I was incensed by yet another reference to the accursed Pardeys. Fortunately, the Bronze Age sailing couple did distract my wife from her disapproval of the dinghy idea. I would learn in the future to quote the gospel according to Pardey if I wanted to get an OK from my wife, but at this point I just saw it as a lucky break. "So you think we should get a rigid dinghy with a sail?" I said.

"That is better than RIB, which cannot be rowed," Janna said.

That was all the approval that I needed, and I started surfing Craigslist for a local hard sided dinghy that could be used as a tender and a sailboat. My dream dinghy was the small Walker Bay with the sailing kit, but the ones on Craigslist were all priced nearly as much as a new one at over $1,500. I found an Optimist sailing dinghy offered for $700. When I mentioned the Optimist to my wife, she approved of it because its dimensions were vaguely similar to the Pardey's tender, but she cautioned me to make sure it would fit on our boat Penelope. I took some sloppy measurements the next time I was on Penelope, and I called the Optimist seller with glee.

The seller agreed to meet after work. He lived in a nice suburban home in Metairie near Lake Pontchartrain. Metairie is a suburb of New Orleans that is immediately west of the city. His driveway was littered with small boats. He had a derelict 20 foot sailboat on a trailer. A Laser sailing dinghy on a trailer. "Do you want a Laser? It's going for $2,000. You can race it in the Olympics." he said. My dreams of being in the Gold medal race tempted me, but it looked bigger and heavier than the Sunfish in Antigua. Plus, it did not look like a tender that you could row three people in. The long and narrow Laser did not resemble a tender in the way the fat and short optimist did. I said, "No, I have my heart set on the Optimist."

He led me around the garage to show me the orange hull sitting out in the elements, then he showed me the single sail and main sheet, the little aluminum boom, the bigger 8 foot mast, and the spirit (pronounced "sprit") pole that held up the upper triangle of the four sided sail.

"I like it. Can I take it out for a test sail?" I said.

"This is a kid's boat. It's for seven year olds. I'm selling it because my son is in college," he replied.

"I want to use it as a dinghy for my 30 foot sailboat." I said.

Having ascertained that I was truly crazy, but I might have that much money he replied, "I have been trying to sell this boat for three years. I guess a test sail is OK."

We loaded the 80 pound dinghy and spars in the back of his compact pickup truck and rumbled to the public boat launch a couple miles from his home. He and I rigged the boat, I put on my life jacket, and let loose the dock line and the wind at my back easily pushed the little sailboat off the dock and towards the broad waters of Lake Pontchartrain. The owner said, "Wait you forgot..." but the wind took the rest of his words. It seemed to sail fine, and I was ready to tack back to the slip before leaving the protected cove. The problem was it appeared that I had a better downwind boat than an upwind boat. The optimist only would slide from side to side as I attempted to tack. The wind just blew the little bathtub backwards. This was an embarrassing show of my lack of sailing skill, being unable to beat back to the dock. Moreover, I lacked a paddle. Eventually, I was faced with the choice of being blown to the Mississippi sound to the east or beaching the boat on the rocky shore. I chose the rocks. I roughly tied it up.

The owner scrambled to the mound about eight feet above my rocky shore and said, "You forgot the dagger board. You can't tack the boat without a keel." That restored some of my lost pride. Just a little bit. A man in a little powerboat took pity on me clinging to the rocks, tossed me a line and towed me to the ramp. After confirming the offer with my wife, I told the owner that I would take it for $600 (in 2011 dollars). Further, I said that we had a deal if he would deposit the new (for me) dink at my sailboat a few miles away.

We put the Optimist on the Penelope, but it was impossible to move it to the foredeck. The Optimist got caught in the spreaders. The 14.5 inches on the side of the optimist could not clear the narrowest point between the spreaders and the cabin top. Thus, instead of lying upside down in the foredeck as intended, it was dangerously pushing out the spreaders, which could compromise the integrity of the rig. I could just imagine the Penelope hobby horsing through the chop while the Optimist took out the spreader and lifelines before going overboard. Thus, our lifeboat would float away as the rig collapsed. However, this revelation did not dampen my enthusiasm for the purchase.

The seller who was overjoyed to part with the tub cluttering up his garage and yard suddenly got greedy when we sat down in the mahogany cabin of the Penelope. "I don't see why I should sell this boat for so little. It is worth at least $2,000," he said.

I'm not totally sentimental when it comes to deal time and am always ready to walk if the seller gets really greedy or annoying. At this point, I only felt committed to my verbal offer, but my love of the Optimist pram was draining away. "The $600 you agreed on is all I'm going to pay," I said. Look at the other boats in the marina. Mine is one of the few that is used. That means that most boat owners are letting their boats rot, and those boats are practically worthless to their owners. There aren't many buyers for sailboats, and I'm one of the only people who is willing to buy them. I never pay anything close to full price. I paid one-quarter of book value for the boat you are sitting in."

"I don't think the price is fair," he reiterated.

"It's the $600 we agreed on or nothing. As you can see, the Optimist is too big to serve as a dinghy for my boat. How many people have looked at the Optimist?"

"You're the only one. I'll take $600, but it is not fair," the seller grumbled. I wrote him a check. We signed the papers, and he drove his truck back to his boat storage facility/house in the burbs.

I had an alternative use for the dinghy. I had gone through every podcast of Noel Davis' *Furled Sails*, which stopped production in 2010. In that podcast, Noel talked about his adventures, and interviewed participants, in the Watertribe's Everglades Challenge race for small boats. In that race sailboats, kayaks, canoes, and hybrids of all three types of boat went 300 miles from Tampa Bay to Key Largo. The key limiting factor for the size of the boat was it had to wheeled or dragged from above the high tide marker, and all mechanisms used to drag the boat to the water had to be kept on the boat for the entirety of the race. That meant no big one ton trailers. Thus, all boats were small and weighed less than a few hundred pounds.

The optimist is stuck in the shrouds of Penelope.

The organizer of the Everglades Challenge mentioned in one of the *Furled Sails* podcasts that they added a class for electrically powered boats using solar or wind power. I thought I could modify the

Linus Wilson

Optimist to fit into that class. Moreover, I envied Noel's descriptions of how he could work on his trailerable boat after work in his spare time. I liked working on the Penelope, but the three-hour drive each way was a little bit daunting and made it hard to do small projects.

I could not buy a trailerable boat because our homeowner's association banned boat trailers. (It was truly a unique subdivision in Louisiana, where everyone has a few boats on trailers.) My wife as part of her job often asks children about the sports they play. The modal response is hunting and fishing. The latter sport usually involves a trailerable motor boat or skiff.

Hiding a trailer was out of the question. The only access points to our fenced in or walled in back yard was through our kitchen door or the fence door which could only be accessed by our neighbor's driveway. Neither the kitchen door nor the backyard door was big enough for a boat trailer, and only the kitchen entrance had any semblance of privacy. I could always increase the width of the fence door to the back yard. For some reason, I thought our neighbors would not have appreciated us backing a trailer into our back yard by way of driving over the grass and roses in their front yard. Therefore, the Optimist which could be placed on a roof of a car was the only option for me to store a boat at my house.

I drove home from New Orleans and rented a van from my hometown. Then I drove back to NOLA, extracted the Optimist from Penelope's spreaders, and deposited it in my garage on its side where it resides to this day.

My first project was to repaint the Optimist gray with blue trim. I guess at the time I was dead set on preventing rescuers from finding my overturned hull. The original color of orange and white contrasted with the gray and blue sea just too much.

My father-in-law, Tom, visited and put some wood on the back for an outboard motor mount. He also put handles on the back which were good both for holding the boat and chaining the boat to a dock. The handles were also good for chaining an outboard to the boat. Those alterations alone doomed our optimist to never being legal for Optimist class dinghy racing. Then, to finish off the defamation, I bought letter stickers, and my wife and I settled on the name "Munchkin" for the Optimist. I thought Poodle would have been a good name since the Lilliputian size of the Optimist was only exceeded by the size of my four pound poodle. We also called both Sophie, my baby daughter, and our poodle Daly, muchkins so the name "Munchkin" seemed to apply to all of our little dependents.

There are few statements of love more sincere than allowing your loved one to put a roof rack on your car. That was the heartfelt gift that my wife gave me. I bought a roof rack for an insane amount of money for her 2003 sedan and had it installed. Now it was time to put the boat in the water, but what body of water? Vermilion Bay, a barely protected arm of the Gulf of Mexico, lay over an hour to the South. The map revealed Lake Martin to the north and Lake Peigneur to the south; both seemed wide enough to sail our little boat.

A quick Google search of Lake Peigneur revealed great YouTube videos of a vortex of the apocalypse, sucking in oil platforms, huge barges, trees, and anything nearby. On November 20, 1980, the vortex of destruction turned a lazy canal flowing to the Gulf into a 150 foot waterfall plummeting into the depths of the earth. As my mutton chop bearded colleague later told me the story, "Salt domes are all over Louisiana. Tabasco sauce is made in Avery Island, Louisiana because that property has a salt dome which is used in the sauce. Lake Peigneur was over a Salt Dome which was mined for years."

"Boy I sometimes complain my job is hard, but when those men said they were going back to work in the salt mines, they were not kidding," I interjected.

"Salt domes are also near oil," he continued. "Lake Peigneur had an oil mining operation that drilled into the salt mine. The salt mine dissolved when water leaked into it, and all the water drained into the salt mine."

Even Odysseus of Greek myth who has a bad reputation for wrecking his boats with the loss of all hands but himself, had enough sense to avoid whirlpools. (Surprisingly, his captain's license was never revoked because he blamed all his troubles on "Poseidon", the god of the sea. That is definitely the ancient Greek's version of "the devil made me do it.") Odysseus sailed near a multi-headed, man-eating monster, Scylla, to avoid a whirlpool, Charybdis. I had learned enough to decide that Lake Peigneur was my Charybdis. In light of nautical tradition, I opted for Lake Martin which was famous for the modern day Scyllas. Lake Martin was the home to huge alligators which were the subject of many swamp tours run through its Cyprus lined banks.

On my drive up, I witnessed a 12 foot long, one-headed Scylla sunning itself in the ditch beside the gravel road that surrounded the nature preserve. Several Cajuns had stopped to get out of their cars to snap pictures of the beast not fifteen feet from its ample jaws. I rumbled on slowly in my wife's car praying that my newly practiced truckers hitch knot would hold the 80 pound wing named Munchkin from taking flight before I got to the boat launch. The logistics of the trip were complicated.

I wanted my wife to sail the Opti too, but someone had to care for our infant daughter. Since it took me four hours to load up the car with gear and Munchkin on top of the car, having my baby daughter and wife wait in the car did not make much sense. Moreover, I had to take out the car seat and fold down two-thirds of the back seat. That was necessary to get the mast, boom, and spirit pole in the trunk and sticking out into the passenger seat. I called my wife when I got to the launch, and she met me there soon after with Sophie.

I was still unpacking when she arrived. I took out the boat first after giving her the option of the first sail. I then struggled for a half hour to rig the child's boat while getting in the way of power boats being loaded and unloaded into the swamp. The wind was at my back as I sat in the bottom of the boat ignoring the hiking straps and gripping the sheet just a little too hard. I rammed into several cypress stumps as I tried to cut the corner into the more open waters of the Nature Conservancy's bird sanctuary. I took the boat on a beam reach trying to avoid the artificial bird nests that littered the center of the lake. When my heart raced too fast I headed up into the wind. I found running off made my heart race more if I failed to let go of the sheet. The cypress trees made the wind fluky. Sometimes it would be 15 knots and at others the boat would be becalmed, and I would have to swish the tiller back and forth to get forward momentum. After about twenty minutes, I started the slow process of tacking back into the boat ramp. The tacking seemed to move more quickly than paddling canoe style and I eventually made it to the edge of the launch where my wife and baby were watching my slow progress.

My wife took a turn. She had no troubled taking it out and back on her own while I watched out for hungry alligators salivating over our baby. I mostly watched tourists load into the couple of swamp tours running next to the launch. "That was fun," my wife said after gliding back to the cleat. "Don't you want to sail more. You were only out for 20 minutes," I said. "Nah, I want to go back home. It is about time to feed Sophie again," she replied. Thus, she left me with the four hour process of reloading the Opti back into the car, driving home very slowly much to the chagrin of many a pickup truck driver, and unloading the car in the garage.

I rigged the optimist in the back yard.
There was too much grass in my backyard to sail well.

That was the last time she sailed the Opti. I would return a dozen times because I had regressed to youth sailing. Solo sailing our 30 foot boat still seemed too likely to end in $10,000+ in repairs. My wife still was the primary person at the helm of the Penelope every other weekend especially during the critical periods of docking and undocking.

6. GETTING THE RIGHT BOAT

By summer 2013, Sophie was two and walking around. I had solo sailed Penelope to Mandeville, Madisonville, and Slidell in Lake Pontchartrain; to Covington, Louisiana up the Tickfaw River off Lake Maurepas, Lousiana; and to Gulfport and Biloxi, Mississippi. Janna and I had sailed her to Biloxi, Mississippi the previous summer. My Dad, Daly, and I had sailed to Ship Island, Mississippi and had dinghied out to the old Fort Massachusetts there.

In the course of about three years, Janna and I had put about $30,000 into the boat, and she looked great. The new paint job, the new main sail, the autopilot, the chart plotter, the slab reefing, new lines and sheets, new alcohol stove, new plumbing, and on and on made her a comfortable cruising boat. Tom and I had put in thousands of hours between us installing gear, fixing things, and sanding and varnishing teak.

From time to time I would look at ads for other boats and visit them. I called one old man with health problems who said that he had taken his boat to the Bahamas from Lake Pontchartrain by way of Lake Okeechobee. I did not like his boat, but I liked his idea. I could get to the Bahamas without having to go all the way around the tip of Florida or even further out by way of Key West. That made it seem too easy.

I had a sabbatical coming up of up to one year. I was sure that Janna could take off three months unpaid from her practice. Sophie would not even be in kindergarten by the time we left. I could sail the boat on my own most of the way to the Bahamas, and Janna and Sophie could join Daly and I.

Unfortunately, I could not see Penelope taking me towards that attainable dream. Penelope could not take me there because Janna and Sophie were part of that dream. Janna likes to shower every day. Penelope has no inside shower and was not big enough to put one in. The head was not a separate compartment. Its privacy was achieved by a clever combination of using the v-berth door and closet doors to close the door on the head. If a shower were installed, the water would go into the closet and flow under the doors onto the sloping floor of the hull into the rest of the cabin. I had some ideas of how to modify it to accommodate an enclosed shower, but Janna was having none of it.

We both wanted a full keel sailboat. We hated the fin keel of Penelope. There are only two major builders of full keel boats on the market at that time, Pacific Seacraft and Island Packet. When an Island Packet 31 came on the market in spring 2013, Janna took a look at it. She loved it. The Island Packet 31 had two private berths—the quarter berth in the starboard stern and the v-berth in the bow. Most importantly, it had a private enclosed shower in the head. The galley had a three burner propane stove and oven. Thus, the eating arrangements would be more like cooking at home. I liked the Island Packet's polycore decks, which eliminate the deck problems that most sailboats have with their balsa cores being rotted by water. Moreover, I was impressed by its 70 gallon water tank capacity. I had added a water tank to Penelope, but it only held 30 gallons of water after that.

The Island Packet also is a very wide boat. Thus, it is more spacious than its length on deck suggests. The Island Packet 31 had twice the interior room of Penelope because of its 11 foot beam compared to the 8 foot beam of narrow Penelope. Penelope was a much better upwind performer. For reasons explained in the previous chapter, I had been disillusioned with tacking upwind. If I planned to travel close to the wind, I wanted to use the engine.

A boat's draft and mast height dramatically affects ones cruising ground. A boat with a 5.5 foot keel and a 55 foot mast will have trouble entering many protected waters. A boat with a mast over 65 feet will find almost no protected waters open to it and will have to only transit ports reserved for ships. Smaller sailboats tend to have smaller masts and drafts and this makes them safer than larger boats, but the correlation between these things is weak. Manufacturers more catering to the weekend racer will tend to have higher masts and deeper drafts so their boats can compete for trophies in light air.

The fixed keel version of Island Packet 31 sailboat has a four foot draft. The Gulf of Mexico is shallow, and the shallower the draft, the better are your boat's overnight options. Equally important was

Linus Wilson

because its bridge clearance was 43.5 feet, the Island Packet 31 could get under the low bridges in the Okeechobee Waterway.

We were smitten with the boat, but not the price. So we looked at other Island Packet 31 sailboats from as far away as St. Augustine. I also looked at Westsail 32 sailboats which have full keels and were made in the late 1970s. I thought they were too heavily built and would be hard to dock solo. They also lacked the more modern designs of flat sterns and nearly vertical bows that increase waterline length and hull speed.

Even if money was no object, which unfortunately it was, we had no interest in bigger boats say in the 35 to 50 foot range. Janna adhered to the Pardey's notion that big boats are too big for their owners to control the sails or manage the anchor tackle. I agreed. When we earned our ASA 106 certification, Advanced Coastal Cruising, we chartered a 42 foot Gypsy sailboat. Everything about the boat made me feel overwhelmed. The loads on the huge genoa sheet winches were frightening. Not only did it take great effort to winch up the main, but also it took great strength to crank the mainsheet, which on Penelope could be pulled by hand. Neither Janna nor I attempted to dock the beast as we were at anchor the whole trip through St. Vincent and the Grenadines. If we had taken such a big boat into the marina, which we never did, a solo sailor or a couple would be unable to fend off effectively on such a big, heavy boat. If the motor could not precisely put the boat where you wanted it, the boat would do great damage to itself and other boats.

We hauled out and sea-trialed another Island Packet 31 outside of Louisiana, but rejected it because of issues raised at inspection. In addition, the caretakers of the boat hired by the man in his seventies who owned it, had let their dozen cats run through it and pee everywhere in the cabin. It did not smell of urine the first time that I viewed it, but, during the sea trial and inspection, it smelled. If the owner sold it, the caretakers' lucrative work of providing dockage, sanding the teak, and maintaining the engine would have sailed away. I did not want to buy a stinky boat.

Slow Boat to the Bahamas

Eventually, after months of negotiation and plans to take our search to Texas, we bought the 1988 Island Packet 31 in New Orleans for $41,500 or $8,500 less than its initial offering price of $50,000 in the summer of 2013. There were far better deals to be had out there on sailboats, but we wanted the right boat for us. We did not want to invest in a boat with a design that we ultimately did not like. We were disappointed that this boat was a sloop not a cutter like most other Island Packet 31s, but life is full of compromises. A sloop is a sailboat with a mast and a single headsail. A cutter is a sailboat with two headsails on an outer and inner forestay and a single mast.

We also paid a slight premium for the boat being local. Most of the boats we had seen had broken gear that would have made delivering the boat more difficult. Trucking boats involves the boatyard expenses on both ends and the potential for damage from the packing, unpacking, and the hurricane force winds at highway speeds. I believe delivery captain charges are over $200 per day. Some gear is likely to break on a delivery trip, too.

The week after we closed on the Island Packet 31, we sold Penelope. By the summer of 2013, I believed that upgrades to Penelope added $0.10 per dollar of upgrade expenses. That is, the rate of return on those upgrades was negative 90 percent. Ouch!

No one makes money buying boats, but the problem with Penelope was that the boat from 1969 was competing with boats 20 years her junior with the same length on deck of 30 feet. Those Catalinas, Hunters, and Beneteaus were probably not as solidly built as Penelope or well maintained, but they were going for just over $20,000 and they had bigger interiors and roller furling headsails. Roller furling wraps the jib or more usually the genoa around the forestay when not in use. Instead of having many different size hank on sails, a boat with roller furling can get away with just one furling sail. A roller furling set up makes increasing and reducing the sail area much quicker. Over pricing Penelope would mean that we would pay slip fees for as long as it did not sell. I think most people tend to overprice the things they sell, and they ultimately recover less money than if they had priced their salable items lower initially.

We listed Penelope for $15,900 with a broker and she had an offer for $15,000 the next day. Our neighbor on our dock had just sold his smaller classic boat, and was looking for another classic old boat. He had seen all the work we had done on Penelope and knew that he was getting a lot of boat for the money. I was glad to sell her to an active cruising sailor instead of the typical boat owner, who lets his boat rot at the slip. The new owner had taken his little boat to the Florida Keys before selling it.

After the brokerage commission, we got about $.50 cents for every dollar we had spent on Penelope. That number does not include slip fees or the value of the 1,000+ hours of Tom's and my labor. What we did get for our money was the chance to sail a great boat for three years. I also got an education in boat repair, and we had a floating condo in New Orleans. I can't really run a rate of return calculation on Sophie or our dog. To a lesser extent, I think the same is true of a boat we enjoyed. We saved the money we got for Penelope to pay for expenses while we went on the big trip in 2015.

7. GETTING THE KINKS OUT OF THE SAILS

Our Island Packet 31 had a good set of sails, but its electronics were not working. The air conditioner compressor was burned out. As before, Janna and I bought a lot of gear that Janna's Dad Tom installed. Tom installed the air conditioner right away and put in two VHF radios—one in the cabin and one at the cockpit. He also put in the new Garmin chart plotter and depth sounder. I added a shower sump so the stinky soap water would not coat the bilge. (Charter a boat without a shower sump that is used at anchor and on mooring balls, and you will know why this is essential. Dirty soap water lines the bilge, and rotting human skin washed off smells awful.) I replaced the broken freshwater pump and installed a new autopilot. We had

Sintes Boat Works redo the bottom paint, replace broken seacocks, which open and close water thru-hulls, and add a few new seacocks.

We changed the name of the Island Packet 31 to Contango. Contango is a finance term. It refers to a commodity whose futures price declines as the date of delivery, the exchanging of money for the commodity, approaches. Most commodities that have storage costs experience contango because taking delivery on something like wheat means you have to rent out storage space. You might not like the name, but at least it is better than Wet Dream or Aqua-holic!

One of the scariest things that can happen on a sailboat was for a furling head sail to come unfurled in high winds. Unfortunately, I found that this was an issue with our continuous line roller furler. Janna was wary of this possibility before we bought Contango. When I solo sailed Contango from New Orleans to Mobile Bay on route to Perdido Key, Florida in June 2014 as part of a summer cruise with Janna, her sister Diana, and Sophie, the roller furler came accidentally unfurled in moderate winds of 5-to-15 knots half a dozen times. None of these episodes was dangerous, but they made it clear that using our headsail with that furler was risky. It is instructive that it took us a year before we identified this problem.

On the trip back, we used an ATN Gale Sail which came with the boat and fits over the furled headsail and kept the genoa furled because thunderstorms were likely that day. We also were lucky the genoa had been furled all day. We did hit a thunderstorm with 30 knot gusts that turned the sky purple.

Janna told me to douse the main, but I resisted, saying if she would not let me install a third reef, which she had been vetoing, then we should keep up the second reef. We both won the argument. Running downwind towards our destination, trying to douse the double reefed main we ripped it at an upper batten. I made crude repairs to the main with sail tape and a needle at our destination of Biloxi, Mississippi.

The sailmaker in New Orleans repaired the tear after I ordered a $150 replacement slide. At the same time, he put in a third reef point. I installed the deck hardware to lead the third reef clew line back to the cockpit later that summer. In addition, I installed an external trysail track prior to that trip. A trysail is a heavy weather sail that is very tough and small. It is used in place of the main sail.

I don't think there are any continuous line roller furlers on the market that day for genoa sails. The code zero for light air drifter sails uses a continuous line set up. The code zero sail cannot be reefed. My furler was meant to be reefed, but the old unit was unreliable. Single line roller furlers were all that was on the market for genoa furling in 2014. Over the summer and into the fall of 2014, I tried everything to make it so our old furler could be reefed without unfurling accidentally. I tried new cleats. I tried rope clutch arrangements that kept the line under tension. Unfortunately, nothing worked. It kept coming unfurled.

We got a new single line roller furler. Installing the new, single line roller furler alone was the hardest installation or repair that I had ever done. It involved me making two trips to the top of the mast with my solo Mast Climber. The first climb was because I had stranded the halyard. I was inexperienced with turnbuckles and the aluminum tube got in the way of adjusting it. If the furling tube were not there, it would have been easy as adjusting the backstay, but it was not. Everything is under tremendous tension and I had to use lines, blocks, and winches and levers to move the forestay into place. It had to be done before we sailed for the Bahamas, and it was by the end of September 2014.

8. ENGINE GURU

If you are departing on a long voyage, have your engine work done by an incompetent novice--yourself. In October and November 2014, I tackled all the regular engine maintenance. Besides changing the oil and filter, all the engine maintenance was completely new to me.

Slow Boat to the Bahamas

I replaced the old impeller after watching a salty looking, but well spoken, bearded sailor do it about six times on YouTube. Glenn Damato's memoire *Breaking Seas* of his somewhat impulsive and quickly aborted round the world sail details how he bought seven spare impellers that did not fit on his engine, relying on a parts guy to order the correct impeller. (Damato's memoire was a great book on how not to embark on a long cruise.) He nearly lost his boat when his impeller broke underway on a lee shore. Because he had not installed the new spares, he did not know that they did not fit. I was going to test my spares for the common maintenance items before I left for the Bahamas. As with Mr. Damato's engine, my engine would give me more than one adult diaper moment on the trip.

The old impeller was in good shape and I saved it for an extra spare. You have to loosen the alternator and salt water pumps to remove and replace the impeller. I put in a new paper gasket to seal up the pump, reinstalled the belts, and the engine ran fine spitting out water with no leaks.

Unfortunately, the alternator then light went on. Horror! After extensive reading of the Seloc and the sailboat electronics manual and the recurring temptation to call a mechanic, I realized I just needed to tighten the alternator belt. *Sailboat Electronics Simplified* by Don Casey recommended having a turnbuckle to tighten the alternator belt between the pulleys since levering the aluminum alternator with a screw driver could damage it. Oops! I repented before I did any real damage and bought a small version of the hated turnbuckles, which had tortured me installing the furler, at the local marine store and tightened the belt until the arm was on its farthest away setting. Hey, what does not hurt the belt makes it stronger, right? I would get the answer to this question in the Gulf Stream in January. The tightening worked and the annoying light disappeared.

"I have one word for you." The graduate leaned in, and the venerable old man said, "Antifreeze." Antifreeze is a hot topic on the cruiser forums. Many say you must, must, must use the orange stuff which lasts longer and is supposedly better. The only problem is if you start out with the yellow-green stuff you have to flush out the freshwater cooling system by a complicated process. If you don't, the orange stuff causes the neon green stuff to create a chemical reaction that clogs your freshwater system. I opted to stay with the yellow-green liquid already in my engine because my to-do list was plenty long. I bought the 50-50 premixed solution because I thought a recipe of 50 percent anti-freeze and 50 percent distilled water was a recipe that I was bound to screw up. It took forever to find the antifreeze drains and get them working. Eventually, I replaced the freshwater coolant which came out pretty dirty, but this may have been dirt on the drain hose not dirt in the fresh water cooling system. The coolant had been changed by the mechanic when we bought the boat over a year prior. The engine said to change the coolant every three months or 1,000 hours. We had exceeded the three months, but not the hour recommendation.

The last piece of engine maintenance scared me the most. Changing the fuel filters seemed fraught with risk. If I did it wrong, I could cause the engine to die at random times without warning like when the boat was right next to a rocky jetty with no sails up and a current and breeze drifting me towards the rocks. The key thing was to correctly bleed the engines.

The routine maintenance of changing the diesel fuel filters frightened me. I had heard possibly this apocryphal story of Larry Pardey, the hero of bearded sailors everywhere. (The two-time circumnavigator is the only one of the hairy lot of them who has sex with any frequency. We know this because of the references to such episodes in the excellent Seraphin series of memoirs co-written by him and his wife, Lin Pardey.) Supposedly, the man who sails an engineless cutter once bled a diesel engine by sucking on the fuel lines.

I had no desire to use diesel as mouthwash. Therefore, I asked the Island Packet sailboat's Facebook group if I really need to change the diesel filters myself. To a man they all said, "yes." A fellow owner of an Island Packet 31, my boat, gave me detailed bleeding directions with pictures. With Keith White's generous help, I tackled the filter change.

Unfortunately, there are two filters on most Yanmar diesel engines. The primary filter can be made by any diesel filter manufacturer and is separate from the main engine. The secondary filter is part of the Yanmar engine. The bleeding is done at the engine and not the primary filter so I could at least use Keith's and the Seloc manual's bleeding directions.

As it turns out, I had one of the worst kinds of primary filters because it was so difficult to change. The moderator of the Facebook group, Hayden Cochran whom I would meet in the flesh in a few months and used to have a Dahl filter, recommended that I replace my Dahl primary filter with the screw-off Racor. I did not follow his advice because I was having trouble identifying components of the engine. I did not want to remove some irreplaceable part of the fuel system to upgrade my filter.

The problem with the Dahl is that it takes four or five hands to change it. So, unless you are an octopus, this poses problems. Janna and I figured out how to put a new element in the Dahl filter. Fill the bowl with clean diesel, and tighten the thing back on. To get it done, we both were in excruciating pain, using upper arm muscles that had lain dormant for decades to do so. Moreover, I spilled diesel on Janna's jeans. She did not immediately change them and suffered from a rash in that spot for two weeks. Unfortunately, changing the primary filter was the easy part.

I could not unscrew the secondary filter. I tried all kinds of wrenches, stuffing my tool pile with new oil filter wrenches, strap wrenches, and pipe wrenches that did not work. One problem was the wall to the quarter berth, preventing me from getting any leverage on the lip that I was supposed to unscrew. There was just one small access panel. I drilled a 4 inch hole in the wall and bought a sealable port hole for it. The extra access panel did not work. I tried turning counter clockwise, per the Seloc manual instructions, with every conceivable tool including tapping the ring with a hammer and a big screwdriver, but nothing worked. Finally, I called in the mechanic, who used my hammer and big screwdriver and simply hammered in the opposite direction. Then, the bowl unscrewed easily. I had been tightening the bowl—not loosening it. He bled the engine quickly and left. I wanted to test it myself. I used the screw driver and hammer and loosened it, and then tightened it. I used the hand bleed pump hundreds of times well after any trace of air came out of the bleed screw. The engine started up and did not die. It's amazing what you can accomplish when you pay a mechanic!

9. HIGH LIGHTS

How many sailors does it take to change a lightbulb? Two. One to do the job of the sailor who chickened out. A few weeks before departure, I thought I should check the running lights. All of them were burned out including the dreaded anchor light at the top of the mast. I quickly replaced white, red, and green running lights, which are at deck level in the stern and the bow. I used overpriced LED lights to conserve battery power on the trip. Next, I tackled the running light twenty-feet above the deck about half way up the mast. I strapped into the Mastclimber and jumared my way up. A jumar is a one-way rope clutch used by mountain climbers to ascend fixed ropes. It is both a noun and a verb among climbers, kind of like Google and to Google. I ended having to replace the whole light and spent over a couple hours up there trying to not look down. Still this was not much higher than I had to go to put in the top of the trysail track.

The dreaded anchor light remained, which had been in my nightmares for weeks. Unlike the pictures of a confident sailor standing over the mast on the Mastclimber's package, how high you get depends on the angle of the halyard. I had both LED and regular incandescent bulbs in my pack. You may not get your head above the mast if you can't get the upper jumar high enough on the mast. In particular, if the sheave is not overhanging or your angle of ascent is not very gentle, the top jumar will get stuck next to the mast before you can raise it to the top. I tried as wide an angle of ascent as I could from the main halyard, climbing from the port amidships cleat. As much as I rotated the top jumar on the halyard, I could only get one-and-half feet from the top. With the jumar scratching the mast and sticking on the mainsail track, I tried to lift myself high enough to see what I was doing, but I changed the light bulb primarily by feel as I had an extra anchor light for practice. I could not see any light coming out and it was never clear if the bulb was putting out light after I phoned Janna below with my cell about turning it on. I tried some tests with my multimeter leads which were awkward, but they indicated there was a complete circuit. I put the old-style incandescent bulb in because I worried I would have to rewire the light for the LED to work. In the daylight, I could not see any light. I slowly descended because jumaring down is practically as hard as jumaring up. Because of my fear of heights, I was only comfortable with sliding each jumar six inches at a time. I told Janna it was not working. Moreover, I thought the only way one could get higher was to use the spinnaker halyard and maneuver around the radar reflector which had caused me to chicken out on that approach in the past. Janna went up quickly on the spinnaker halyard and reported the bulb was already working, and she did not have to do a thing.

Not willing to mess with success, we left the new energy sucking incandescent bulb in. Unfortunately, the anchor light is the most used bulb of the four essential lights. The others are bow running, stern running, and steaming. Those other three are only turned on for night sailing when you are likely, in the case of running lights, or sure, in the case of the steaming light, to be motoring and are charging full batteries. In contrast, the anchor light is on from dusk to dawn when unplugged outside of a marina and a prudent mariner probably would not run the engine while he or she sleeps! Unfortunately, the most important light to have an energy efficient LED bulb only had the energy-sucking incandescent bulb. I was willing to live with it because, if I had waited for the boat to be perfect, I would never have left the dock.

I arrived the previous day to prepare the boat for departure, loading the last bits of gear. The weekend before we had put up the Bimini and set out jacklines and harnesses.

I had all of spring semester 2015 off from work and did not have to start teaching until the August 2015. I could have had the whole 2014 to 2015 academic year off, but I did not want to live on the boat during hurricane season, June 1, to November 30. Thus, I taught in fall 2014. Moreover, we believed Janna could not get more than three months off. Nine months away from Janna and Sophie did not seem like a pleasure cruise. The plan was that I would get the boat as far as I could before Janna and Sophie had their three month break from February to May 2015.

10. COLD COMFORT

On December 9, 2014, I got more fuel in the morning and filled the tank completely full. I was careful to set and throw all the dock lines on their nails or well onto the finger slip because any line in the water would become ruined by marine slime long before I got back. I left before nine and was at anchor before 2PM. This long trip started with a leg of less than twenty-five miles. The whole task of getting to the Bahamas seemed hardly possible. I took comfort in the trip to Perdido Key last summer and my own calculations that even a slow pace would put me in the Bahamas in a couple of months. It was a lonely motor in light winds across the eastern expanse of Lake Ponchartrain. After clearing the swing bridges at Highway 11 between Slidell and New Orleans, I following the green buoys that kept deep draft vessels out of the eastern shallows known as the middle ground.

I tried out a new anchorage that had been mentioned in Claiborne Young's *Cruising Guide to the Northern Gulf Coast*. Published in 2000 its pre-Katrina recommendations were sometimes hit and miss. The other Rigolets (pronounced RIG-uh-leez) anchorages mentioned in that book, which I had experimented with were very exposed. They were smaller and more shallow than advertised. Who knows how much these marshlands had changed in the fourteen years since the book's publication! I had ended up doubling back to the shallow, mosquito-infested, fishing-focused, but friendly Rigolets (Bait and Seafood) Marina when Claiborne's anchorages did not pan out. Still, I wanted to avoid marinas as much as possible to gain experience before entering the reef strewn waters of the Bahamas. The soft mud of the Gulf coast with Tow Boat US at the ready seemed a safer place to learn than those exotic islands. The Double Bayou Lagoon lay near the end of the Geoghegan Canal which was at the start of the Rigolets and near the Rigolets Marina which was also in the Geoghegan Canal. I dropped the 17 pound Danforth with 30 feet of ¼-inch chain and 90 feet of rode in fifteen foot depths in the big rectangular lagoon about 1,000 feet northeast-to-southwest and even longer northwest-to-southeast. Rode is the name for rope used on an anchor chain. There was a big shelf that dropped off to 30 to 40 feet on the southeast end which I avoided. (You have to put out less rode if your anchor is in shallower water.)

I could not deploy the 22-pound claw attached to the 5/16-inch chain because the Maxwell 800 windlass without the motor jammed so easily and free fall mode would not work reliably. That 200 feet of new 5/16-inch chain would be stranded in my anchor locker and would never be used until I got a new windlass in January.

The high was a brisk 60 degrees but overnight lows were to be near freezing. So I ran the new Honda EU2000i companion generator with the help of the Smart Start for my air conditioner/heater. It did start my Marine Air heater, but I got error lights on the generator, indicating overloading when I tried charging the batteries, using the AC outlets, or running the water heater. The latter really made the generator roar in disgust. Around 9 PM, I noted my carbon monoxide alarms started reading dangerous levels of CO_2. The levels were not high enough to set off the alarm. I shut down the generator anyway because dying of CO_2 poisoning in a Louisiana swamp was contrary of my goal of reaching the Bahamas. The problem was there was no stable place on the stern (the downwind side) to place the generator

Linus Wilson

that did not have a lip above the exhaust. The only stable place was in the cockpit seats with a lip above the exhaust or the helm seat that made me turn the exhaust perpendicular to the wind because it was wide, not long. I put on a lot of layers. Daly and I snuggled under many covers and a sleeping bag until sunrise.

The anchor alarms on my phone and the Garmin chart plotter went off all night. Since I was all alone, I kept on stretching out the drag alarm beyond 300 feet. The hazards were far away, and they were alligator reeds and mud anyways. When I pulled up the chain and rode, I found out why the alarm went off so often. We were anchored to crude oil jelly. My chain and anchor were covered in the black gold. No wonder no one had recommended this anchorage since the Deepwater Horizon oil spill of 2010. Crude oil jelly has very poor holding power. Luckily, that was the only anchorage bottom I plumbed made of petroleum jelly. I did not know whether I should have staked a claim or filed an environmental complaint.

Dolphins dove and jumped under the bowsprit as I worked. A couple rolls of paper towels was enough to remove the offending stuff from my anchor tackle as the autopilot steered straight ahead in the Rigolets. I would clean a few links and then run back from the bow to the helm in the stern on my jackline tether to change the course. At one point, the dolphins suddenly disappeared. I looked up and we were headed straight for the reedy shore. I ran back and changed course as the depths had dropped from 60 feet to 6, but the disaster was prevented.

Daly was cold and his synthetic wool jacket and warm blanket were not enough to keep him from shivering in the 40 degree weather and the stiffening breeze. Therefore, I put the toy poodle down in the cabin with his bed, and he was much warmer and more content there. He usually hates to be in the cabin when I am not, but I visited him periodically to get warm when the coast was clear.

Layers kept me warm in the cold December trip east along the Gulf coast. I would bundle up in long underwear, jeans, and my foul weather bib. I always wore two pairs of socks. One of which was wool over. On top, I had a t-shirt, long sleeved shirt, a wool sweater, a fleece, and my foul weather jacket. I had a fleece hat, which I wore under a wide-brimmed hat for the sun. I often needed a fleece blanket on my legs if I was stationary. My feet would still get cold and I would periodically move them up and down to get them warm, being careful to not sweat from the exercise. As a survival show junky, I knew sweat or any water will lead to chills and hypothermia. If I had to move like when I was pulling up anchor or putting the halyard on the mainsail, I would take off a layer. I would peel off layers as the day wore on, but would end up putting them back on as the sun set. I wore gloves, but I would have to take them off when raising the anchor or handling wet lines. Even my sailing gloves would become soaked by this activity. Those leather and synthetic material sailing gloves would be useless for the rest of the day or until I put them in the oven or over the heater if I got them wet.

That cold morning, I did some jumping jacks to get me warm but not sweaty after the night without a heater. I'm hardly a tough guy. OK, I am a wimp. The 40-degree temperatures would be nothing to a northern or Canadian sailor, but I am better suited to 90-degree weather than 50-degree weather. I was headed south for the winter after all. I had more warm and waterproof clothing in reserve. I had the wet suit and the survival suit packed away. I did not use the survival suit, which makes its wearer look like an orange version of the green character Gumby, but the wet suit would get some use in the next week.

The CSX railroad bridge loomed at the end of the Rigolets and the entrance to Lake Bourne. It was clear that it was partially open inexplicably blocking trains and boats from passing. I had to call on the VHF to convince the bridge tender to open it more. Lake Bourne, which is less of a lake than the estuary Lake Pontchartrain, greets you as you exit the Rigolets. Lake Bourne is an indentation in the coast that is really part of the Gulf of Mexico. That day it was rough and cold with winds around 15 knots and seas of 2 to 4 feet. The Mississippi Sound, which stretches from Lake Bourne to Mobile Bay, is

Linus Wilson

wide open and often rough. Where there are southern barrier islands, they are often distant leaving a lot of fetch for swells to build. Between those low-lying, uninhabited islands, the swells and winds are not block for hundreds of miles. I had seen worse conditions in my old boat Penelope and conditions got better as I moved east. Nevertheless, as I experienced more of the Gulf Intracoastal Waterway (GIWW) in Florida, I would grow to appreciate this stretch of water much more.

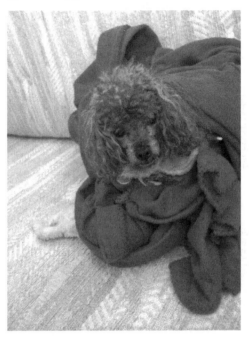

Daly is wrapped up in the cabin because it was too cold for him in the cockpit when we left in December.

I spotted twenty fishing boats clustered in a small area. I also passed a Coast Guard boat working on a buoy, but saw little else. You are much more likely to hit a buoy than another boat along this lonely stretch, especially on a weekday in December.

On the long trip, I rewired the interior lights. After finding all the LED cabin lights that I bought would not work in our old cabin lights, I learned from a sailor on the Island Packet forum on Facebook that you have to switch the positive and negative wires to get LED's to work. I busied myself on the long lonely day in the Mississippi Sound rewiring the cabin lights. At the end, I had bulbs that used one tenth the electricity of their prior bulbs, allowing the boat to be more self-sufficient.

I was annoyed that Gulfport's Small Craft Harbor strongly encouraged if not universally required all boats to dock at their fuel dock before assigning a slip. That required docking twice and each docking is an opportunity to have a trip ending collision with a stationary dock. I understand it encourages visiting boats to fill up at their fuel dock. I told them it was a policy that was unfriendly to visiting sailboats, which are much less maneuverable in tight spaces than their gas and diesel guzzling counterparts. The attendant was unsympathetic, but he said he would talk with his manager.

I had kept up my distant membership with the New Orleans Yacht Club after we moved out of Municipal Harbor in New Orleans in the hopes that I would get some free dock space from other Gulf Yachting Association clubs. When I finally got a hold of the Biloxi Yacht Club, they said I could dock for free. This is the first and last time I got that freebee from a GYA club for my $30 per month dues. I was happy to press on the extra thirteen miles as I remembered their docks were pretty straightforward to get to from the Deer Island Channel that runs along the Gulf of Mexico side of Biloxi's casino strip. I arranged for a rental the next day as I had work commitments to go back to on December 11, 2014.

A fortysomething bespectacled man, tooling around on his sailboat, greeted me at the dock and caught my stern line. I thanked him and asked him if he wanted to go for a drink at the yacht club bar. He declined. I found plenty of company up there. One old timer, Otto, who was in good spirits and well known to everyone there, told of his trip to the Bahamas in his classic double ender sailboat. When I told him about my plans to take the Okeechobee Waterway to the east coast, he said that he went to the Bahamas by rounding Key West. He said, "The ICW. No way! I sailed in the Gulf of Mexico the whole way."

I got back to the boat a couple of days later, and brought eight gallons of diesel. 7.5 gallons of which I emptied into the tank. While every day I always raised at least the third reef of the main, I preferred to have the engine running at least at idle in all but the stiffest of fair winds to make miles and not overpower the boat. It's no secret that the Island Packet 31 is a heavy weather boat, and it does not respond much to weather or winds below 10 knots. (Some of the following passage was written in double speak, and I have put translations in parenthesis.) I'm sure my conservatism (yeller bellied chicken soul) and lack of sailing effort (getting potato chips in the cabin) constrains the boat from getting the fastest speeds under sail.

On the night before left Biloxi, I came with some duct hose from Home Depot and used that and tape to try to direct the generator exhaust overboard. However, the generator did not like this, and it generated too little electricity to light up the AC panel in the boat. When I tired of fiddling with the new duct, it only would run the outlets and the battery charger. If I turned on the marine heater/air conditioner, its overload light went on. I ran the space heater off the extension cord on the dock. In the morning, I ran the generator to charge the batteries until it ran out of gas. The hose attachments did not work at the Biloxi Yacht Club dock. So, I would have to refill my water tanks someplace else.

I left Biloxi just after sunrise as I had over fifty miles to reach my anchorage at Dauphin Island, Alabama. Unfortunately, the charging light came on when I first started the engine, and it would not start without both batteries 1 and 2 turned on. Previously, either battery 1 or battery 2 would have been sufficient to start the engine. I disengaged the propeller and revved the engine, and this got rid of the charging light. I had left the sausages on the burner, and, by the time I stopped my fiddling, smoke came out of the cabin. I turned off the burner and enjoyed my burnt sausages before leaving.

I backtracked somewhat, moving west on the Deer Island channel so I could sail south of that island in the charted deep water. This would allow me to be in the lee of the light north wind. More importantly, I could avoid two hours of buoys and sport and fishing boats flitting by in the narrow channel. The motor sail past Horn Island, Petit Bois Island, and the uninhabited west end of Dauphin Island was uneventful in the 5 to 10 knot winds. The Mississippi islands unlike the islands all along the Florida coast or Dauphin Island, Alabama for that matter have no roads connecting them to the mainland, and no one lives on them.

The trickiest part of the day was the entrance to the Laffite Bay anchorage. I had been there last summer on the way to and back from Perdido Key, but it was always a white-knuckle entrance. If I kept my bearing exactly, the four-foot keel would nearly hit mud at low water and float just above it at other times. I made it in as the sun started its descent at 3:15 PM. The payoff was a 360 degree protected anchorage, which is exceedingly rare and would not be seen again until Naples, Florida. Vacation houses all with their own docks for small motor boats line the sides. Unfortunately, the generator problems continued to make the cabin cold or the air toxic. The Honda generator could only run the space heater and the battery charger without overloading. Running the Honda for more than a couple hours caused CO_2 levels to register on the two alarms in the cabin. I had to shut it down and wait for levels to drop before contemplating turning it on again.

11. WRAPPING UP

In the morning, the charging light persisted until 30 minutes after I started the engine. When the mechanic came by last, I had him increase idle RPMs to 1,000. Strangely, that day it was idling at 600. Likewise, at full throttle (for me) the engine was only at 1,600 RPMs when before a similar speed and engine noise would come from 2,200

RPMs. I could not find any explanation for this change. My uneducated guess was a wire to the RPM meter was loose.

There were two tidal stations in Dauphin Island that I found. They each had wildly different tidal stages at my 7 AM start. Neither were particularly close to my anchorage. I came close to running aground on my previous tracks. The forward depth gauge was 3.0 and the Garmin went down to 3.5 feet. (Unfortunately, I know from previous experience that the Garmin shows 3.1 to 3.2 feet when hard aground.) Janna joked over the phone that I was at "Dolphin Island," and, ironically, she was right. The dolphins were playing on the northern shores when I came in and went out. There was an east head wind around ten knots, which made for a nasty chop as I crossed the unprotected ship channel. The seas went down to one-to-two feet in Bon Secour Bay, the southeast side of Mobile Bay and backed from east to northeast to northwest, giving me an increasingly better sailing angle.

I got more diesel and water at Homeport Marina in Gulf Shores, Alabama. I remembered this dock was right off the GIWW on the north shore of the canal, making it an easy docking when it was not busy. It also was connected to LuLu's the restaurant, owned by Jimmy Buffett's sister and a cheeseburger in Alabama sounded good at noon. I lowered all sail and tied it up in preparation. I put out a 25-foot port stern line, a 100-foot port bow line, and a 25-foot port line on the bow cleat. I backed in and tossed the attendant the port stern line. Then, as the west northwest wind blew my bow farther away I walked the bow line aft and tossed it to the attendant. After tying up, I filled up with diesel, gas, and water and paid my bill. I thought I would give Daly a walk after lunch. He never got to leave the boat as it turned out.

I asked if I could stay where I was for lunch but the gas guy said I had to move if I wanted to go to LuLu's. Unfortunately, a giant ice machine separated the docks right next to each other so that one could not merely walk the line and boat across. I was port tied facing east and LuLu's was just to the west of the fuel dock. I balanced on the edge of the dock holding to the outside of the railing on the north side of the canal, and tied off the port stern line to LuLu's dock. The mostly west northwest wind tended to oppose my purpose. To give the dock guy something to do, I had him walk the bow line back. I find most people are completely clueless about using lines to move boats in close quarters, fending off. Nevertheless, they are almost always opinionated. Unfortunately, as I could taste the burgers and fries the cleat hitch at LuLu's came untied, and I had no time to retie it before the boat drifted west and off the dock. I jumped aboard quickly and awkwardly ducked under the Bimini to get securely in the cockpit as the attendant held the bow line. I had an extra line that I left on LuLu's dock, which I intended to retrieve on my next attempt.

Unfortunately, there would be no next attempt. The gas attendant was startled by this and reacted by untying the line amidships. Then, he kicked the bow and said, "You gotta to uze ur engine to go to LuLu's!"

I protested, "I lost my dock line. My engine is not on. You should have waited for me to start my engine before untying my line! Where is the bow line?" I pleaded.

"It is on the boat."

I frantically tried to start the engine. First, I had to locate the keys. Then, I had to wait 15 seconds for the glow plugs on the engine to warm up or the diesel will not fire. Nevertheless, when I tried to start it, it would not turn over. By this time, the boat was drifting far downwind sideways. I ran to the cabin to switch the battery from 1 to using 1 and 2 simultaneously. The engine fired up, but then I heard a clunking noise. I revved the engine and the propeller stopped. I saw the bow line had been violently ripped off and the other end surely was dangling from the propeller. The attendant had not put the bowline on board. He threw it in the water, and it had dragged onto the propeller. I could not imagine how he could have done more to sink my boat save taking a blow torch to it or cutting the engine water hose with the seacock open. He untied my lines with the engine off. He threw one line in the water and lied about it. Then he kicked my bow off the dock without my permission. I was in big trouble.

I unfurled the genoa half way to get more steerage, but tacking back to the dock disappearing hundreds of feet away was out of the question. I was alone, and the boat makes sluggish progress to windward. Moreover, it was likely that the current, which runs as much as 2 knots in that canal, called Portage Creek, was pushing me much faster than the wind. In which case, I would have to out sail the current upwind. In a tree-lined canal with fickle breezes, this was mission impossible in a solo sailed Island Packet 31. I called my wife Janna and had her call Tow Boat U.S. As it was, frequent gybes made my motion erratic as I was trying to use my phone while managing two genoa sheets.

Janna suggested dropping the anchor. I told her that was a bad idea in this case. I knew from experience that the canal, Portage Creek, was frequented by large, fast sport fishing boats and tugs with barges. In either case, dropping an anchor would likely lead to being dragged with horrible consequences.

Tow Boat US called asked for my location and course asked if I wanted a tow boat or a tow boat with a diver. The diver would cost $100 but the tow was free because of our annual subscription. I was pretty sure that I could free the prop if I could stop the boat safely. I was trying to make for a boat yard about half a mile downstream as a dock of refuge on the north shore, but I did not turn hard enough. Instead, I flipped the bow with my late turn so I was floating backwards onto the rock jetty, which was just east of the opening I missed. "I'm sorry I can't talk right now. I'm fending the boat off the rocks."

The operator replied, "We can't come out if your boat is on the rocks. We have to call the Coast Guard if lives are in danger." Our engine had broken down right outside our marina about six months earlier when we left for a day sail, thinking the day's fog had cleared. Janna called Tow Boat US, but they called the Coast Guard, whose base was 100 yards from our slip, because the Tow Boat US boat could not go out in the fog. So I was familiar with this tactic. I relented because I knew Tow Boat US would abandon me if I did not pay for the diver.

"Do you want a diver?" she persisted.

"Fine, I want a diver. I want a diver! I have got to go, I'm using my boat hook to keep the boat off the rocks!" I said.

She replied, "The boat with a diver will come in 45 minutes."

I pushed the boat off the rocks and drifted further downstream. Another dock opened up, but it was still under construction, and it had metal bars used for foundations still sticking out. Coming close to that dock would likely do more than scratch the tender fiberglass. I steered away. Rocky shores on both sides loomed ahead. I steered the disabled boat too close to the trees on the north shore and the rigging took out at slow speed some small overhanging branches, now twigs, raining down on deck. As the boat scraped near the clay shoreline, I spotted a huge decrepit line with a knot at the end that I could tie a smaller line to. I grabbed it, and a little crab scurried out. I secured the smaller line to the starboard bow cleat, and the boat was stopped on a soft bank. However, if a fast or large boat came by, Contango could be cracked up by the trees jutting out from this bank in response to such a boat's wake. No large or fast boat came on this cold but sunny Sunday in December. I would learn that the Coast Guard had delayed a barge that would have passed. When I passed through Portage Creek the next time, I noted that tug and barges regularly tied up their steel, not fiberglass, hulls to similar lines along this stretch of canal.

I put down the boarding ladder, stripped down to trunks, and tried to inspect the damage. The 58-degree water was way too cold. I needed the wet suit. I put on the wet suit and mask and held a safety line so the current did not carry me away. I unwrapped most of the remaining line, but a large section needed to be cut off. I found that a mini hack saw worked better than the serrated sailing knife, and I had all but a sliver cut off when the Tow Boat US driver came by. I went to the bow to brace the boat against his wake.

He had about four good teeth in his mouth. "I heard ya haad sum trouble with yer prop." I let him do the last little bit, and paid him.

Linus Wilson

While he was suiting up, the Coast Guard's fast but small boat came by while I braced the boat again.

"Are you OK?" the coast guard man asked.

"Yes, we nearly have the line off the propeller," I replied. The glum twenty somethings from the Coast Guard hung around for 5 minutes, but soon decided this was too boring and left.

Luckily, for me the Tow Boat US and Coast Guard boats were the only boats that I saw on Portage Creek after the Homeport Marina fuel guy threw my line in the water and kicked me off the fuel dock. On our summer trip, several dozen large boats would have passed this way in an hour's time.

By the time the line was cleared, the engine was running, and the paperwork was done, it was 3:30 PM. Backtracking and docking at LuLu's to retrieve my lost dock line would mean that I would have to stay at the marina whose staff nearly wrecked my boat, or I would have to traverse the canal after sunset. I was not willing to do either and gave up on retrieving my lost line. (I repeatedly tried to contact Homeport Marina about the incident, but they ignored my calls and online queries.) Instead, I made for the anchorage at Ingram Bayou, which was 7 miles further east on the GIWW. The tow boat man followed me for a few miles, but my slow boat was doing fine under its own power. So he sped off in another direction. Miraculously, my weird RPM readings disappeared after clearing the propeller, and were back to 1,000 at idle and 2,200 at full speed ahead.

Ingram Bayou had an upper anchorage and a lower anchorage. Both anchorages were excellent. The upper anchorage was smaller and slightly more protected with near 360 degree protection and very close shores. However, it was only big enough for one boat to swing, but I found two boats crammed in the upper anchorage. I backed up and turned around, towards the lower anchorage, which could easily fit five cruising boats. I had it to myself. Because there was no wind penetrating this anchorage, which only had southern exposure to a breeze, I was disturbed by how the line never went taught. Thus, I set the 17 pound Danforth twice.

12. TOP SECRET

I got up before first light and left before dawn while fog hung around. East winds prevailed, and I thought the GIWW around Perdido Key was too narrow for barge traffic, but this hypothesis would be proven wrong before the trip was over. I only saw one cruising boat on the GIWW this day. I called ahead to the Pensacola Beach Yacht Club, another GYA member club, but they said visiting cruisers from other GYA clubs had to pay a fee rivaling marina fees. This annoyed me, and I pressed on. The whole of the Santa Rosa Sound looked like a good place to anchor, except for the prohibited areas along the Gulf Intracoastal Waterway east of Navarre, Florida's bridge. The winds turned southeast and Claiborne Young's guide raved about a section just east of the prohibited area. He said it was a favorite anchorages of barges because it was so big. I could not see that from the map, but with the current southeast winds it looked like my best bet since I would not make Ft. Walton Beach before nightfall.

The Navarre Bridge only offered 49 feet of clearance, condemning most cruising sailboats to go into the Gulf of Mexico. The Island Packet 31 with a mast that poked 43.5 feet in the air, and a VHF antenna that only reached 46.5 feet could clear 49 feet.

As I approached the prohibited area, strange helicopters buzzed this way and that. Their side rotor winds would rotate perpendicular to the ground as they hovered or move 90 degrees when they moved forward. Something about the way they moved made me think they were unmanned, and were very small drones.

I tried not to pay attention as it was clear this was a military base, and I was the only boat they had probably seen all day. Woe to the boater who is alone with bored members of the military. I had twice been boarded by the Coast Guard on Penelope because I was the only boat out on Lake Ponchartrain that day. "How many crew members do you have, sir," they would ask.

"One," I would reply, "My four pound toy poodle Daly." Of course, they found nothing to cite me for, but I had to slow down for a half hour to facilitate the warrantless inspection.

The strange drones buzzed quite close, and I could imagine the NSA's visual recognition database kicking into gear. A gray aluminum boat that appeared to be manned by seal team six zoomed past, considering my snail like progress. "He must be going so slow to monitor our secret installation that was built right next to the Intracoastal Waterway. No boat goes that slow unless they are conducting surveillance." I imagined their commander saying. In reality, I was motoring at top speed.

I dropped the hook at the recommended anchorage, which looked too small for two 30' boats let alone barges. Soon a very muscular, fit, clean-shaven, and short-haired twenty year old paddled up to my boat in a yellow kayak. As he checked me out from six feet away, I offered him a beer since Jimmy Buffett was playing, but he declined slyly catching himself before saying, "I can't drink because I'm on duty." This undercover seal said, "I just love to paddle here to watch the Osprey Helicopters! Don't you?" he said inserting this piece of counterintelligence.

I replied, "No, I'm just travelling to the Bahamas. I had to anchor here because it's getting dark." That satisfied him and he paddled off. There was no need to arrest me right away. It's not like I could beat them in a high speed chase. Perhaps I would lead them to further insurgents. I texted Janna, "If I disappear after tonight, it is because the U.S. government is detaining me at Guantanamo."

I had been soured on marinas after the treatment I got from Gulfport and Homestead, two places that I had paid transient fees in the past. I reveled in the ease of anchoring. It was quicker and less stressful to drop the hook and pick it up than docking in a slip and undocking in the morning. Moreover, I was saving money.

Unfortunately, this place would dampen my enthusiasm for anchoring soon enough. At 3 AM, the anchor dragged closer to the military base's beach to the south, and I reset in the dark relying on the

Garmin for guidance in the blackness. (I blamed it on the seals and their covert ops.)

At 6:30 AM, as I was making breakfast, the first squall of the trip came up and a north wind pushed us dangerously close to the beach. The loads on the rode were so big I could not pull up without the engine, but it was hard to keep the boat turned in the right direction while I was hauling rode at the bow. The bow likes to turn away from the wind when there is slack on the rode. I threw out my back when the bow surged, and the whole business became much harder. Eventually, I wrapped the 5/8-inch rode over a sheet winch and was able to inch away from the beach slowly. When I got the anchor up after a 45 minute struggle, I faced an hour and a half of hand steering in the aptly named section of the GIWW called the narrows in the squally morning.

I regretted that I had not made Ft. Walton Beach, Florida when I passed it because it looked like an inviting place with several sailboats anchored. After 8 AM, the skies cleared, and I entered the wide waters of Choctawhatchee Bay. I had a fair west wind of 10 knots, but my bad back made me refrain from raising any sail. (This was the first day that I failed to raise sail.) I wanted to find someplace on the east side of the long bay so that I could make Panama City the next day. A long canal awaited me at the end of Choctawhatchee Bay with no overnight options if I completed the long Bay in one day. I felt too weak to anchor, and the marina options in the cruising guides were limited.

I found this very inexpensive marina not listed in the guides on Lagrange Bayou on the north east side of the bay. I thought that the marina would be sheltered from the north winds forecast, making docking easier, but actually it was very breezy when I came in. The dock master recommended that I go into a slip that only had a 10 foot turning basin. There was no way I could get in there, and I told her that from the cockpit. Unfortunately, that was the deepest water she had. I requested the other side, which had openings and a seemingly unlimited turning basin to the southwest. She assented. Unfortunately, as I throttled up to make my turn, I ran hard aground in the mud. The Garmin read 3.1 feet.

A small powerboat with pretty good sized outboards was fueling up at the fuel dock, and they offered to pull me off. The women in the boat saw my yacht club burgee, and she said she was a former member. She mentioned some folks in the club you could not help but meet, asked about my trip, then they tried to pull me off. I was pretty sure my status in the second most prestigious yacht club in New Orleans out of two was as low as you could get. I did not race, and I was the only one willing to use the dungeon showers. Thus, having been discovered aground in a Florida bayou could not hurt my reputation.

They tried one way and the other. They asked me to use my engine. Finally, after a twenty minute struggle, they got me off. The marina manager had me tie up at the end of the pier, which was their fuel dock, and she went inside. Alone, I was free to struggle with the embarrassing task of untangling my bowsprit and anchors, which the wind blew at low speed into the lifelines and anchors of another boat. I finally got the lines—a long starboard bowline in front and a long starboard bowline in back—tight. After I tied a smaller amidships line tight, I could pay the marina manager. A few fenders were added on the starboard so the boat did not scrap too much on our three feet of slip space. I looked at the Garmin and it read 3.6 feet. Thus, only six inches separated Contango from the muddy bottom. I hoped that I would have enough water to leave this place in the morning.

Daly walked on land for the first time since leaving Biloxi. I bought a year's nonresident, saltwater fishing license. (There were so many variations of fishing licenses!) Then Daly and I lay down in Contango. The rest felt so good. Lying down was what my back needed.

I woke at 5 AM. I had another work commitment in Lafayette, Louisiana. To meet it I would have to drop Contango off that day in Panama City and drive a rental car back this weekend. The depth sounder on the Garmin chartplotter showed 3.3 feet and the boat looked to be several inches lower than the previous night. I made haste to get off the dock. Luckily, I slipped off the lines and motored off without incident. A gentle north breeze turned my bow away from the dock into deep water. I had escaped Lagrange Bayou!

This is a view from the cockpit of Contango in the "Grand Canyon" section of the Intracoastal Waterway west of Panama City, Florida.

I crossed the remainder of the Choctawhatchee Bay and entered the long ditch with steep sides known as the "Grand Canyon." I got a boost of 1.5 knots from the current, with my paddle wheel knot meter showing 5 knots and the Garmin showing 6.5 knots. I saw a floating steel drum in the channel because birds used it as resting place. It's a good thing that I'm a nature lover! Trees were often falling down, and two unlighted nun and can buoys would certainly spell doom for a boat transiting this canal at night.

It was a calm day with shifty winds, and I came out in St. Andrews Bay. There, I reserved a space at the Panama City municipal marina for four nights. At $1.50 per foot this was my biggest marina bill yet. Two of those four days I would be in driving back and forth from Lafayette. Since my back was still sore, I asked for someone to catch my lines. A good sailor came out in foul weather gear with the city's logo, caught my stern line, and walked me back on the floating dock right next to the marina office. I felt like Panama City had rolled out the welcome mat!

13. THE FOG OF CREW

On my trip from New Orleans to Panama City, I reviewed the applicants for the offshore passage to Clearwater, Florida. One of the things that disturbed me in my trip planning was that the Intracoastal Waterway disappears along the "Nature Coast" or "Big Bend" section of Florida, which is southeast of Carrabelle and northwest of Tarpon Springs. My Dad teaches high school English and was not retired like many men over 65. He said he would crew if he did not have to close on his new house. Unfortunately, as the weeks passed it looked more and more likely that his closing would take place between Christmas 2014 and New Year's Day 2015. This was exactly when I was likely to be crossing the Big Bend of Florida.

To me he was a great crew member. He followed directions, moved well on the boat, and I loved spending time with him. However, being on a boat was more a fatherly duty and clearly was not something he would seek out for himself. We had never sailed when I was growing up. I can recall few instances when we ever used a boat. We might have canoed once or twice.

I had advertised on this site, which seemed more focused on Brits than Americans, Crewseekers.com. Unfortunately, it's no secret that Americans have not been the most adventurous sailors.[1] Just look at "America's" reining America's Cup team with an Australian skipper

---

[1] Of course there are exceptions such as Matt Rutherford, an American, was the first man to solo non-stop circumnavigate the Americas. He sailed through the Northwest Passage and rounded Cape Horn in a 27 foot Albin Vega sailboat. That was a boat which I would not consider for crossing Lake Pontchartrain.

and English tactician. The San Francisco Bay defense of the 34th America's Cup was broadcast in the U.S.A. on a fledgling cable network, reflecting the lack of interest despite the closeness of the competition. Sailing in the United States has been in decline since the 1980s with little end in sight despite the success of a U.S. born Silicon Valley billionaire winning and retaining the America's Cup. Interest in the States is so low that the "American" defender chose to defend the 35th America's cup in another country, Bermuda. The Vendee Globe has not had an American compete in years with most of the sailors from France. One will find in the Bahamas that as many half the cruising boats are Canadian flagged. At the George Town Cruisers' Regatta, about 25 percent of the boats were Canadian flagged. Canada has one-tenth the population of the United States, and the trip from Canada to the Bahamas is likely much longer than any trip from the U.S. Gulf or East coast. Just look at the glut of sailboats that sell here for $2,000 or some other ridiculous price tag. You won't find those prices in the UK or Australia. Thus, I had poor luck finding a crew matching website focused on Americans.

I got three applicants. Applicant number one sounded younger than forty. He lived in New York City and worked for Accenture Consulting. "I only have one week's vacation," he said. "I need some firm dates, and I'm more interested in larger boats doing Atlantic crossings."

I replied, "You might consider airplanes if you want to cross the Atlantic in a week."

That was a conversation killer. "I have another call coming in," he said.

The second applicant, a native born South African living in St. Augustine, Florida said, "I have 30,000 sea miles. I have rounded Cape Auglhus at the bottom of Africa, and have crossed the south Atlantic three times. Once I did it in my own 52 foot ketch, visiting St. Helena." He said. "Do you have any offshore experience?"

Linus Wilson

"I crewed on a delivery trip that crossed the Gulf Stream from New Smyrna Beach, Florida to Myrtle Beach, South Carolina," I replied clearly outgunned. I can hear the mutiny cries already. "Do you mind if I ask how old you are?"

"Seventy-six."

"Are you retired? I consider being retired a plus because you have a flexible schedule. I also like that you are based in Florida."

"I am retired, but I am very busy," he replied tersely.

I had read many horror stories about unrelated crew members. One of the most frightening accounts was that in *Imperfect Passage* by Micheal Cosgrove where his crew member with an inflated sailing resume threatened to kill him in the South Pacific and steal his boat. Therefore, I tried this crude quiz of Mr. 30,000 miles' sailing resume. "I have a quick question that will be easy for such an accomplished sailor as yourself. What kind of knot would you use to tie a dock line to a dock?

1) A figure eight
2) A bowline or
3) A cleat hitch."

He was taken aback by this question, repeated his resume, and did not answer presumably because he was offended. I pressed, "If you wanted to tie up to a cleat…"

He answered, "A cleat hitch." That was not exactly a roaring success, but he became so agitated I did not press with another question. I mentioned the logistics of coming onboard and he became easily angry and argumentative. He seemed difficult to get along with and may have mobility issues. I told him I would get back to him.

My third applicant scored much better. For his privacy, I will call him Dean, because like James Dean's iconic role, I would later think that he was a "rebel without a cause." Dean could have played the part of my father-in-law's alter ego. A long lost twin brother who appeared similar superficially, but did everything the "good brother" would not do. Dean physically resembled my father in law Tom vaguely. Tom, says "fudge" when swearing. The strongest thing Tom drinks is Coca-Cola. He is kind and soft spoken. Dean drinks, swears, takes big risks, and would later brag that he does not want to live into his seventies, which is very unusual for a guy in his early sixties. Dean was not an evil twin, just a bad boy. He lived fast and hard, but I had no reason to believe that intentions were anything but noble.

Dean told jokes, stressed that his schedule was flexible, and he would even be interested in crewing on the Okeechobee Waterway canals if things went well. He had a 44-foot sailboat in Lake Ontario, but always wanted to do an offshore passage. Dean got the cleat hitch question right and another easy sailing question correct. I offered him a position right away, but warned my Dad, Larry, may also come along. He booked a flight December 27, to Panama City, Florida right away.

Dean and my Dad favored departing from Panama City to Clearwater. Dean wanted the longest possible offshore passage. Thus, a 44-hour passage from Panama City to Clearwater was preferable to a 30 hour passage from Carrabelle to Clearwater. My Dad liked Panama City better because it was closer to I-10, which was the way he, my Mom, and I would be passing after Christmas on the way to my parents' home on the west coast of Florida. Unfortunately, Panama City would keep us on the water longer. That was more time to burn fuel, catch bad weather, become sleep deprived, get sea sick, break stuff, have crew injuries requiring evacuations, and be out of reach of Tow Boat US.

I knew from my delivery trip that it did not take very strong winds to turn the open ocean into a mini rollercoaster, which made moving around a test of strength for a guy in his late thirties. My potential crew members were both in their sixties. Moreover, hopping along the coast from Panama City to Carrabelle made it more likely that my crew would jump ship. It was better to have them sail for the part that I needed them right away rather than squander their time and patience with stuff I could do easily alone. I primarily wanted crew to have the chance to sleep on the passage. Finally, you have to steer around the dangerous shoal waters of Cape San Blas if you depart from Panama City to Clearwater.

Apalachicola, Florida was an intermediate departure point with Gulf of Mexico access through Government Cut. Government Cut near Apalachicola was a very narrow 50 feet. That is probably not enough room to safely turn around Contango if conditions are too dangerous. I knew from the delivery trip that a bad cut in the wrong conditions can be very scary. On the delivery trip, we saw five-to-six-foot seas offshore and got beaten up in the entrance canal to the South Carolina ICW. However, the worst wave was a breaking wave that hit us when we exited the New Smyrna cut on a sunny day. The East Pass near Carrabelle is more than a mile wide and is one of the safest access points to the Gulf of Mexico along the GIWW. The East Pass by Carrabelle was the cut I wanted to take,

I had two days to get to Carrabelle once I got back. My parents would be driving by on December 22, or December 23, to take me back home to celebrate Christmas in Lafayette with Janna and my four year old daughter Sophie. The weather was not totally cooperating. A drizzle made everything wet. At least on this leg of the trip, I had some waterproof ladies lavender gardening gloves. Thus, my dainty hands did not get too cold and wet as I handled sheets and lines. Also my back was totally healed from the strain I had in the Santa Rosa Sound a few days earlier.

The ten-knot north breeze and forecasted one-to-two foot waves convinced me that I should sail outside of the ICW channels to Port St. Joe. There were really no recommended anchorages or marinas within striking distance of Panama City during the daylight hours. Thus, Port St. Joe outside of the Intracoastal Waterway was my best bet. Once at Port St. Joe, there was a canal that would allow me to join the GIWW and avoid the Cape San Blas shoals. I was a little apprehensive of leaving the GIWW, but the wave forecast was good, the Panama City Ship Channel was wide and deep, the St. Joseph Bay opening to the Gulf was miles wide, and there wasn't an Intracoastal

Waterway in the Bahamas. I'd better toughen up now despite my wearing of lavender gardening gloves for warmth!

I was out of the Panama City Marina before dawn. The Gulf was deserted until I saw some shrimp boats near St. Joseph Bay. I docked along a long concrete pier in the rain, throwing the dock line to the marina attendant. This was a nice Marina, and it was in easy walking distance of restaurants and a grocery store. I walked Daly to the beach facing St. Joseph Bay a few hundred yards south of where I docked. There was a sailboat with its keel sticking out of the two feet of water it was sitting in. It was clear someone had tried to heal it with a halyard dangling from its side, but that effort evidently failed since it was still high and dry. I thought it must have been run aground by some tropical storm or other severe weather event. I later asked the bartender at the marina restaurant about the boat, and she said some guy just abandoned it.

After sunset, I saw a huge 50-foot trawler come in. It was steel and its bow loomed 10 feet over the water. A 5'3", 170-pound man in a t-shirt and shorts got out in the rain and started talking to anyone who would listen about his trip. I was wearing my foul weather top and jeans and fleece in contrast. I was interested in what he had to say and pressed him for details. He had just bought this boat in Tarpon Springs and crossed the Gulf. That was just a little longer than the Carrabelle trip I planned after Christmas. He was a retired Navy man, and his wife was aboard this rugged looking ship of dreams, which was more a work boat than pleasure boat according to my eye. He said they saw seven foot seas and he was shocked how rough it was. To illustrate this point, he showed me a blue tarp that must have retailed for $5. "Those seas and winds shredded my tarp!" Obviously, he was new to boating not on the government's dime if he would worry about such a loss. You can't buy a key chain at West Marine for less than $12. He was bound for Pensacola.

"Why did you sail around Cape San Blas? Why did you not stop in Carrabelle?" I asked.

"We've been to Carrabelle. We have never been to Port St. Joe. What is Cape San Blas?" he replied.

"Did you have any trouble around the shallows near St. Joseph's Island that form's Cape San Blas?" I pressed.

He said, "No."

I would be avoiding that cape even if he did not. Daly and I left the next day a 6 AM in darkness. To my surprise the sun never seemed to rise as we maneuvered around the marina and under the high fixed bridge which was the gateway to the Gulf County Canal and the quickest way back onto the GIWW. A pea soup fog dogged me the whole way and my running and steaming lights stayed on until Carrabelle. I would periodically ring Contango's bell, which is usually stowed in the cabin. However, if any boat was travelling fast in the other direction, this would have been unlikely to warn them. Fortunately, I saw no one in the canals that day.

The last long leg to Carrabelle proved challenging. The tide was going out, and I fought a 1.5-knot adverse current based on the discrepancy between the paddle wheel knotmeter and the GPS speed. The narrow canals mostly maneuvered through cypress swamps. Somewhere in the fog I crossed into the Eastern time zone, and my iPhone clock moved an hour forward. I passed a rare small town. White City had a public dock by its boat ramp that could serve as overnight refuge. A thunder squall blew through as I crossed Lake Wimico the only open water on the GIWW on this stretch between east St. Andrews Bay and Apalachicola. I did not have much sail up in the generally windless canals, so that squall posed little problem. The Coast Guard had been warning of dredging in Apalachicola over VHF channel 16, and I was nearly driven into onto a buoy by the dredger. I chose the shallows over hitting the buoy and almost ran aground as a result.

14. THE PIRATES OF CARRABELLE

The protected waters of St. Georges Sound did not feel so friendly, with the rain, a 15-knot east headwind, and the shifty currents. I saw an open oyster boat bobbing in the three-foot waves and slowed to see if they needed assistance. They did not and continued working, ignoring the conditions. When I came parallel to the East Pass, a four-foot swell rolled the boat in the fading light, but at least the sun peaked out from behind the clouds. I think I was trying to call Carrabelle Marina, but instead I called ahead to C-quarters Marina. C-Quarter's gruff attendant was nervous that I would come at near 5:30 PM when he planned to leave. I arrived at 5:10 PM. Since they had one row of slips right off the river channel, docking was relatively easy. A man with long gray hair came to watch the last of the docking and chided me. "You've run aground. You are too close to the back of the slip," said the prophet.

"No I'm not. My depth gauge shows that I'm in six feet of water," I replied.

I paid the scowling attendant for a week since he said I would get the 7th night free.

Unfortunately, for me the long haired man was proved right in the morning as all the water had drained from the back of the slip and the rudder was clearly in the mud. Since I was tied up, I could use the dock lines to dislodge the rudder. Clearly, C-quarters had inflated their dockside depths. When I pointed out that my rudder ran aground overnight and dockside the depths were 0, the new attendant just ignored me. I should have demanded a refund and gone to another marina, but I expected my parents soon. They only had 1/3-length finger slips. That meant that I had to pull the boat so that only 1 foot of the stern was parallel with the slip. This forced me to slink around the Bimini and solar panels balancing over the water in a precarious maneuver that would tempt me and my crew member to put weight on two things that should never be used for support—the aluminum frame of the solar panels and the aluminum frame of the Bimini. This made the boat very hard to get on and off of. I was only able to unload Daly and my bag with the help of my Dad. He held the dock line tight as I passed the loads through the side of the Bimini.

We had an enjoyable Christmas with Janna and Sophie in Lafayette, Louisiana. My Mom, Dad, and I left early on December 27. Their closing would be in a few days, and my Dad could not come on the trip. On the way home for Christmas, Google maps had routed us through the Apalachicola National Forest. It was scenic, but remote. Nevertheless, it also was a fast route devoid of traffic. After my round trip with the rental car less than a week before, I knew how bad traffic could be on that section I-10 and other roads. Also Carrabelle was surrounded by that forest. Diverting around it would lengthen the trip. My Mom on the other hand was freaked out by the lack of strip malls *et cetra* and approached me with the paper Rand McNalley Atlas, saying we should take another route.

I was nervous about making it on time. Carrabelle was the final destination of the day for them. Unfortunately, the logistics of our trip meant that I would drop both of them in Carrabelle at a room we arranged through C-Quarters. Then, I would drive back west three hours to Panama City. If I were late for Dean's 9 PM flight, we would start on a bad foot and may be driving back to Carrabelle in the wee hours of the morning. The drive to Lafayette demonstrated to me that my parents refused to drive 70-miles-per-hour on 70-miles-per-hour freeways, and they drove similarly slower than the speed limit on all other roads. Moreover, they like to stop at fast food places and rest stops every hour for a 20-minute stroll and bathroom break. Thus, if Google maps says that it takes 8 hours and 30 minutes for the typical car to drive from Lafayette, Louisiana to Carrabelle, Florida, then you can bet my parents will take at least 13 hours.

There would have been a confrontation on the drive to Lafayette, but my car was still at Bucktown Marina near New Orleans. I drove them the short distance from Mobile to New Orleans when they were hinting I should share a hotel room with them. I got in my car and drove home that night. My parents found a hotel and arrived in the afternoon of Christmas Eve.

Slow Boat to the Bahamas

I impressed on them the importance of less frequent stops, which speeded us up from their ideal pace, but three factors ensured I picked up Dean horribly late. My parents refused to let me drive. (I have not been in a stationary or moving traffic accident since I was 17.) In addition, it rained half the time, and they responded by driving even slower than usual. Thirdly, my Dad left his briefcase in Lafayette and only remembered that he left it when we had driven an hour away, adding two extra hours to the already long trip.

I was so upset that I had dealt with the uncertainties of travel by sea and was ahead of schedule, but my parents insisted on making me late by the mundane and eminently more predictable car travel. By the time we crossed the Florida border, I started talking about a rental cars. Unfortunately, it was a Saturday afternoon and most car rental places close at noon on Saturday afternoon. Airport locations won't pick you up or drop you off. Moreover, I was having trouble finding a car rental place near Carrabelle. As it turned out, it was my parents' car or walking at that stage.

I tried to lower their expectations for what a room in Carrabelle would be like. "Compare it to camping out in a tent. In that sense it is not too bad." At least that form of expectations dampening worked, and when we arrived, they did not refuse to stay at the dinghy place on offer. (If they did not stay within walking distance of the boat, then there would be a roundtrip in the morning where I would pick them up and I would be driven by them back to Carrabelle. The logistical problems still make my head spin.) They handed over the keys to me at 8:30 PM when the Panama City airport was 2 hours and 30 minutes away. I dropped off Daly and put in the new battery that I bought before Dean occupied the berth above it. With such a long drive ahead to Panama City, I phoned his home to verify that he had taken the flight. His startled wife said he had, and I assured her I was on my way to pick him up. I found him at the deserted airport after 11 PM. I was over two hours late. He was a little annoyed but did not dwell on it.

I soon realized what I forgot to ask him, "Are you a smoker?" It turned out he was. He never smoked in the cabin, and it was not a big issue. Nevertheless, I probably would not have invited him had I known. He said he had applied to many boats for a while, but this was the first one that accepted him primarily because I forgot to ask if he smoked. I warned him about my toy poodle. He said he a couple dogs, and that it was not a big deal to him. Nevertheless, Daly was agitated and unusually awake in his presence and slept four days straight after Dean left.

Dean convinced one of the grim fellows working at the Marina to lend his truck to Dean. He drove me to a greasy spoon in town for breakfast, and the grocery store, which was 200 feet away from the boat. Dean was the son of an English father, but spent most of his childhood in Canada. His many stories of rebellion and getting kicked out of boarding schools underscored that he had a deep dislike for his father. This was despite the fact that Dean was in his sixties, and his father was likely dead. He was well spoken and intelligent. It became clear that he had the best schooling that money could buy. Still, he had the rough edges that I had observed in some men from rich backgrounds, who went to boarding schools—a rowdiness and surprising vulgarity. Despite his posh upbringing as the Brits would say, he had a very working class job and worked his hands, which seemed to be an extension of his rebellion. He worked as a cabinet maker and a shop teacher before retiring.

I mentioned that he was in the same profession, cabinet maker, of John Guzzwell, the Canadian man who built a 21-foot boat, which he solo sailed around the world. Supposedly, fellow Canadian Larry Pardey was inspired to build the 24-foot wooden cutter Seraphin in part by Guzzwell's book *Trekka Around the World*. Dean had not heard of John Guzzwell or his book.

Dean discovered things about my boat that I had never figured out. He discovered the aluminum containers in the fridge were vertical ice cube makers. In the silverware, he found strange metal bars which were pot holders to secure the pots in rough seas while on the stove. I changed the oil with his help as we were bound to go over 100 hours since the last oil change on the way to Clearwater.

We discussed the weather report. Either tomorrow or the day after looked more promising than anything I had seen since arriving. The winds would be light and shifting on December 29 and 30, but there would likely be some rain, seas would mostly be one-to-two feet. On December 30 and 31, northeast winds 10-15 knots, building to 15-20 knots early on the 30th. Seas would build from two-to-three to five feet. The northeast wind would give us a beam reach, which is the fastest and easiest point of sail. To my surprise at the time (but now it seems predictable) Dean said, "I like waiting because we will have better sailing weather, but it's your decision." I was leaning toward leaving the next day, the 29th, but I stupidly agreed to leave the morning of the 30th.

I had told him earlier in the day, "I don't care if we motor all the way. My concern is getting the boat to Clearwater in on piece. Until my wife arrives, this is a delivery trip. Sailing is secondary." My decision of when to leave was not true to that statement.

We were balancing off the side to go to a local watering hole when my cell phone holster scraped against the Bimini frame and fell straight into the water. It was completely dark, but that really did not matter. The visibility in the muddy Carrabelle River was less than a foot. It was a big loss. Not only had I lost my only cell phone, but also the iPhone was my primary source for weather information, and it was a backup chart plotter. I used the weather apps Boat Weather and Windfinder several times a day for the latest weather information for where I planned to sail. The Navionics app was used for on the go route planning and distance estimation. I would also find that app worked far out of reach of cell phone signals because it used the GPS network. The Garmin chart plotter at the helm and paper charts were backups for the Navionics app.

When I got back from crying in my beer and losing games of pool to Dean, I got an inspiration at 3 AM in the morning. I could dredge the bottom of the river where it fell with my fishing net taped to a boat hook. I knew exactly where it fell. On the first attempt I brought watery brown mud and a couple of clam shells. I dipped again. The net glowed and was singing or rather the iPhone was playing "Rebel Yell" from my music stash. Since I had dropped two iPhones in the water before. I had started using the waterproof case made by Lifeproof. There was water inside the case but the phone still seemed to be working.

I dried it off the best I could and placed it in rice until morning. That cure did not work the last time I submerged an iPhone, and I soon learned it would not stop a deterioration of performance this time. The phone and wireless internet features did not seem to work. I wanted to go into Tallahassee, the nearest city with a car rental place, to see if I could replace the SIM card or trade in the iPhone for a new one.

I had a separate portable WIFI and used that to book a car in Tallahassee. They said they did not pick up renters in Carrabelle, but they would go as far as the Walmart in Crafordsville, Florida. I had no idea where that was, but I asked the marina for a courtesy car or a ride. One of the less intelligible employees gave me the number of a taxi service in town, said there was no place to rent cars in Carrabelle, and said someone else who worked at the marina could get me a ride. The friendliest of C-Quarters staff picked me up and 45 minutes later and dropped me at the closest outpost of civilization, according to Enterprise Rent-A-Car, the Crawfordsville Walmart. I asked her about the Clearwater pass, which she said was "a piece of cake" and told her of our plans to leave the next day. She said she had her "six-pack" Captain's license and had made the trip several times.

I thought I got a ride because I had stayed eight nights at the marina. Nevertheless, when we approached the mecca of bulk purchasing, she for the first time mentioned money, "You know a taxi ride here would cost like $40 or $50 dollars," she said. "You are lucky I had some errands to run in Crawfordsville."

I remembered bitterly how I was rewarded by tipping the fuel dock attendant at Homestead Marina and was not about to get out my wallet. Moreover, I would not have dropped my phone and be renting cars and considering buying replacements had it not been for C-quarter's inflating their dockside depths. When I had told her that I ran aground the previous day in the slip her response was "so what?" I paid this marina more than any other marina on the trip, to that point, and I all got a shallow slip that was almost impossible to get on and off the boat from. Now one of C-quarter's pirates is trying to shake me down at the end of a free ride over 30 miles from my boat.

I tried to be diplomatic and keep my options open. "Thank you again. It was very kind of you to give me the ride. Can I get a ride back when I'm done?" I asked.

"I'm not sure about that, but I'll give you my number," she said as she carefully wrote out her cell phone number.

I bought a disposable, pay-as-you go phone and a bag to dry out cell phones while I was there and used it to call for a ride from Enterprise.

In Tallahassee, my visit to the AT&T store was not encouraging. I was less than one year into my two year contract. A replacement phone would cost $550 and an upgrade would run $750. I paid $300 for my last phone because I was at the end of my two year contract. "You can always call up Apple," the AT&T salesman offered. With my phone continually doing strange things and Google maps freezing up, I got lost easily in the strange city of Tallahassee. I had to relearn old skills of looking at street addresses and asking for directions. I was driving like it was 1999.

Apple would replace a water-damaged phone for $250. Unfortunately, I would have to go into an Apple store. The nearest Apple Stores were in Tampa or Jacksonville, and I could not reach either store before they closed. Moreover, same day appointments were not available at either store. I got an appointment with the Tampa store on New Year's Day. If we left tomorrow as planned, then we should arrive in Clearwater, near Tampa, on New Year's Eve. I dropped off the car and begged, pleaded, and threatened to be dropped off in Carrabelle. This was the closest Enterprise, and they did say they sometimes dropped off renters in Carrabelle. All the protests to the national office did not help.

At 3 PM, I was cooling my heels in the Walmart in Crawfordsville, Florida. An ultramarathon separated me from Contango. I tried to find a taxi in Crawfordsville but had little success with the yellow pages. I called the marina employee who said that if I paid her $150 she would pick me up after her shift. "I guess I have to get back to the boat." I replied. That was extortion. Could I really expect better from C-quarters Marina? My parents said the room they had smelled of urine, their dockside depths were 0, and their staff engaged in piracy. Next, I called the number of the taxi service in Carrabelle. They could drive me back for $50. A pleasant newly retired lady picked me up, and I gave her $60. I was back by 4:45 PM, and the extortion lady was on duty. I paid the marina for an eighth night, and the pirate begged for money. I gave her $20 as an insult to her profession, and she complained more.

I told Dean, who had wisely stayed in town during the Walmart odyssey, that we would leave the Pirates of Carrabelle in our wake the following morning. The weather forecast on the VHF had not changed—10-15 northeast in the afternoon of December 30, and 15-20 overnight early on December 31. Unfortunately for me and Daly, but fortunately for Dean because he reveled in the big wind and seas, the weather forecast would turn out to be wrong.

15. BAD PASSAGE

I wrote down a watch schedule that I had Dean read. When I had previously crewed on an offshore delivery trip, inexplicably the skipper failed to write down the watch schedule. He had it in his mind, but there was no adherence to it. The crew coverage was chaotic, and we did not get rest during the day in preparation for the nights. To me, the most important part of having a crew member was that both he and I would sleep. Dean had the 6 PM to 9 PM and midnight to 3 AM night watches. I would have the 9 PM to 12 AM and night watch. During the day, we had two hour watches.

I also wrote the following:

"All hands for docking and reefing. Motor runs after sunset and until sunrise even at idle. Double reef at night (no more sail) maybe less. Genoa turned to no more than 100% dusk to dawn. Never go forward without another sailor. Clip in at all times on night watch. Boards should be in at night and most of the day."

Since I was pretty sure only my wife would choose to put up less sail than I would, I needed some mechanism to restrain the impulse of the typical sailor to put up a lot of sail while I slept. What shocked me was that Dean never attempted to violate these written rules.

Over the last few days, I had introduced myself to the skippers of the trawlers docked a C-quarters. They were primarily doing the Great Loop, heading southeast towards Clearwater. None of them thought the weather window we saw was good enough to cross. It struck me that sailboats are better in rough seas than most trawlers. They wanted to wait for a complete calm, and a couple despaired that they would not cross to Clearwater that season, which was odd since we were still so early in the season.

We got up before 6AM in the darkness and were off before sunrise at 7AM. The East Pass posed no problems and, for most of the daylight hours, we had almost no wind. We steered to the course recommended by the chart book between the East Pass and Clearwater. "Why don't we steer straight for Key West? We can be there in a couple days." Dean said as we got in open water.

"I like to sleep. I'll sleep more if we go into Clearwater, and hop along the coast, sleeping every night. Besides, we would cross shipping lanes into Tampa Bay if we pushed farther south." I replied. "I think going in the ICW to the Okeechobee Waterway is a good

Linus Wilson

plan." I also had enough fuel for Clearwater, not Key West. I was not sure that we had fair finds all the way to Key West.

On my previous delivery trip, I was picked up as crew in Ft. Lauderdale in part because the owners of the new boat, a husband and wife, had changed their minds about cruising straight away. They had been sailing with the skipper after picking up their brand new Oyster 36 sailboat in Tampa. They planned to cruise the Caribbean right away after earning their sailing certifications. That offshore trip made them change their plans. The skipper never said why. I was only confident in the trip to Clearwater. I figured a lot of bad stuff could happen if it was extended to Key West. Besides, the skipper warned, "It always takes a lot longer to leave the Key's than you expect." I had many weeks and months ahead to ponder what he had meant by that. I thought it is better to get to the Bahamas slowly than to never get there at all because of some major breakdown offshore.

When out of sight of land, I wrote down hourly GPS fixes. I despaired that I had estimated distances on the Navionics app, which was not operational because the iPhone had started turning itself off at random times. I finally just stuck it in the drying-out bag from Walmart, and gave up on it. I would just have to trade it in in Tampa. Dean busied himself, figuring out how to program a route into the chart plotter. He put in two waypoints and we had a countdown of the miles to go and an updated bearing to steer for as the GPS told us how many feet or miles we were left or right of the line drawn between two waypoints. In many things, I am a semi-Luddite, scorning technology, and I had neglected the features of this piece of technology. Prior to this cruise, I had used paper charts and a parallel ruler for route planning. Unfortunately, my spiral bound chart books, which were my only paper charts from Pensacola, Florida to the Bahamas, made it nearly impossible to use a parallel rulers. Moreover, plotting courses in open water is OK, but in narrow channels, such plotting is fruitless and very time consuming with a parallel ruler. Thus, I had given up on the paper planning and relied more and more on the iPhone app and the chart plotter on the trip up to Carrabelle.

Slow Boat to the Bahamas

As the sun set, I reefed down the main to the 2nd reef and genoa to 100 percent. We seemed to be entering a huge bank of cloud as darkness descended. After 10 PM the wind noticeably picked up from the northeast to over 10 knots. We switched watches at midnight and Daly and I retired in the v-berth. I did not sleep long. Around 1:00 AM, Daly's growling woke me up. All the extra stuff that had been stored in the quarter berth before Dean came aboard was put it in Janna and Sophie's side of the v-berth. Now, the rising seas had started to make this mountain of food, clothes, and gear unstable, and Daly was rightly worried about it crashing down on his head. I put Daly on a settee cushion to shield him from the potential projectiles in the forepeak. When I poke my head up, a big wave soaked me, and I had to retreat to wipe off with a towel.

When I emerged for the second time, I saw the five-foot beam-on seas that Daly had been feeling while I snoozed.

"The wind has picked up to over 20 knots. The boat is doing a great job in the conditions," Dean said.

That last phrase worried me more than the former.

The boat would rise then crash. Every minute it seemed we would get a set of three big waves, each bigger than the preceding one, and the boat would jerk sickeningly down. Before long, I could feel a set coming before it arrived. The wind speed indicator went from reading 20, 22, 23, 20, 24, and 21. I was taking it all in when Dean to my shock yelled through the howling wind, "I think we should put in the third reef. The sail shape on the second reef is awful."

I of course agreed. The 1st and 2nd reef points for this boat from the factory come from the end of the boom. That meant that the reefed sail's clew's angle of pull is far less than the 45 degrees that is ideal. This problem is the worst for the second reef, which has a very narrow angle of pull perhaps five-to-ten degrees. When Janna came aboard later in the trip, she got the idea of securing a sail tie tightly between the end of the boom and the second reef's clew line. That would widen the angle of pull and improve the upwind performance of the main with the second reef in. But tonight I was glad for any excuse to reduce sail and was not worried about the "poor sail shape" that bothered Dean with so much wind. We needed some sail up or the ride would be much worse than not sailing. However, I did not want to dangerously overpower the boat.

I went back to sleep. I took a sheet, a couple pillows, and my eye mask, and curled up on the leeward, the starboard, settee next to Daly. The v-berth by this time had become such a war zone that I had to close up with its privacy door. I set my alarm for 2:15 AM, and Dean and I reefed the Genoa down to 75 percent before he went off watch. This was the first high winds that I got to test the new single line roller furling reefing system in.

It worked great. On the whole trip, we never had the accidental unfurling problem that plagued our previous continuous line roller reefing. Dean suggested heading into the wind to reef, but I favored reefing underway since the motion from changing points of sail was likely to be awful in the building seas. While the furling line was a tiny 5/16-inch, twelve braid line, we found that if we wrapped it around the sheet winch and hand tailed the line, it came in easily as long there was slack on the working sheet. I have never been able to just yank on that furling line to reef. This is in part because I had to add a kink to the guides at the bow. The kink lifted the first furling line eyelet a foot higher than the other eyelets. I made this change while sailing in the Mississippi Sound because otherwise the line would jam in the furler because of an improper angle. Since that alteration early, I never had it jam on the whole trip. Dean wanted to take the kink in the guides out, but he just became angry when I asked him not to and explained why I had raised that eyelet so high.

Very early into my 3AM to 6AM watch I became nauseated. There was no horizon in the infinite cloud we were encased in. All I could see were the big waves nearby or the boat with my headlamp. Turning it off did not help as there were no stars or moon to use as light sources.

Slow Boat to the Bahamas

As the wind speeds stayed between 20 and 24 knots and the seas built to six feet, I realized the 200 watt aft solar panel had popped out of both of its top forward elbows and was waving with each crash down a wave. Only the wire inside the frame was holding it together. It would be a great loss to lose it. Moreover, there was no easy way to just "cut it away." I made a decision to get some dock lines to tie it more securely to the boat so it did not break off. The adrenaline staved off some of my seasickness as I stood up above the cockpit seat, clipped in, clinging to the Bimini and desperately trying to secure a knot as we rose and crashed down the occasional seven-foot seas. This process burned over an hour, tying two lines to either side and then to the stern cleats.

I did not have to throw up. I attempted to minimize my motion sickness by closing my eyes for a minute and then standing up to look around. I saw other lights on my first night watch between 9PM and 12AM. No fools except us were out between 3AM and 6AM in this angry stretch of the Gulf of Mexico.

I gratefully curled up on the leeward settee with Daly from 6AM to 7:30AM. I snoozed with all my foulies on. Foulies is a sailing slang for rain proof foul weather gear. When I awoke and considered shaving, I noticed that my Scopalamine seasickness patch was gone. It must have been washed off by the wave that hit me at 1AM.

I was surprised by the nausea because the delivery trip had nearly as bad weather, but I never go nauseas. I was reading and doing math problems throughout that trip. Those were two activities that should have contributed to sea sickness. On that trip, my patch was always on.

After putting on the patch back on at 7:30 AM, I got hungry before 8 AM. I prepared sausages, eggs, and pancakes for Dean and me. I ate heartily. Meanwhile, the northeast wind was easing in the first light of the morning to 15-to-20 knots then to 10-to-15 knots. The gray waves got smaller and smaller as we entered shallower water and got in the lee of the land.

Linus Wilson

I called Clearwater Beach Marina, and we entered the Clearwater Pass without incident. It was a culture shock as many pleasure and tourist boats were moving around inside the breakwater. There are two channels that run north to Clearwater beach marina. The deeper one is about two miles out of your way. We threaded the needle through the shallower more direct one and avoided the clear signs of shoaling in the channel. Clearwater Beach Marina has a large turning basin, but it also has many tourist boats. An endless procession of fishing tours, dolphin tours, pirate tours, the cigarette boat tour, the shark tour, *et cetra* would come by as I tried to line up for the slip. Up to this point, I had never seen any tourist boats. Now a new tour boat would pass every three minutes, disrupting my docking attempts.

I put my feet up after breakfast. It was still gray as we approached Clearwater, Florida, but the wind and waves were subsiding as Dean and I approached the end of the overnight passage from Carrabelle, Florida.

The turning basin was south of the north-south facing slip. A 15-knot northeast wind was blowing. In my experience, backing into the slip is the hardest with a strong wind blowing in the direction you want to back up. I would come from the east and try to turn around and back in, but I would get blown way off my intended target. Dean tried to convince me to go bow in, but I refused. After about 40 minutes of this, I tried approaching from the west in forward. This time the wind blew my bow so that I was in a good position to back up, and I had enough precision to line up the slip. I backed in and tossed a stern line to another boat owner who came by. The original set of gawkers had long gone, tiring of the spectacle. I had pre-tied and flaked the bow and stern lines on both sides prior to entering Clearwater Pass. Dean would just stand at the bow next to a piling and not wrap a line around it. I had to go forward to do the obvious. He later remarked he had only used docks in Canada. He had never been in a slip, which is different from a dock because it has pilings on the port and starboard. A dock only has pilings on one side. Dean was all abuzz, untying lines that I had tied and putting on new ones while muttering things about spring lines. I did not disturb him as we were safely in the slip. It was 1 PM on New Year's Eve, December 31, 2014, and was time to take Daly for a walk. Half the trip to the Bahamas was behind me, and I was happy.

16. THE HANGOVER

Clearwater Beach was really a break from everything that came before. The weather was warmer. For the first time in the trip, Daly and I were mostly moving south when we left Carrabelle. Tourists lined the streets with t-shirts, touting their home towns or the last beach they had visited. They were talking with all different regional accents. The public beach was just across the street from the marina, and several beach shops touted towels, sunblock, and new bathing suits. The skippers buzzed around their boats and were generally friendly. We met one skipper, Rod, who was sailing a big, white, 47-foot cutter called *Si Bella*. He said in his Texas drawl that his wife and he had faced 10-13 foot waves in the Gulf of Mexico, and he was bound for South America before the end of the season by way of the Bahamas.

Linus Wilson

I turned on my phone after removing it from its magic drying bag and it worked perfectly the rest of the day. It looked as if I could skip going to the Apple Store and losing more money on New Year's Day. We rested most of the day on New Year's Eve. We went out for drinks at a high rise hotel, but retired well before midnight. Only Daly's barking woke me to the fireworks going off at midnight. I rolled over and went back to sleep. I needed to rest up for 2015.

I was going to rent a car, but Dean found another sailboat owner who lent us the keys of his truck to work on repairing the solar panel mounts. On his first day in Carrabelle, he shook them side to side to demonstrate that they lacked some essential rigidness. I'm sure the retired shop teacher would have given me a "D" on the project. "We can't do anything about that now because there is no West Marine," I had said. "Let's just be gentle to them and we can think of strengthening them when we get to Clearwater." Now in Clearwater with the sea proving his prediction right, he was eager to work on it. $400 later we added supports to make the frame stiffer and screwed in the four elbows on top to the aluminum frames so they would not pop out so easily. The day reminded me of the weeks I spent with Tom, making improvements to Penelope and later Contango.

By the afternoon, Dean seemed to be overtaxing himself, especially with the tapping of screws over his head. I tried to encourage him to stop and take a break, but he pressed on stubbornly. Dean talked about he and his wife had a lot of health issues. He worried that they could not get the medical care they needed if they cruised outside of Canada with their 44-foot boat.

Dean was not the last sixty-something sailor with a big boat that I would meet who balked at foreign travel because of ongoing medical issues. In Marathon, I met a sailor on rugged, new 52-foot sailboat. He said they weren't going to the Bahamas because it was too hard to get the prescription medicines his wife needed. In Lin and Larry Pardey's 25th anniversary edition of *Cruising in Seraphin*, they wrote "Some people of 70 are more fit than people 30 years younger, but it is rare for a couple over 65 to be in perfect health." When I was in Clearwater beach, Lin and Larry Pardey were closer in age to the retired cruisers who are the norm, not the exception. That makes it easy to forget that this couple finished sailing around the world in Seraphin before either reached her or his 41st birthday.

I grew up in central Ohio and spent most of my school age years there. I was offered full tuition and room and board to attend Ohio State as an undergraduate and their Ph.D. program in Economics. I turned down both offers, but I have always religiously followed their football team. On New Year's Day, Ohio State's football team was in the first ever playoff semi-final with the best program of the last decade and probably of all time, the Alabama Crimson Tide. I promised Dean I that I would buy him dinner at a sports bar playing the game. Nevertheless, he was under no obligation to stay and watch it after dinner. The game was bound to go on after midnight because of a 9 PM kickoff, but no one scheduling the game seemed to care that I had been going to bed typically at that hour. I tried to get Dean to head back to the boat, but he stuck it out to the end. Ohio State did beat the number one team, but the game dragged on until 1 AM. My team eventually beat number 1 Alabama by a score of 42-35.

The net result was Dean and I were very tired when it was time to head out the next morning, January 2. On the previous day, I had doubled the dock lines so it would be easy to pull them aboard when it was time to leave. I started up the engine at 8AM and asked Dean to stand at the bow. Before I knew it, Dean had thrown off the working starboard bow lines that kept us from hitting the boat in the slip to port. When in a slip, half the lines are slack and half are working. The working lines if removed will free the boat to be blown by the wind. The slack lines if removed will have no effect on the boat in the short term. If you first remove the slack lines, you can react more quickly when the working lines are removed, but, if you remove the working lines first, then you have to remove the slack lines before you can put the boat into gear.

I yelled from the helm, "Why did you do that? I never told you to remove those lines. You never remove the working line first." I was shocked that he did not understand this basic principal of leaving the slip. In retrospect, his blunder occurred because he had never been in a slip. On a dock, as opposed to a slip, there was never one side (port or starboard) that was the slack side and another that was the working side. To leave the dock you have to untie the lines on the one side of the boat where the dock is. His boats were never tied up on both port and starboard.

"You never told me what to do," he protested. He was upset. I asked him to step aside while I fended off the boat on the port and retied the working starboard bow line. This was an easy undocking for me solo since my bow was pointed out of the slip and the wind on the starboard (the east) would push my bow in the direction I wanted to turn.

"OK, take off the port line on the beam and bring the line onboard. Next, take off the port bow line. I'll take off the port stern line," I called from the helm.

With those lines aboard, I said, "You need to quickly bring aboard the starboard bow line. I'll bring aboard the starboard stern line." I brought my line aboard, but he was slowly hauling the 100 foot line a foot at a time on board. He chose to pull on the short side of the dock line. Had he pulled on the long side of the dock line he would have had 10 feet instead of 90 feet on board. Alternatively, he could have used his hands to pull the doubled line over the piling. Another faster option than he chose would have been to take one half of the line the short side or the long side and take the whole flaked out mass behind the piling with his arms and back onboard. As it was, it would take him 5 minutes to complete the 10 second task while the stern drifted into the dock. I asked him to step aside and I pulled the line over the piling. I ran back to the stern and motored out saying, "I could have solo-sailed out easily."

Of course, that virtually ensured that was what I would be doing soon. I was having serious doubts about coastal cruising with Dean. Attempting the Okeechobee Waterway canals with him seemed even more risky. They would be much less forgiving with rising and falling water and potentially other boats in the lock be pushed by very powerful forces. He would tell my mother that he never had solo docked his boat. Perhaps his wife or buddies did all the line handling, and he was glued to the helm. I did not trust his skills at the helm enough to experiment with marina docking. He seemed to have little understanding about the influence of wind at slow speeds. That might have been because his boat's bow thrusters allowed him to move his bow much more precisely than I could ever hope to on a windy day.

I have had two complete sailing novices, my Dad and my sister-in-law Diana, aboard who knew enough to fend off when the boat drifted into another boat. They certainly took direction better than he did. I think it is often easier to have inexperienced crew because they are receptive to direction than an experienced sailor. Every boat is different. What works on one boat won't work on another, but many experienced sailors will be offended if they are told not to do what worked for them in the past. I think many skippers would say they select crew based 90 percent on attitude and 10 percent on experience.

I had planned to take the GIWW south from Clearwater, but the previous day I read that there were six swing bridges between Clearwater and Tampa Bay on the Intracoastal Waterway. That was bound to be slow and frustrating. Therefore, in 5-to-10 knot east winds and one-foot waves, we exited Clearwater pass and sailed in the Gulf of Mexico. It was a good motor sail without incident. Dean tried to contact his golfing buddy who lived near Venice, Florida, and my parents' new home, to no avail.

We entered the deep and wide Egmont Key Channel. I saw a large ship on the other side of Egmont Key. I left the marked channel in deep water and started altering my course. Dean said, "That boat is at anchor. I can't believe you are taking evasive maneuvers! I sail past huge container ships all the time on Lake Ontario," he said.

"Thanks for spotting that. You are right! It is always helpful to have an extra set of eyes," I replied. He was still fuming. I thought but did not say, "It is clear you are much more of a risk taker than I am.

We'll see if I go farther taking fewer risks with my small boat than you go taking big risks with your big boat."

I had wanted to anchor at Jewfish Key, an anchorage recommended by a charter company that I used a few years back. Unfortunately, we arrived their late in the day at 4 PM. Because it was a holiday weekend when Florida was packed with tourists, we found it full. I tried dropping the hook in a less crowded section, but the depths were much shallower than my charts indicated, and we were briefly aground. Desperate, I examined some orange and white floats that looked like crab pot floats, but I thought may have been mooring balls. (I did not have enough experience with mooring balls at this point to know they are much larger than crab pot floats in most cases and are usually white with a reflective blue stripe.) Having examined the size of the line attached to the float with the boat hook with Dean at the helm, I decided that even if it was a mooring ball, its line was too insubstantial to tie Contango to it. We motored off.

I was then scrambling to find a marina or anchorage we could reach before dark. I got a hold of one nearby marina, but it was clear we would only come in after sunset. Plus, the fee was $150. It seemed like a recipe for disaster. I then realized that the old wisdom "Never enter an unfamiliar harbor at night," did not apply to Sarasota Harbor or Marina Jack's slips. I arranged to get the most overpriced mooring ball that I would see on the trip. Marina Jack, where Janna and I had docked when we bareboat chartered 33 foot Hunter, ran the Sarasota mooring field. My parents just sold their house in Sarasota, and my charter had took me along this stretch of the GIWW.

I called up and reserved a ball for $45. Picking up a mooring is often low risk in an uncrowded mooring field. This overpriced mooring field was practically deserted. Dean did a great job driving us near the mooring and I picked it up and secured the boat relatively easily. Unfortunately, my boat hook got caught in some barnacles on the float and the momentum bent the retractable hook so that it could not close easily.

Slow Boat to the Bahamas

Dean was disappointed that I would not deploy the dinghy. "It takes two hours to prep the dinghy and put on the outboard, and nearly as much time to bring it back on deck. We'll get into Venice early tomorrow and stop at a Marina," I said. His golfing buddy, who had not yet got back to him, lived near Venice anyways. I did not feel obligated to enter marinas after dark to make a grumpy crew member happy. If he wanted to jump ship that night, I would have gotten out the dinghy just to be done with him, but he was not ready to say he was leaving that night. On my delivery trip, we stopped at no marinas, after I went on board, even after all my clothes were soaked with bilge water that had flowed under the settee storage.

Dean had begun to accuse me of having no other applicants for the crew position and intimate that I would have never been able to cross without him. I thanked him for coming and I appreciated it. I reminded him that I had solo sailed from New Orleans to Carrabelle, and I could have set my alarm every 15 minutes overnight on the Carrabelle passage. Alternatively, I could have waited a few days until my Dad closed on his new house. Another option was that I could have hired a captain to join me on the passage.

The next day my love affair with the Intracoastal Waterway turned into a love/hate relationship tipping towards hate. The GIWW was teaming with boats that bore the name of one charter company or the other. In the narrow channels, there was very little I could do to stop a collision if one of these inexperienced tourists lost control or did something stupid. I hated going through the swing bridges. In particular, the Blackburn Point swing bridge looked about 25 feet across and had a very strong opposing current as we passed. On the way, Dean's friend finally agreed to meet him, and Dean said he would be leaving the boat.

We docked at the Crow's Nest Marina right next to the Venice Inlet. My parents were there when we docked as the current delayed our arrival. I asked Dean to not participate in the docking, and I backed in along the inside of a long dock, throwing my line to the attendant. Nevertheless, the boat was facing a dead end in a narrow turning basin. Dean chatted with my Mom ashore while my Dad and I worked the lines. We used a long line on the port bow cleat to flip the direction of the bow so that the boat would be tied up on the port side instead of the starboard side. Thus, the bow would face out of the marina instead of into the marina. After that we unloaded Dean's gear and drove him to his friend's gated subdivision near the I-75 freeway. His friend was not at home, but we dropped Dean at the clubhouse for the golf club where he said his friend would catch up with him. I thanked him for coming and kept the invitation for him to come back aboard open. Privately, I told my Mom there was a 95 percent chance he would not come back.

17. THE KEYS TO THE BAHAMAS

I was impressed by my parents' new house. It was within walking distance of a big park, restaurants, the beach, and shopping. They were consumed with their renovations. I asked that they drop me off early so that I could get an early start south the next morning. I talked to a cruiser from Kentucky in a trawler next to me. He said one of his favorite places was Marathon, Florida in the Keys.

That gave me an idea. I could sail under the Seven Mile Bridge by Marathon and bypass Key West, giving me a faster route to the Bahamas from the Florida Keys. My Dad was willing to take off a week of work to go through the Okeechobee Waterway canals, but the last stretch of the GIWW showed me that I preferred the more open waters of the Gulf of Mexico to crowded narrow channels. Most of my sailing experience was in the wide open and often deserted Lake Pontchartrain and Mississippi Sound not the pleasure boat heavy and narrow ICW on the east and west coasts of Florida. In such canals I had no time to route plan or do much of anything. It was draining without a ton of crew. For the last two days, Dean was on strike most of the time.

Slow Boat to the Bahamas

I switched the anchors. I anticipated anchoring in the Pine Island Sound, and I wanted the 22 pound claw to be on the anchor chain and rode I could deploy. I had lost faith in the Danforth and put it on the Maxwell 800 windlass side, which I could not deploy because that windlass would not let go of the chain quickly enough. Overnight my carbon monoxide alarms went off. I think the boat from Kentucky or another neighbor nearly killed me, running their generator in a marina for reasons I could not divine. I walked Contango to the very end of the dock to get as far away from the other boats and fumes. I waited for the CO2 readings to go down. My CO2 alarms had never gone off when I ran the Honda. I had always turned it off when my sensors read anything.

I left at 7:30 AM with my parents looking on. (I hate audiences, but it went OK.) Also, they brought me a McDonalds breakfast sandwich that I saved for later, homemade pizza, and oatmeal cookies. I was done with the Christmas Turkey so the home cooking was appreciated. The Venice Inlet posed no problems and was much deeper than charted so I planned to use it on the way back. It was a pleasant day with southeast winds of 5-to-10 knots. I unfurled the genoa part of the day.

A small boat with two 300 horsepower outboards seemed to be adrift then seemed to follow me along the coast as I came out of Venice. It would not respond to hails. Finally, it motored off in the other direction after I said my GPS position as part of my hail. It probably was a small fishing boat.

Dean made it official with a short text saying that he would not be joining me in a few days down the coast. I was relieved, and, by this time, I was in full route-planning mode for a Marathon trip. I texted him to tell him I was in Marathon after I arrived. I never got a response. If he can't forgive his father 50 years after some slight, I suspect there is little hope that he'll forgive me.

My calculations indicated that I could cut out a week of travel. Further, my Dad would not have to miss a week of work to handle

Linus Wilson

lines with me. In addition, I paid over $2 per foot in Venice to go to the marina. It was likely that I would pay over $3 per foot on the east coast. While the GIWW ends in Ft. Myers, Florida, Naples and Marco Island are easy jumps down the coast with lots of facilities for boaters. Thus, a trip to Marathon would most naturally go from Marco Island to Marathon, not Ft. Myers to Marathon. South of Marco Island is the Florida Everglades swamp. There is little in the way of people there or facilities. The ports are shallow and running aground is a big risk. Further, there will be a lot of mosquitoes if I attempt to anchor in the swamp. I wanted to stay in deep water and avoid the Everglades.

Sailing from Marco Island to Marathon is about the same distance as sailing from Marco Island to Key West. This is because you have a kink in your course on the way to Marathon in order to stay well offshore of the shifting sands of the Cape Romano and Cape Sable shoals around the Everglades. The benefit is that you sail in slightly shallower water (30 feet instead of 50 feet) closer to shore. Moreover, Marathon is over 50 miles closer to a reasonable jumping off point to the Bahamas.

The Island Packet Facebook group moderator Hayden Cochran posted a pdf file guide that he made of route planning to the Bahamas. I downloaded it and asked him questions about things that worried me about crossing from the Keys. In particular, I worried that the Atlantic side of the Florida Keys were in the Gulf Stream. He got back to me very quickly assuring me that they were not. The Hawk Channel, which is favored by sailboats for its greater depths, wider waters, and lack of bridges, was separated by a reef from the Gulf Stream. Most boaters are very careful about entering the Gulf Stream because it can create huge disorganized waves when a strong North wind blows. The Gulf Steam is an ocean current which runs two-to-three knots northward. It separates the U.S. from the Bahamas.

With that last objection to the Florida Keys route to the Bahamas overcome, I was convinced that sailing overnight to Marathon was the best way to go. Over 20 knot winds were forecast for as early as Wednesday night. If I could reach Marathon on Wednesday morning, January 6, I could have small seas and light winds.

Slow Boat to the Bahamas

Sailing to the Keys meant it made more sense to cross to Bimini in the Bahamas instead of Grand Bahama, West End. My plan to enter from the West End on Grand Bahamas was predicated on the idea that I would take the Okeechobee Waterway to Stuart and then go south along the east coast until I was south enough that I would not be fighting the north moving Gulf Stream. In contrast, if I came from the Florida Keys south of the Florida mainland I would not need to go so far north. Bimini was the closest large port in the Bahamas to the Florida mainland. (The anchorage of Gun Cay near North Cat Cay is a few miles closer to the U.S. than the larger settlement of North and South Bimini.)

My decision to avoid the Intracoastal Waterway was confirmed by all the boats that I encountered on the Pine Island Sound and the mouth of Charlotte Harbor when I left the nearly deserted, but pleasant, Gulf of Mexico. The first recommended anchorage had a tricky entrance. Nevertheless, it had many masts poking out above the pines. I passed that one up. When I came up on the anchorage at Useppa Island across from Cabbage Key, it was deserted. I dropped the hook in 11 feet of water. Two other sailboats dropped the hook, but we had plenty of room and calm water all night.

I liked the northern part of the sound. When I cruised east north of Sanibel Island towards mile zero of the GIWW, the cruise was marred by a long narrow channel with shallows on either side with strong currents. This stretch was referred to by the cruising guide as the "Miserable Mile." A moniker that is well deserved. I stopped at Naples because I thought it would be easier to get diesel there and then continue on to Marco before sunset. This was a mistake.

The marina that seemed easy to access from the chart turned out to have a fuel dock that was in the depths of the marina and not visible from the private entrance channel. I decided to turn around after sailing into the channel. However, its twenty-foot width channel was too small to turn around in. Thus, I tried to back out.

Linus Wilson

Despite there being "NO WAKE" signs everywhere, small skiffs with at least 150 horsepower on the back of them would kick up three feet of water in a regular procession. The Naples Police boats would cruise around, ignoring these displays. Naples is where old CEOs live out their retirement years in frustration because they have so few people to boss around. What is a 6'6", Viagra-popping, septuagenarian to do but take out his frustrations by running his two 150 horsepower outboards at full throttle in the canals that form the water world of Naples, Florida!

These continuous wakes would cause me to drift in the shallows and scrape bottom. A half hour later, I won Contango's freedom. Unfortunately, the next fuel dock was a further four miles up the channel away from the Gulf of Mexico outlet. I had to circle this easier access fuel dock four times before the traffic and squally winds would let me in. I found a side of the dock where the northeast wind pushed the boat into the dock and tied up. An irate gas pump guy came out. "Is your boat disabled? You can't stay here overnight. You will have to dock again to get closer to the pumps." The pumps were four feet away.

I replied, "I have no intention of staying here. I just want diesel and water. Just take this stern line and walk it to the pump," I said. He took it begrudgingly.

"You can't dock here overnight," he accused.

"No problem," I said. "This is a fuel dock, and I stopped only for fuel."

He went off to pump 200 gallons of gas into a powerboat scowling as I tied up Contango.

I went to pay for my 14.5 gallons of diesel. "Don't you touch my dock lines as I'm leaving," I warned the attendant. "This is a sailboat. It is not as maneuverable as a powerboat with an outboard. If you untie or even touch my dock lines, I will pursue criminal and civil complaints, suing you and your marina for damages." I left no tip. I gave Daly a three minute walk and threw out my trash, while the crazy fuel guy fumed. I filled the tanks with water and motored off. This would be the last fuel dock Contango was tied up to on the entire trip.

By this time the sun was setting, making it to Marco Island before dark was not possible. It was only seven miles down the Gulf. Thus, anchoring at Naples would only add an extra hour-and-a-half to the trip. Moreover, leaving straight for Marathon right away was a bad idea, because I would probably reach that unfamiliar port before sunrise. The canals around the mansions in Naples make for 360-degree protected anchorages. I choose one of the bigger intersections near the entrance and exit canal and waited until 9 PM the earliest I could leave without risking a night entrance into Marathon based on my calculations. I anchored in six feet of water and had no trouble passing the charted four-foot depths by buoy 13 to get in and out of the anchorage, but that may have been due to the tidal stages being relatively high.

It was very dark when I exited the anchorage. Night sailing in a buoyed channel, I learned from the delivery trip, in which we ran the boat through the ICW all night long is best done if a light is shined on each one of the day marks or nun and can buoys. The shorter nun and can buoys are the hardest to find because they are so low in the water. That is the easiest when you have at least two crew members on watch. You want one at the bow with a light and one at the helm. When Janna and I did our night sailing certification, American Sailing Association 106, Advanced Coastal Cruising, all the lighted buoys in St. Vincent and the Grenadines, were burned out or sunk. Thus, we totally relied on the chart plotter. We were in a wide channel entering a wide bay. Therefore, identifying the buoys did not matter.

Unfortunately, in Naples or the ICW, you want to identify all the buoys so you don't hit them or stray from the channel. I was able to find buoys 13 and 12, as I came out of the anchorage with my headlamp. The light shone on 10, 9, and 8. I motored on and then slowly with red buoy 6 flashing in the distance. I shined the lamp on 7, marking my turn from south to west. I searched for the 5, and it quickly came into view to the starboard. I felt the 2 foot swells coming in opposing the east tailwind. You could not react to what was coming except by feel. I aimed the autopilot between the flashing red to port and green to starboard. When on top of them, I aimed the headlamp on them and their reflective numbers sparkled. The swells subsided as Contango cleared 1 and 2 flashing beacons, the green and red beacons, respectively.

My sailing plan had me sailing more or less due south until I passed latitude 25 degrees 40 minutes north. That would keep me offshore to avoid the dangerous Cape Romano shoals. The light winds were not so light—10-to-20 knots. My spreader flag rope, which was pretty flimsy, broke in the breeze, stranding the yacht club burgee up high. It was held by a single eye. I thought that I may have to get out the Mastclimber to recover it, but I would postpone that for a calm anchorage or a marina slip. The spreader flag halyard would become more important when I entered the Bahamas because that is where the yellow quarantine and courtesy flags are hung.

After Marco Island's lights dimmed into the distance, I started taking fifteen minute cat naps setting my alarms ahead. I used the leeward settee with a sheet and two pillows on it. Between 1 and 2 AM, I spotted a white light abeam moving astern near the Cape Romano Shoals to my east. It could have been the light marking the southernmost shoals. By 2 AM, I had turned towards Marathon. I napped most of the time, just waking up to look all around for any light. Then, having checked the heading and progress, I would reset my alarm and curl up with Daly. It was not until 5:19 AM that I woke to see another light. I was up from then on more or less. I was 20 miles west of Cape Sable when I rounded it around 6 AM. I spotted several small commercial fishing boats in this area as dawn started piercing the darkness at 6:20 AM. The winds started moderating to 10 to 15 knots from the north and I let out the 3rd and 2nd reefs.

With the sun, brought the views of crab pots way offshore, which made some in the Facebook Island Packet forum say I should avoid Florida Bay north of Marathon. If I refused to sail in waters with crab pots, I would never leave the slip in Lake Pontchartrain. I showered and shaved. Shaving was a breeze with the small waves. Showering proved more difficult. I had to steady myself with one hand and hold the soap with the other. The shower head would spray away from me into the head sink from its high perch with each wave. I needed three hands! The lowest point in the head was on the port, but the shower sump drain was on the starboard side of the head. After drying off, I turned the boat 180 degrees to get the shower to drain into the sump.

18. STUCK IN MARATHON

Entering the Seven Mile Bridge approach, you have to pick your way via GPS through the shoals and crab pots. I passed under the bridge and I saw that the entrance channel to Boot Key Harbor had a line of boats going in and none going out. I naively believed that I could pick up a $22 mooring ball in Boot Key harbor. I did not reserve it ahead because the guide correctly said you had to hail the municipal marina when you entered the harbor. Marathon is a city not a Key, the Florida term for most of its islands. Outside of Key Largo and Key West, it is the biggest town in the Florida Keys that are connected to the mainland by the celebrated Highway 1. Marathon is made up of Vaca Key on the north and Boot Key on the south. A scratchy connection said on the VHF that there was a wait list of over 20 people for a mooring ball. Moreover, you could not get on the wait list over the phone. You had to appear in the marina office in person to get on the wait list.

The eccentricity of Marathon's process, not talking over the phone of the mooring situation, meant boats come into Marathon completely unprepared and desperate to find a berth. This is good for overpriced marinas in Marathon, but bad for unsuspecting boaters. I let Contango drift in the deep water before the channel before calling Burdines Marina about a slip. They charged about $3 a foot. Ouch! I would be paying nearly $100 a night.   I planned to go to one of the Yanmar dealers to get oil filters so I did not feel like passing up Marathon.   Burdines was close to those Yanmar dealers and West Marine. The boat yard with the filters would not provide dockage.

With the prospect of the $100 per night charges, I thought I should cruise around the harbor, call other marinas, and think about anchoring. Mostly, I started this ill-fated tour of Boot Key Harbor because I chickened out from docking at Burdines because of the narrowness of turning basin for Burdines' slips. I was multitasking— driving, looking at the cruising guide, calling, and looking at my Navionics app. With 200-plus boats in the harbor packed like sardines, multitasking and steering was tough. I passed the "anchoring area." It had a dozen boats with a scope of 1-to-1, instead of the recommended scope of 5-to-1 for all chain and 7-to-1 for rode. In short, it was an underwriter's nightmare.

I tried turning around in the middle of the mooring field, but this proved impossible. Finally, I saw open water and I made for it. I wanted to try the south channel out of Boot Key Harbor, Sister Creek. Then, suddenly, I was anchored by my keel as my speed dropped from two-knots to zero. I had ran into the two foot deep water, because I was looking at the depths in Sister Creek instead of verifying the depths right in front of me were enough to pass over. At least I got to rest! I was unlikely to drag in this anchorage!

I had Janna call Tow Boat US.   Within 10 minutes a twentysomething with dreadlocks and a long beard came alongside in his 8 foot long fiberglass dinghy and patchwork one horse power outboard. "It looks like you ran aground on the sandbar. Do you want a tow?" he offered.

I was just enjoying my contemplative perch before he interrupted. I sat up and said, "Sure, if it is a *free* tow. I was told it would be an hour before the tow boat came out."

"Sure! No charge. Just trying to help a fellow boater." He tied on his ¼ inch tow line to the bow and the tiny boat and motor pulled until the line was taught. There was no movement. He could not

Slow Boat to the Bahamas

budge the boat. He gave up and added before departing, "You should get a $1,000 fine for disturbing the sea grass." Where did that come from? All I saw under my keel was sand, but I let my dreadlocked savior have the last word.

Tow Boat US's representative arrived 45 minutes later. He easily towed me off after carefully scouting the depths around me. I signed the boat paperwork while underway, trying to dodge incoming boats. Then, I handed it back to the Tow Boat US skipper with both our boats making 2.5 knots. I had not learned my multitasking lesson, and called Burdines to verify that I still had a slip. They did, and they explained my slip was in the middle of the east row of slips.

The docking was uneventful because Burdines had almost no wind despite the 15 knot breeze blowing into the harbor. I backed right into the slip as if I knew what I was doing. All the fending that was needed was my neighbor had to poke port stern of my boat so that I avoided his big set of dinghy davits hanging far outside of the outermost piling.

A lot of people got stuck in Marathon, and it wasn't because of the sand bar in the middle of the harbor. Marathon had a lot of live aboard sailors as well as cruisers. The waitress and the ice cream shop lady would talk about their sailboats. The net was introduced by some guy who said he came there for a weekend twelve years prior.

My 31-foot boat was pretty small in Marathon. Most sailboats were 40 to 50 feet long. At $300 per month, the mooring balls in Marathon were a lot less expensive than such big boats could get being tied up to a dock. Marathon was this water world of greatly patched dinghies and hippies both young and old. The suburbanite amenities of Publix supermarket, Office Max, Home Depot, and the AT&T store were all within walking distance of the dinghy dock. The 360-degree protection of Boot Key Harbor was another inducement.

The library, TV, internet, sail makers, and boat builder's workshop in the municipal marina helped too. It was as if the cruisers and live aboard sailors were in charge. For once, there was a marina unconcerned with catering to the sport fishing boats. The cruising sailboat was king in Boot Key harbor.

I was not stuck there after I got the tow. I was paying $300 every three days instead of every thirty like most boats. I had somewhere to go, the Bahamas. When the 25-plus knots sustained winds would go, so would I. The corrupting influence of cheap mooring balls had not turned my cruising boat into a floating condo. To me, Marathon, for all its virtues, was a place where cruising dreams came to die into a suburban normalcy, albeit with a tropical backdrop.

The next day, I used Facebook messenger to meet Hayden Cochran and his wife Radeen after he posted that he was in Marathon. He and his wife had a slip a couple hundred yards from Contango on the other side of Highway 1. He met me out on the highway, thinking I was lost instead of just running a little late. Hayden's slip was exposed to the coming North blow, but they entertained me for an hour. Radeen and Hayden were so nice. They kept their 35-foot Island Packet in pristine condition. Where a layer of grime covered Contango and the varnish flaked off, their seventh coat of varnish was smooth enough for me to check my stubble. No bit of clutter disturbed their cabin or cockpit.

I asked them about crossing the Gulf Stream. Hayden recommended leaving from No Name Harbor from Key Biscane near Miami. I objected that that was too far north and I would be turned much into north setting Gulf Stream. I thought that what worked for Hayden's 35-foot boat may not work as well for my smaller 31-foot boat because boat speed increases with length. In retrospect, I think he was correct that that was the quickest and best crossing location to Bimini. "You owe it to yourself to spend a month in Miami anyways," He said. "Miami is one of my favorite places. You can anchor in the canals and dinghy to Miami Beach. My ideal type of cruising is where you can anchor for free and land your dinghy for free on a public beach." At the time, I thought that going north to Miami would just divert me from the trip to the Bahamas. Since this was a six month sabbatical versus a retirement cruise, I thought I had to choose Miami or the Bahamas. Nevertheless, that was a pretty good endorsement which I would remember.

"I want to cross from no higher than Key Largo," I stated. Radeen suggested that mid-Key Largo would not be good. Her quick calculation showed that anchoring off Rodriguez Key just east of Key Largo would give me a trip of nearly 80 miles and was too far south. "Another popular departure point is anchoring off Pumpkin Key. Boats then access the Atlantic from Angelfish Creek," she said. The Angelfish Creek mouth departure point made sense to me at about 25 miles south and 50 miles east of Bimini. That was a rough ratio matching the average 2.5 knot current of the Gulf Stream and my boats safe pace of 5 knots.

Fresh off running aground, I said, "I'm a little afraid of the Bahamas. In the Gulf Coast, we have a lot of mud sometimes sand, but seldom rock or reefs. How do you avoid reefs?"

They replied that you needed to follow the charted waypoints very carefully. "I'm a bit worried that I'll have limited access to weather reports after I leave the U.S. I rely a lot on the national weather service's marine forecasts," I said.

"We use Windfinder for wind, passageweather.com for waves, and Chris Parker for weather routing. His e-mail service is very reasonable if you don't have a SSB," replied Radeen. I used the former, but had not used the latter two. I signed up for three months of daily Bahamas and Gulf Stream crossing e-mails for $95 from Chris Parker, an independent meteorologist. I also started using an app downloading GRIB files which show wind speed and direction forecasts.

Hayden added, "To cross the Gulf Stream, you are looking for a front that disrupts the northeast trades, and hopefully gives you south or west winds."

In addition to all the good advice, they gave me a small wetsuit which fit neither one of them, but looked like it would fit my 5'3" wife Janna. They invited me to a potluck a few days hence, but I said, "I probably will leave by then. I don't have the budget to pay Burdines $3,000 a month."

"You have to wait a day after the blow for the waves to settle down," Hayden cautioned. The north winds were already starting to pick up. The north-facing marina, unlike mine, was very exposed to the blow. I felt bad about delaying Hayden and Radeen from any preparations they wanted to make. I would not wait. While the high winds blew, I refilled my diesel and water tanks and provisioned at the nearby Publix grocery store.

The first day that I landed in Marathon, I met a cruiser while getting on the waitlist at the municipal marina, who was filling a bladder tank with the marina's freshwater hose. I asked him about it, and he said it that it was better than lugging five gallon water jugs. Five gallons of water weighs 42 pounds, which is heavier than my heaviest anchor, the 33-pound plow. Lifting 42 pounds from a pitching dinghy onto a pitching boat is a recipe for back problems. Water is much heavier than diesel, and, with Janna aboard in the Bahamas, water would go a lot faster than fuel. We could go through ten gallons of water per day. I started working on gathering the supplies for his bladder tank system. I ordered a 32-gallon tank which would fit in but not overload my 600 pound capacity roll-up inflatable dinghy. Since once full, the bladder tank would far too heavy to carry, 267 pounds, I also needed a pump to pump it. I ordered the bladder tank online from West Marine and overnighted it to Burdines since the Marathon West Marine did not have that tank in stock. I bought a wash down pump and garden hose adapters for it at the local West Marine.

I needed to get a certificate from a U.S. vet verifying that Daly was healthy and up-to-date on his rabies vaccine. The regulations I read indicated that this statement had to be filled out 48 hours before arrival in the Bahamas. This was almost impossible given the difficulties of getting the dog to the veterinarian and the uncertainty about Gulf Stream crossing weather windows. Janna thought it was more important that I get a certificate signed than getting it dated 48 hours before arrival. She encouraged me to get one while I was waiting for the weather to pass.

I asked the closest vet over the phone if they could fill out the form, but leave the date blank. Their scheduler said that was impossible. Instead, I got an appointment with a vet 5 miles away, and did not discuss the issue of not dating the form. Daly was in his beloved Sherpa bag while I peddled my tiny fold-up bike with 16 inch wheels, smaller wheels than most kindergarteners' bikes. I had trained Daly to get in his Sherpa bag, dog carrier duffle bag, for a treat. He can spend hours in it without barking. It's a home away from home for him. We got to the vet and she filled out the form, but she dated it January 8, 2015, that day's date. She refused to leave the date blank. Oh well!

I started pedaling back but a tire was low. I pumped it and the whole tube burst. Now I was peddling with 4.5 miles to go and a completely flat tire. I peddled a little while until I came on the airport where I thought a bus would run. The "bus" was a taxi service. As it turned out, the cab was only $6, and I had him drop us off at West Marine because I needed more log books, charts, and a water jerry can. I peddled home on my clown bike with packages and dog. I was only lacking my dignity. The water bladder tank was waiting for me at the marina. I was ready to sail northeast towards Key Largo the next day.

19. HAVING A BALL IN KEY LARGO

I cast off before 7:30 AM unsure of a destination except northeast up the Hawk Channel. A small craft caution was in effect, but any breeze approaching 15 knots, ideal sailing, is given a caution rating by the national weather service. Of course, since I was in the trade wind belt, where easterlies of 15-to-20 knots were the norm, I would have to wait a lot if I waited for westerlies or calms to proceed east to my crossing point at Key Largo. I bucked the east winds. At least they only averaged 10 knots, and I made decent progress motoring into the seas in the Hawk Channel.

Linus Wilson

Having missed out on the mooring in Marathon, I used internet searches to research more about mooring balls. I discovered that NOAA dive buoys are free. Most are located on the Atlantic sides of reefs, but a few are closer to the Keys. The Hen and Chickens reef buoys was one example. I discovered in my Google searches that there were three free buoys at Indian Key, which could provide some shelter to the east wind.

Before getting out of radio contact with Marathon, I asked for advice on entering the John Pennekamp Coral Reef State Park in Key Largo. The cruising guide said it was a tricky entrance. More worrisome, the mooring balls charted depths were five feet. Instead of mud or sand under your keel, there would be a boat-crunching coral reef. The moderator responded to my question after the net on another channel. He said the depths were indeed five feet, and his deeper draft sailboat had been fine. He warned that the entrance was narrow, and *securite* calls on the VHF were necessary to warn other boats transiting the canals of your presence. I had hoped to make John Pennekamp, but it was looking like I would be transiting the long and tricky entrance at dusk. It was definitely a place I did not want to enter at night.

Instead of pressing on, I picked up the most protected buoy at Indian Key. This time I used my new "heavy duty" boat hook, and all went well. I was the only boat to pick up a mooring.

A small, fast fishing boat eyed me on the mooring or perhaps the crab pots near my mooring. The grandfather seemed to be taking his grandchildren for a ride. He picked up another ball slightly farther from shore. However, in five minutes, they left. I'm not sure why on such a small boat that he did not just tie up at the Indian Key dock a few hundred feet away. There were some ruins that I was missing out on shore, but I was not energetic enough to deploy my dinghy for the first time that day.

I fixed the spreader flag halyard while there by taping two clothes pins to my super-long when-extended boat hook. The clothespins caught the frayed yacht club burgee. I pulled it down and taped and sewed the new bright orange 550-pound paracord to the frayed line and ran it through. I was ready to hoist my Q flag in Bimini when I got my weather window.

Chris Parker's e-mail emphasized the risk of squalls on Monday, January 12, if I departed in a few days as I had been thinking about. He seemed to indicate that I would have much better weather if I waited a few days longer.

Janna had booked her and Sophie's plane tickets into Nassau, Bahamas on February 1. About half the population of the Bahamas lives in New Providence Island, where the capital of Nassau is located. That was by far the least expensive flight and easiest way to join me since flying into Nassau had the fewest connections. Nassau was only two days sail from Bimini. Thus, I did not have to worry yet about them arriving in Nassau before me. I could be choosy about my weather window.

Overnight, the winds picked up to about 15 knots and started the howling that would fill my ears for several more days. Nevertheless, the boat's motion was OK since I was in the lee of Indian Key. There was a small craft advisory with the 15-20 knot winds from the northeast, but I pounded through the 3 foot swells to John Pennekamp State Park in the Largo Sound. I toyed with the idea of a fifty-mile day to Miami, but not in these headwinds and seas, which took 1.5 knots from my speed-over-ground. A shorter day was welcome, and besides I was now within a few hours sail of Angelfish Creek, my southwestern waypoint for the Gulf Stream crossing. I mused that the delivery skipper's comment about "We always staying longer in the Keys than we plan for" might have had to do with the trade winds. If you go to Key West, you have to buck the northeast trade winds for 150 miles to get back to the mainland. In that sense, my coming into Marathon saved more time than I first anticipated relative to sailing to Key West.

I cancelled my satellite TV subscription for my residence back in Lafayette that day, ducking in the cabin for better sound quality. It was really the only bill we escaped when we were gone, and the cruise created a lot more. It's expensive and cumbersome cruising and maintaining a house at the same time.

I came into the entrance canal's buoy 3 as a huge tourist boat operated by the park rounded the corner. I turned around and did circles waiting for it to exit. It was far too big to share the channel with. After coming into the channel, I transited the South Sound Creek bordered by mangroves. Thankfully, I only saw small recreational fishing boats as I looked for brown water. The water here was clear enough to read. The entrance to the moorings on the northwest side of the Largo sound was not really marked, and I just tried to pass over the five foot charted depths with a close eye on the depth sounder. These moorings were only slightly more popular than those at Indian Key. There were two with small, old trawlers on them. Mine would be the only sailboat. I did not find that to be a particularly good sign with respect to the depths in the mooring field. I picked up a mooring after several attempts as the wind and my distance from the bow often kept me from getting close to my target. At least I had plenty of room to miss in the mostly vacant mooring field. No other boats would join us for the rest of my stay. While the Largo Sound has 360-degree protection from the winds, I found it too long to get rid of the chop. The location of the mooring field also was not helpful because it was the most exposed to the prevailing easterlies.

I changed the oil and filter with the new vacuum pump, with an eye to the upcoming crossing. I had stocked up on filters in Marathon. The most valuable thing about the dipstick vacuum pump was the directions that indicated that you must mark the length of the dipstick so you know exactly how far to lower the skinny, dipstick hose. Lowering the hose no more than 2-3 inches more than the length of the dipstick, I could hear when the hose started sucking long before I saw the black fluid rising through the clear hose.

That task done, I hoisted and splashed down the inflatable dinghy for the first time in the trip. I carried the 25 pound Honda 2 HP and loaded other gear so that I could check in and pay the dive office. Leaving Daly on board, I got dinner at a sports bar across the street from the park. I got some more hose attachments for my water bladder system at the Ace Hardware across the street. Then, I bought a new tire and tubes at a pawn shop next door to the hardware store. The dinghy ride back in the dark was pretty frightening in the two-foot chop of the Largo Sound. Unfortunately, the tubes and tires for my fold up bike were the wrong size. Daly was happy to see me though, and we had a bumpy night in Largo Sound.

Contango on a mooring ball in the Largo Sound.

It was Sunday and the pawn shop and Ace hardware were closed. I wanted to exchange the tubes and tires, and create a screen. At Home Depot in Marathon I had purchased screen but it would not work with the snaps that Dean had suggested. I wanted some thin wood with which I could staple the frame of a screen. Daly got a walk that day and rode in the dinghy in his Sherpa bag. After dropping off Daly, I walked over a mile to West Marine, and got the last bit of adapters for my water bladder system. I filled the bladder with hose water, attached the alligator clips on the pump to battery four under the v-berth, attached one end of the hose to the pump and the other to the bladder tank. I had used 20 gallons since Marathon. I kept the remainder and used it to top off the tank after that night's shower.

I met Roger and Mary that day at John Pennekamp's marina. If you don't like the moorings, you can tie up at the marina. Roger was an engaging Canadian eager to share Gulf Stream crossing gossip. They had a well-maintained Albin 27 and he dreamed of seeing the Bahamas on their great loop cruise. I mentioned Chris Parker's views. One surprising thing was that the meteorologist thought light north winds constituted good crossing weather. Roger and I thought you would never cross the Gulf Stream with even a breath of north wind.

The John Pennecamp mooring field is about half a mile from the dinghy dock if you go under the "No Motorized Vessel" bridge by the kayak rentals. It is a mile if you don't violate the convention. My two horsepower Honda cannot actually outrun a kayak if the kayaker is using his or her paddles. Nevertheless, the dirty looks from the kayak rental guys convinced me to take the long route to the dinghy dock and showers during opening hours.

In the morning, I found that one of my dinghy oars had fallen off overnight. The dinghy oars on this West Marine dinghy just clipped in and the slightest pressure would push them out of their plastic oar locks. I should have brought them onboard overnight. I scanned the mangrove line downwind until I could make out an unusual white straight object. I did not motor straight to it but went along the coastline from east to west approaching it. Each bit of foam dashed my hopes, but where I saw the white line the oar was floating in the shallows.

The weather reports indicated that the early morning hours and early afternoon of Wednesday January 14, would make for the best crossing weather in the foreseeable future. I needed to do my laundry, get more groceries, refill the diesel tank, get more diesel oil, and exchange my bike tires. There was no diesel, groceries, or coin laundry within walking distance. Moreover, the only place open late enough to see my team in the national championship game was miles away. I had to do all that day, January 12, 2015, so that I could anchor or pick up a NOAA mooring near my Angelfish Cut waypoint, which was several miles north. I had to leave the park at daylight on Tuesday, January 13, because it would be too dangerous to leave the unlighted mangrove canal at night.

The prospect of the Bahamas looming made me dash to enjoy my last bit of suburbia. We all know that to live the suburban lifestyle to the fullest, or survive, you need a car. Therefore, I rented one more car, in the morning.

I first went to the pawn shop to exchange my tubes and tire. The owner was a man with many guns for sale. He had poster of Osama Bin Ladin, the then-killed Al-Qaeda terrorist believed to be responsible for the destruction of the twin towers in New York City. Osama Bin Ladin in the picture said "Impeach Obama." The pawn shop owner was about 5'8" 320 pounds with a Hawaiian shirt with the top 3 buttons undone and gold chains peeking out from the forest of gray hairs. The large man started acting erratically when I tried to exchange the merchandise bought on Saturday. "That is pretty stupid buying the wrong size. The size is on the side of the tire," he responded. Then, he said, "I can exchange the tubes, but I cannot exchange the tire, because the tubes are on the same SKU but the tires are on different SKUs."

"OK, let's exchange the tubes," I responded and he took my tubes. I wasn't going to argue. He was obviously well armed and crazy.

"OK, I'll buy your 16" tire," I said.

"What are you going to do with that 12.5" tire?" he questioned slyly.

"I'll keep it," I said.

"What do you need with it? Give it to me!" he demanded.

"Why would I give you a tire that I paid for and have a receipt for, which you won't exchange or refund. This is a free country I can do what I want with this 12 inch tire, but I won't give it to you," I said.

Hands reaching under the counter he said, "Get out of my Goddamn store!"

I beat a hasty retreat with my new 16" tubes and 12" tire. I put the tire next to the trash in the park later on. A passerby picked up the obviously new tire. I bought a 16" tire at the bike shop next to West Marine. Roger and Mary were there renting bikes and declined a ride back, preferring to pedal on their temporary wheels. Roger said they did not plan to cross on Wednesday. They probably would head north. The Alabama couple next to Roger's boat were making their pre-departure preparations.

The skipper on the boat from Alabama was shopping for diesel engine oil too. Roger said, "The prices here are outrageous. I bet we could buy the oil for half price at Walmart."

"I don't know if there is a Walmart nearby, but I have rented a car. I know you can pick this up at one of the auto stores in Key Largo for much less. Roger declined but the man in the trawler from Alabama that I had met next to Roger's boat gave me $20 to pick up some for him. I offered him a ride, but he always looked at me with great fear as if he had been cornered by a wild eyed man in a strait jacket and a knife in his teeth. He made an excuse and said he and his wife would walk.

I got the oil 40 percent cheaper than at West Marine at an auto parts chain. I got groceries at Publix. Then, I reiterated my offer of a ride when I gave the trawler skipper the oil and his change, but said I had to unload my groceries. I wrapped the groceries in plastic bags. If it was not the sea spray, the showers were going to make everything wet. I got delayed with other things and it took three hours to get back, and the Alabama couple had left on foot without me according to Mary.

I took my laundry to the coin laundry. All the marine fuel docks closed at 5 PM, but the gas station next to the laundromat had diesel. I unloaded the laundry and fuel, filled the diesel tank, and took the dinghy back to watch the big game. My team, Ohio State won the national championship by a score of 42-20, beating the Oregon Ducks. The game was not close, but Ohio State turnovers gave Oregon hope. I got home after 1 AM.

It rained late into the night. Chris Parker was right about the squalls on Monday, which stretched into the early morning hours of Tuesday.

In the morning, I scouted the deep water in the dinghy by sight in the unusually glassy Largo Sound. I found that, instead of cutting to the channel straight from the mooring field, I should make an equilateral triangle. I should go to the south east end of the mooring field, make a sharp turn to the charted five foot depths, and make a sharp turn and backtrack to the 23 and 22 buoys. One of the powerboats left their mooring before me and followed a similar course.

I dropped off the car and Enterprise drove me back. When I tried to come back to Contango around the long motorized vehicle route, the outboard engine sputtered and died. I was sure I ran out of fuel, and I stupidly did not take extra because I had lashed it to the deck in anticipation of leaving. About 0.8 miles from the mooring field, I started canoe paddling to the dinghy dock and the kayak shortcut. The tourists gawked at the idiot in the dinghy sitting in the bow paddling with one oar when any reasonably coordinated person would have used two. "Perhaps the engine just stalled and I did not run out of gas," I thought. I looked in the tank and there seemed to be still plenty. It started right up with a pull of the cord. Throwing caution to the wind, I motored past the kayak dock and straight to Contango. After an hour or so of unloading the motor and hoisting and lashing the dinghy to the foredeck, I was off the mooring.

Linus Wilson

20. CROSSING THE GULF STREAM

The Albin 43 owned by the Alabama couple would overtake me in Hawk channel and turn into Angelfish Creek. That was the last that I would see of them.

I was headed for some NOAA mooring buoys on the Atlantic side called the North Patch. These were completely unprotected. I wore my life jacket with PLB and portable VHF strapped to it despite the extreme heat. After six failed approaches, I picked up the only white mooring ball I could see. There were several other buoys charted, but, evidentially, the others had succumbed to Poseidon's wrath. This was the worst motion I would experience anchored or moored during the entire trip as the boat bobbed side to side in the four foot swell. Finally at 6 PM, with my Scopolamine sea sickness patch on, I called it quits. There would be no way I could rest here. I threw off the mooring line and motored towards the shallower water next to Old Rhodes Key, which is just north of Key Largo and Angelfish Creek. I should have anchored by Pumpkin Key as Radeen suggested, but, in the dark, I anchored at 7 PM on the less protected Atlantic side in the ten foot depths. The motion was much better, and I got some sleep. I set my alarm for 11:00 PM.

There was no wind when I weighed anchor at midnight. I pulled the slack rode and chain in without the aid of the engine. If there was some current or wind, it might have steadied the boat more. As it was, I only had a fitful three hours of sleep. I found my second seasickness patch had fallen off and put it on again. The sky glowed in the direction of Miami as if dawn would break from the northwest at midnight. As I started moving I could make out two boats leaving Angelfish creek to the south. My starboard bow was facing their red port lights. The buddy boats were hailing on 16 and switching channels to chat.

One was much faster than the other, and I hailed it on the VHF.

"Wayward Sun, Wayward Sun, this is the sailing vessel Contango. Over," I said.

"Tango, this is Wayward Sun. Over," the man's voice replied.

"Can we switch to 17," I asked.

"Tango, this is Wayward Sun switching to 17," he replied.

"Contango switching to 17. Over," I said. On channel 17, I said. "Wayward Sun, what kind of vessels are you and Kavu? Where are you headed?" I asked.

"Tango, we are Lagoon catamarans, and we are headed for Bimini. Over," he replied.

"I have a 31 foot sailboat bound for Bimini, too. I'm going to slow down, and let you both pass. Contango out," I said.

"Wayward Sun, switching to 16. Over," he said.

We were following the same line between shallows into the Atlantic and the Gulf Stream. There was no reason to run into each other in the dark. I slowed down to four knots. The Lagoons were much bigger boats than my sailboat. Moreover, catamarans can move much faster than sailboats as a general rule. They oddly kept their 360 degree anchor lights on instead of their running lights which are only visible from the front. That misuse of running lights, ironically, made it easier for me to track them throughout the night. I would see their white or yellow stern lights running at the same time that I could see their anchor lights, indicating they were in front of me. Seeing their red lights with the anchor light meant they had fallen behind.

They took an odd course, which I believe was a navigational error. Instead of running straight for Bimini as I was, they first kept their course over ground at 90 degrees, due east, and curved north as they got closer. To move perpendicular to the north current, 0 degrees, one must turn into the current and steer say 120 degrees, slowing one's progress. Instead, you want to steer roughly 90 degrees, but make a course over ground of 60 degrees for example. That way, the Gulf Stream is speeding you to your destination. The whole point of leaving from Angelfish Creek was that you would let the North current speed your crossing not slow it. I was sure their skippers had confused the course-to-steer with the course-to-make, and their much faster boats lagged Contango for most of the trip. They had a curving course well south of me most of the trip, while I took a straight line north of them most of the trip. They only passed Contango after they turned almost due north right before we both reached the shallows of the Great Bahamas bank. They probably traveled over 70 miles once leaving Hawk Channel when Contango took a straight shot and only travelled 55 miles.

To run a straight line course, I had to steer a very different course than my GPS indicated that I was making over ground. When the current was weak, I set the autopilot on a course that was almost identical to my bearing towards my Bimini waypoint. Nevertheless, when the current strengthened I had to have the autopilot steer more eastward. Thus, in a weak current, the autopilot might be set at 60 degrees, east north east, but, as it strengthened, the autopilot would need to steer closer to 90 degrees, east. This is actually really simple to do with two waypoints programmed as a route in the chart plotter. Whenever the GPS says our course is deviating from our bearing to the next waypoint outside Bimini, I would make small adjustments on the autopilot. I would ignore the autopilot's numbers. The autopilot's course indicated the angle we were steering. That was only a gauge of how strong the current was. A higher degree on the autopilot in this case meant the current strengthened. A lower degree on the autopilot meant the current had weakened.

It was not until 1:18 AM that I noted any influence of the current as the depths hit 130 feet. I slightly altered from the breadcrumb trail as to not pass over Fish and Game Reef. At 1:30 AM, I could see the moon peeking out of the eastern sky. This indicated there were clouds ahead despite the very starry sky above. By 1:35 AM, I estimated that the Gulf Stream was decreasing the course made good by 15 degrees as Contango stuck to its bearing to Bimini. 80 degrees

Slow Boat to the Bahamas

on the autopilot made good 68 degrees on the GPS. The boat is making 6.5 knots over the ground at 2000 RPMs. There is no wind. The Gulf Stream is giving us 1.5 knots towards Bimini. I let out the second reef at 1:45 AM because the boat was bobbing around too much with just the third reef out.

After 2AM Kavu and Wayward Sun were chattering about at tug whose side lights I had noticed. They mistook it for a ship, and a posh English lady's voice on the VHF assured them that they were not seeing the ship Meteor. Kavu and Wayward Sun diverted when a large cruise ship passed pretty close to them. They were well south of me. Therefore, I did not need to alter course.

By 2:45 AM, I was in the fastest part of the stream, and, to maintain my 68 degree straight line course, the autopilot steered 90 degrees. Fifteen minutes later I spotted a ship off my starboard bow. I saw two white lights and one red. It was moving to my stern seemingly bound for Florida. At 3:20 AM I had to do several 360 degree turns when I came very close to a ship with many white lights. I was confused by a red light, which I thought must have signified its port bow. I flashed my lights on my main sail to get its attention and called on the VHF. The operator was shaken by our proximity after I flashed my sails, and the ship flashed a light at its mast. "We are west bound. Bound for Miami," the operator said. The red light was a stern light. I was steering into its bow by steering behind the white lights. I needed to steer behind its red light, and it would pass to the west.

After that close encounter, which made me very grateful to be running my engine with the genoa furled, I saw a flash of light in the northern sky and wondered if it was a squall. I took no cat naps this night. There was too much traffic. Through the night, I wore my light jacket, fishing shirt, pants, and offshore life jacket. Daly was content in his life jacket, snoozing on his brown bed.

At 5 AM, I thought I had better get our entry papers ready. I gathered Daly's various forms, the boats papers, and got my passport out of my briefcase. I'm not sure why I did not gather this while I was waiting for my weather windows in Marathon or Key Largo. For some reason, I thought I could do it on the Gulf Stream crossing where I would have little ability to gather missing documents. The passport that I got out of our safe during Christmas was not my passport. Rather, it was the passport of my daughter. That might make it hard to get through immigration!

By this time, I was too far committed to turn around. I would surely lose my weather window, and Contango would be pushed far north to Miami. I thought that I could just get it sent FedEx if I could not check in without it. By 5:30 AM, the air got colder, and the north wind picked up from 5 knots to 10 knots.

While tracking several light combinations, nature called. Since I was in the middle of the Atlantic, way offshore, I threw my biodegradable wad of toilet paper overboard. Poseidon immediately voiced his displeasure by setting off an engine alarm. The cooling water light went off. I shut down the engine. I unfurled the genoa. With this increasing northwest wind I had a nice beam reach and even with 100 percent genoa and 2nd reef main. We could maintain 4.5 to 5 knots easily. I turned on the engine again, and the charging light went on water seemed to come out the back initially, and then the cooling light and alarm went off.

I thought perhaps that I had to change the impeller. I took off the engine cover under the stairs and touched the cooling belt. It was very loose. I was looking to tighten it and then I noticed that the alternator belt had two diagonal slashes in it. I had to tighten it earlier in the trip from New Orleans because it was wearing out. That day in the deepest most dangerous waters of the trip many miles from Tow Boat US and the U.S.A. it broke. I toyed with the idea of notifying someone else of my predicament, but I thought that would only bring trouble. I was sailing fine, and what could another boat do anyways except worry others unnecessarily?

I had one spare alternator belt, and, having changed this belt before, I got out my socket wrench sets and went to work. I started the engine after installing the belt, and fortunately there were no lights.

Slow Boat to the Bahamas

By the time I cleaned up, the lazy swells of 1-to-2 feet had grown to 3-to-5 feet and were continuing to build with the North wind. White caps were showing. I was not yet falling off waves as I was between Carrabelle and Clearwater, but I soon would be. Chris Parker said that we should expect the Gulf Stream to start getting angry at around 10 AM to 12 PM in his last dispatch. It was 8 AM. The north wind had arrived early.

It was clear that the Gulf Stream was slowing down, and I was only 10 miles out from Bimini. One huge container ship's bearing seemed stubbornly constant and it seemed headed for my stern. I tried hailing the westbound container ship north of Bimini, but I got no response after many attempts. A female crewmember on one of the catamarans that I had hailed around midnight gave me the name of a boat that I was describing. Up until this point in the voyage, I had no need for AIS which gives the locations and names of ships. I was happy that one of the catamarans had it. With the ship's name, an eastern European-sounding man answered the hail and said, "Ceentango, vee vill alter course 2 degreez." When I asked for clarification the operator ignored me, but that seemed to do the trick, and the container ship's bearing kept changing and moved to my stern.

By this time, the 5 foot seas were making movement difficult. I furled in the genoa and went down to the third reef. I always tied up the main sail before going into port on this trip so that docking would be easier. This was the only time that I worried about being thrown off the boat despite my harness and firm grip on the boat. The main was tightly sheeted in. Nevertheless, the beam-on waves had me clinging to the main and bracing with my legs for minutes as I struggled to stay on the cabin top. I gave up, tying only one sail tie where I would usually tie three. If I hit my head while being thrown from the cabin top, my harness, my portable VHF, and personal locator beacon might not be enough to save me.

After many hails I got a hold of Bimini Blue Water Marina, and they promised to have a line handler ready. Sailboats were converging from all directions and the marinas could not keep up. The entrance channel was well marked. The water became shallow quickly as the deep blue of the Atlantic turned to turquoise in the entrance channel and tan in the sand bar north of the channel. I had never seen water so clear as the swells sluiced Contango, and the boat scooted into the harbor.

21. BIMINI BLUES

The marina office advised me to wait for the marina representative to direct me into a slip. I backed into a different empty slip than the one he suggested. "Can I stay here instead?" He shrugged, and I threw the marina representative my dock line. He walked me back. As it turned out, there was plenty of room in the harbor of North Bimini to turn around and tie up. Many boats chose to anchor despite Bimini having the least expensive dockage I had seen since Mississippi, $1 per foot. I tied up some lines, gave the office my credit card, and boat details. They handed me the arrival paperwork. I napped until 1:30 PM, thinking there is no hurry to see customs and immigration. That was a conversation which I wanted to be well rested for since I only had my daughter's passport.

I hoisted the yellow quarantine flag and took down the New Orleans Yacht Club burgee from the starboard spreader when I woke up. I filled out all the paperwork. Prior to coming into port, I told Janna of my dilemma, and had her rush home from work to take pictures of my passport. She texted them to me. The cruising guide said that the skipper needed to go down to the government offices 100 yards away with all the paperwork and crew passports. I could not find customs in the low block government complex. I did see a sign for immigration, and I walked in. I was the only person there besides her.

"Are you coming on a private boat?" she asked.

"Yes," I replied.

"How many people are on your yacht?" she asked.

"Just me."

I got out my stack of papers and she asked, "Passport please."

"I mistakenly picked up my daughter's passport, here, but I have pictures of my passport on my phone," I said confidently, showing the passport with a picture of my daughter when she was an infant.

"You must bring your passport. The Bahamas is a different country. You must go back to the United States right away and not come back until you have your passport," she said.

"I can't go back. The Gulf Stream is going crazy right now," I replied with real fear in my voice. "My wife can send my passport overnight, and I can have it tomorrow."

"Then come back tomorrow with your passport," she replied.

I was not too worried about being deported or arrested because she did not even bother to hold onto my paperwork or ask what marina I went to. In all likelihood, I would come back, and all I planned to do was inject several thousand dollars in the Bahamian economy before departing. Moreover, I planned to do the last thing she suggested.

I had my marching orders. FedEx the passport, and I can clear immigration and customs tomorrow. There was one problem with this plan. FedEx does not deliver to Bimini.

Had I understood the shipping situation, I would have sailed straight to Nassau, where I could have picked up the passport at the FedEx office on arrival. You do not have to check in at the first island you come to. Skippers have the choice of where they sail to and which island they check in at. Most goods come into Nassau first, and then are distributed to the less populated islands such as Bimini. Native Bahamians can earn a living just buying stuff in Nassau and selling the goods in the less populated outposts. Locational arbitrage is very profitable there. On the other hand, in the US, if you bought basic goods in stores in Washington DC or New York city and tried selling them in rural areas or the suburbs, you would lose money hand over fist. I was naïve. I thought the shippers UPS, FedEx, and DHL, had conquered the world. I believed that an island just 50 miles from Miami on the doorstep of the U.S. must be easy to send an envelope to. I was wrong.

After finding FedEx did not deliver to Bimini and finding little about UPS shipping there, I asked the marina office about shippers. They recommended DHL. Janna found that the UPS store in Lafayette, Louisiana could accept DHL packages. Their computer said DHL ships in two business days to Bimini. Janna put my passport in a DHL envelope and I planned to get my passport on Friday, January 16.

The skipper of the boat has a lot more freedom than his crew or his dog before the boat's crew clears customs and immigration. The skipper can check in with authorities, pay the marina, and many other things prior to having cleared. In contrast, the pets and crew must stay aboard. That meant Daly was confined to the boat, but I was unlikely to raise the ire of the authorities if I moved around with the Q flag up. At least, no one asked me to stay on the boat.

The next morning I went for a run around North Bimini. Going slow, stopping to rest and enjoy the sights, or shop that took me an hour. I ran up to a big expatriate gated community and ferry terminal with a Hilton being built on the northernmost part of North Bimini Island. Only the western side of North Bimini is inhabited as far as I could tell. Most shops are one-tenth as well stocked as your typical gas station or 7-11 in the United States. For example, there were many days when you could not buy eggs. Luckily, I found a hardware store in Porgy Town that had a car belt that could be used if the Yanmar alternator belt broke as it had broken the prior day. Porgy Town was just north of Alice Town, which was where my marina was located. There was no Yanmar mechanic or Yanmar parts dealer in Bimini. I would have to go to Nassau for that. I also stopped at the BTC store. BTC is the phone carrier in the Bahamas. Unfortunately, the store had no SIM cards. Thus, you could not buy a cell phone or in

Slow Boat to the Bahamas

my case set up my portable WIFI until they got more in. "Try back on Friday," the sales lady said.

The turquoise blue water under my keel revealed many fish and I was tempted to fish while I threw them hot dog bun crumbs over lunch. I even saw a small Dolphin fish so prized by fishermen with its fat head and green, blue, and yellow body swim by. A school of yellow and black fish less than six inches long loved my bread and brought bigger gray trigger fish. My net that saved my cell phone did not succeed in bagging any of these small swimmers and they ignored the frozen shrimp that I had been dragging around since Biloxi, Mississippi.

A wreck on the western shore of North Bimini in the Bahamas.

My air conditioner would not work. I was paying $15 per day for my electrical hookup and was bummed to not get full use of it. I got this HPF error which denotes water circulation problems. I blew out the line with a garden hose and cleaned out the clogged sea weed strainer, but this did not work. Janna's Dad said it was possible the pump had gone bad and we ordered a pump, which Janna would take on the plane to the Bahamas. It was a minor annoyance since the nights were cool enough and the days were not that hot. I swam under

Linus Wilson

the boat and checked to see that both the intake and outtake lines were clear.

My neighbor, a 40-something man from Maine in a 40 foot sailboat, said I was nuts because there were many sharks just 50 feet away by the fish cleaning station at the Bimini Big Game Club Marina.

I thought he was being overly fearful of sharks as most people are. The incidents of shark attacks are practically zero in the United States and are very low worldwide. In *Last Breath* by Peter Stark he reports that there are nine shark deaths per year worldwide, and sharks are not even among the top 10 most dangerous animals to humans. In contrast, snakes are the most dangerous and kill 65,000 persons per year. Nevertheless, war and homicide kill far more people than snakes or all other animals combined.

However, my neighbor had a point. I would see later that there were many sharks that always swam exactly where he said. Those sharks were there twenty-four hours a day, seven days a week.

Janna wanted me to send Sophie's passport home by DHL right away because they would need it to fly to Nassau. I arranged for a pickup through the marina office. The attendant said the DHL guy would be there any minute. The DHL delivery man will be referred to as Tony in this narrative although that is not his real name.

On island time, Tony did not show up for two hours. While I waited I tapped three screws on the elbows of the solar panels, but the fourth I broke the die and could not remove it. I guess it would serve as a permanent screw! I planned to leave on Saturday when I got my passport later that day, Friday. I had topped up the diesel tanks on the first day. I wanted to get my laundry done and pick up the SIM card from the BTC store. So I left for 15 minutes and Tony the DHL guy of course came at that time.

I gave him Sophie's passport hidden in some papers. He mumbled how it was unfortunate that we did not meet earlier. I did not know what he was talking about. It was 1:30 PM—well before the drop deadline. He said the package would not arrive until Monday. I was not impressed with the fact that he did not even know how to fill out the DHL waybill, but a Monday delivery in Lafayette was more than I hoped for or needed. By Saturday, when my daughter's passport was not added into the system, he said the package would not leave Bimini until Monday. (Not leaving Bimini on Monday is a big difference than arriving at its destination on Monday, but we had more time.)

I was not going to miss the delivery of my passport so I camped out beside the marina office before it closed from 4:30 PM onwards. I saw a DHL representative, not Tony, walk by the marina with letters. As I tried to hail him, a white van sped up and took him away down the road. This was infuriating, and I had Janna call DHL in the US because the Bahamas number did not pick up. Moreover DHL only gives an 800 number for the US, which is useless if you are calling from another country.

I asked the marina office to give me Tony's number since they missed the delivery. The new lady at the office did not know his number. I looked up Tony's delivery company in the phone book. The marina gave me the phone book for all of the Bahamas, which was smaller than the phone book for Lafayette, Louisiana. The section on Bimini was only three pages. I started calling airlines in Bimini, but I got no answer. Then, the attendant said that I would not find him "Tony Baritone's number is unlisted." (Baritone was not his last name. I changed it here to protect the real man's privacy.) Because she inadvertently gave out his last name, I was able to look up Baritone in the book. There was one Baritone, and I called him.

"Hello, can I speak to Tony," I said.

"Tony does not live here. He is next door. Do you want his number?" the man offered.

I of course said, "Yes." I dialed Tony and left a message. I got two return calls from him one from Illinois and one from Florida, according to my phone. I could make out little of what he said. First, he said he had my package, but would not deliver it until Monday because the Marina office was closed. Then, he seemed to say that he did not have my letter and would update me on Saturday. I called him on Saturday and he said my passport's package would be on the 10 AM flight.

I got my last tracking update of my passport on Friday at 6 PM. The website said, "Delivery arranged no further details expected." The translation for this odd phrase we found out was that DHL does not provide tracking information once the package reaches Nassau. Once DHL puts the letter in the hands of Tony's company, DHL washes its hands of the whole delivery process.

The cruising guide says that the Queen's English is spoken in the Bahamas. This is not true. Any resident of Buckingham Palace would struggle to understand most Bahamians. I could make out 1 out of every 2 words spoken, and I got two degrees at an English university and lived in the UK for nearly a decade. The cruising guide warns that, in the Bahamas, they drive on the left side of the road. In North Bimini, this does not matter since there is only room for one car on the road.

On Saturday Bimini had several blackouts. The marina next to us, the Big Game Club, was less rustic. I had a very bland fried conch dinner there, which I ate in almost total darkness. I made a screen to fit in lieu of the top two companionway slats, which I would use for the rest of the trip, but I found little evidence of mosquitoes so far.

I ran in the early afternoon in South Bimini which is not nearly as developed or dinghy as North Bimini. South Bimini is accessible by two ferries, which run from the parking lot south of Brown's Marina. That marina is mentioned in Hemingway's *Islands in the Stream*, which takes place partially in Bimini. The ferry takes you over 150 yards of water.

I visited the beautiful marina on the island, and marveled at the schools of fish that swam around its new floating docks while I ate my ice cream and drank Sprite zero from the marina store. There was a nature trail by the marina, which had various plaques about wildlife. I paid particular attention to the one about poison ivy-type trees, who give anyone who touches them awful rashes. I had enough of the trees and turned to the beach trail enjoying the rich shades of turquoise and blue of the water. South Bimini seems to be an expat refuge with unoccupied vacation homes. The owners of these second homes by the sea no doubt fly into the airport, which is on South Bimini. After a long run, I reached the airport and stopped at the only place for refreshments there. I got some junk food and diet coke in the air conditioning and watched a couple reruns of Golden Girls. Refreshed, I hit the trail towards home. I came across a place that sold floating nylon line for my dinghy and got 25' to replace the dinghy's fraying line.

When I got back on the ferry and into North Bimini I visited the museum, which was free and unattended. Because I was listening to his novel *Islands in the Stream*, I was interested in all the pictures of Hemingway and his big fish catches from his boat Pilar. He was still young and vigorous when he visited Bimini. I found the only mosquitoes on the island in that museum and did not stay long.

I did not catch a 10-foot-long fish like Hemingway, but I snagged a 1 foot Triggerfish with a new hand net that I bought. I fed the fish two loaves of bread and I had a few ounces of meat to show for it, but it was very tasty. The skipper on a small sport fishing boat from Coral Gables convinced me that the trigger was so small that it was unlikely to be a risk for Ciguatera poisoning. "The bigger reef fish, which have consumed many smaller fish, are at the greatest risk. You have nothing to worry about that one."

On Sunday, I got the air conditioner working with the advice of Tom. He had me blow water out the through-hull outtake. I had plenty of adapters to hook the hose coming out of the pump to a garden hose. It cost me a gallon or two at $.50 per gallon, but it was worth it. A big bubble accompanied the first burst and the flow gave a few bubbles. It was hard to see the flow since the outtake often is below the water line. I think this first blast of water cleared a clog in

Linus Wilson

the outtake. I also tested the pump by running a line from the pump outtake into the galley sink and turning on the AC. Lots of water came out. The pump seemed to be working fine.

Many boats came in that day, including many trawlers and sport fishing boats. That is a good sign that the weather was pretty calm. I thought that day would have been a good one to start the two-day trek to Nassau. The Abby B and Carina were two sail boats from Maine with crew and skippers about my age, which sailed into Bimini when I did. Probably less than 10 percent of the cruising boats in the Bahamas had a skipper under 50 years of age. I spoke to them, but they always kept their distance. I thought at the time that this was because I was not traveling with my wife or I had my Q flag mysteriously up for days. However, I wonder if the real distance was that they were buddy boating.

Palm trees facing the Gulf Stream off North Bimini.

Slow Boat to the Bahamas

They had left their slips that day, but they returned in the evening much to my surprise. Abby B's skipper displayed a conch he had found but he was worried its lip was not fully formed, and he would have to throw it back. I was inspired by his conch diving and dove for some conchs in the waters of the marina. All the ones that I picked up had holes in them meaning they were harvested.

I paddled in my kayak to the small island in the shallows just outside the channel. It had thousands of harvested conch shells lining its banks. I found some small live conchs but left them. I wonder if the conchs are in danger of depletion as they have been wiped out in the United States. As I lifted myself out of the kayak onto the boarding ladder, having finished my short row, the pull cord of the fanny pack life jacket caught and deployed. I had to get out my spare CO_2 cylinder and repack the fanny pack.

The Abby B was a sailboat one slip over from me from Maine. The skipper was in his early thirties and his girlfriend was in her twenties. Why they stayed in Bimini so long puzzled me. I would have left as soon as my passport arrived.

I introduced myself to a couple from the Hamptons in a small Pacific Seacraft about as long as my 31 foot boat. They came into the marina that day also. The wife assured me that they were not the rich and famous. Instead, they took care of the place for the rich and famous when the latter group left. She worked for the city, which had no problems with revenue!

I convinced her to give me a tour. As I mentioned earlier, Pacific Seacraft is one of two companies that are still in business producing large numbers of full keel sailboats. Island Packet, the maker of my boat, is the other. Pacific Seacraft sailboats are famous for their canoe sterns, which I don't particularly like. (I prefer flat sterns or swim step sterns because they give more space for the length.) The Pacific Seacraft boat was much narrower and it had a 4 foot 11 inch keel. I like my boat's four-foot keel. It has allowed me to get into so many more places. Besides, I ran aground enough with Contango's short keel! Moreover, a narrower boat has less living space. The tour convinced me that Pacific Seacraft sailboats weren't for me.

The owner of the Pacific Seacraft talked about the NFL playoff games. I visited the Big Game Club again and enjoyed the Seattle Seahawks' come-from-behind victory over the Green Bay Packers. The place was packed. I went downstairs and played a few free games of pool with a local. The table had no place to put coins in! I told myself to aim more directly at the ball when I want it to careen off in a different direction this time. It worked, and I actually won a game before tiring of playing.

22. DH HELL

On Monday, January 19, 2015, I held a vigil for the letter containing my passport. I waited outside the marina office most of the day. I called the DHL Bahamas number that Tony gave me. The customer service representative said it would be on the 9AM flight from Nassau. Then, when that did not happen, she said it would be on the 4 PM flight. Neither came to pass. As the day wore on, I started e-mailing every executive, board member, or investor relations person I could find from searching the DHL website about my daughter's passport, which had no tracking and my passport letter that had disappeared in Nassau. I never mentioned that the package Janna sent to me contained my passport.

Most large companies' e-mail addresses either are first name-dot-last name and at the company's website. That was the case for DHL. Most of the DHL executives were German. If they all had been native English speakers, I think I would have received a bigger response. The e-mail that got the greatest response was sent to the CEO of DHL Americas, Stephen Fenwick, who was interviewed in a *Miami Herald* article appearing that day. I also copied an e-mail to the reporter who wrote the story.

Slow Boat to the Bahamas

Eventually, I learned that Western Air was the airline used to transport the DHL packages from Nassau to Bimini. The customer support representative claimed I violated U.S. law, sending my passport back to Sophie. This was a ridiculous allegation, which I had my father research. He found they were completely wrong. Passports are sent by the State Department all the time express mail or FedEx. I stressed it was a violation of my trust to open up and inspect my package. I believed this story was a diversionary tactic to cover for their failures or (worse) to justify thefts or elicit bribes from tourists, who entrusted their passports to them. I made these points forcefully and while waiting at the door of the marina with quite the audience of boats and their crew. I said to her, "DHL is a delivery company that never delivers anything." She never saw anything wrong with their failures, blaming their problems on outside contractors.

A DHL van in front of Atlantis Resort on Paradise Island in the Bahamas.

Most people are afraid of bad weather before they start a cruise, but the worst weather experience up to this point did not compare to the passport problems. This was the lowest point of the trip by far. I commiserated with Janna how I had stupidly given DHL Sophie's passport and we both ended the conversation in tears. We could have delivered these things ourselves with a plane flight and avoided all this misery. I would never trust my daughter's freedom of movement to DHL or any other express mail service. If I ever retrieved our passports, I promised I would personally fly back to the United States to deliver Sophie's passport to her mother. Without my own passport, I could only sneak back into the United States from Contango. I was tied to Bimini as long as the hope of the passports being delivered was held out. The Bahamian cruise was in shambles and looked unlikely to happen.

Because it was the U.S. but not Bahamian Martin Luther King Day holiday, I would have to wait before speaking to the U.S. Embassy. I could report my passport and Sophie's passport stolen if this mess continued. I had no idea what would be the ramifications of that action.

I called Western Air after 5 PM. The representative suggested speaking to Martha in Nassau. The number they gave me did not work that night, but it would work early the next morning. I noticed that DHL linked to social media on their website, and I took my troubles to Facebook and Twitter.

My mother said I had fulfilled my dream of sailing to the Bahamas, but I told her I had not. "My dream was to sail in my own boat to the Bahamas with Janna and Sophie on board. Without Sophie and my passports, that would never happen. I was so gullible to trust DHL."

After e-mailing 50 executives in the wee hours of the morning because I could not sleep, I called Martha at Western Air at 6 AM. Her assistant said she had the keys to the DHL deliveries, but she would be back soon. She called back while I was making breakfast. She said my two packages would be on the 9 AM flight from Nassau to Bimini. I told her that I planned to receive them at the airport, and she said that was OK.

I got a reply from the CEO of DHL Americas Stephen Fenwick, and I laced up my running shoes brought my wallet, fishing shirt, fishing pants, and my floppy Lawrence of Arabia hat. I brought a magazine to pass the time in the tiny airport. I started running after the ferry hit South Bimini shores. Someone offered to give me a ride in the bed of the truck with some other grumpy looking Bahamians. I declined. I had already been taken for a ride by the Bahamas DHL.

The run was lifting my spirits. I arrived at the airport before it opened at 7:45 AM. The airport employees, customs, immigration, security, and police started trickling in at 8 AM. When the waiting room with its 16 seats opened I read my magazine, and introduced myself to everyone from Western Air and told them my packages would be on that flight. After 9 AM, I called Martha and verified that the passports were on the plane. Her male assistant answered and said they were.

The baggage handler was friendly, but the gate agent was visibly angered when I said my envelopes were on the plane. "How do you know this?" she snapped.

When the Western Air flight came in a surprisingly big plane for the tiny airport, I watched carefully for the mailbag to be unloaded. I remembered the DHL man being whisked off by the white van right before he walked into the marina on Friday. I did not want that to happen again. I was going to bird-dog the passports this time. The sour puss gate agent picked up the DHL bag with what looked like two envelopes in it, mine and Sophie's, and placed it behind the counter. "You will have to wait until I get back." The DHL envelopes were put under the green mailbag. The nicer guy, who loaded the bag, came by and got the mailbag. I asked for my packages. He looked at the DHL plastic bag with what looked like it had just two envelopes and said, "Are you Tony Baritone?"

"No, he is the local DHL agent. Those are my packages. He has not shown up for work this morning as usual" I said. He shrugged his shoulders and left with the green mailbag leaving the DHL bag.

Linus Wilson

I was not about to let my passport disappear in another switcheroo as had happened on Friday. I picked up my DHL packages and started walking out muttering, "This is ridiculous!" Picking up Sophie and my passports set off a firestorm. Ground crew members, police, and customs converged on me at once. I gave up the package immediately without fuss and backed off, but a quick explanation was necessary. "I'll wait. That is my property. The local DHL agent tried to steal my daughter's passport and my express letter," I protested. "They only brought it here today because the CEO of DHL Americas intervened. I have been in constant communications with DHL. Those are my packages."

The 6'2", 230-pound, jolly-looking officer took charge. He was wearing a strange uniform to my eyes. He had black epilates, a captain's hat, and a light blue-and-white-flecked, short sleeve shirt.

"Are you Tony Baritone?" he asked.

"No, Tony Baritone is the local DHL agent. He did not show up for work today. The contents of the package are my daughter's passport and my express letter, which are four days late," I said.

"Let's see some ID," he said. I handed him my drivers' license and my faculty ID. "Where do you work?"

"I'm a professor at the University of Louisiana at Lafayette," I replied.

"How did you get here?"

"I came by boat. I'm here for pleasure."

"You're on vacation?" he said and I nodded.

"Did you not see Tony Baritone come by?"

"I have only met Tony once, and I probably could not pick him out of a crowd," I replied.

They searched around for Tony in the tiny area and produced Tony and the gate agent. While pointing at me, Tony came out and said, "This man is a thief!"

"Arrest these two," I said pointing to Tony and the gate agent. "They are running a passport theft ring. They tried to steal my daughter's passport!"

My retort stole Tony's thunder, but the officer told me to sit down, which I did. I was just trying to see the names on the two envelopes that were produced. At least, I got the officer to supervise the process.

Tony said, "He broke international law trying to send a passport through DHL."

"Don't listen to him. The illiterate is dispensing legal opinions now," I said. That produced a gasp from our large audience. I continued, "Tony, you are late for work on a day when the CEO of DHL Americas called to ask why you did not deliver my packages. About half the men in Bimini are unemployed." That got another roar from the crowd, "But, you won't show up for work when your do-nothing-job involves delivering one package a week." I then took a picture of Tony and the gate agent.

The gate agent went ballistic, "He can't take a picture of me. Have him trash those pictures immediately!"

"OK, OK, I'm deleting all the pictures. See," as the jolly officer looked on.

"He must delete the pictures of me!" she repeated.

"The officer saw me delete them."

"You stay seated," warned the officer, and I complied.

Tony and the gate agent slowly entered the details into the computer probably because this was the first time they had bothered with such formalities. My daughter's passport's waybill number was never entered in DHL's computers prior to that. My package's waybill said that no more information would enter the system after touching down in Nassau. Tony gave me several "I'm going to kill you looks." Finally, he had me sign for the packages, and I walked out with my daughter's and my passports.

23. THE ESCAPE

I had a one-and-a-half mile jog to the ferry, half-expecting to be arrested any moment. At the ferry, there were two men smoking what looked like a joint in the gazebo. Seeing groups of men drinking at 10 in the morning on a week day was not uncommon in Bimini, but this was the only time I thought I witnessed drug use. I stayed outside. The last thing I needed was to be associated with people mixed up in drugs. When we landed in North Bimini, one of the smokers tied up the ferry and said, "Here you go, chappy!" to me. I was kind of put off by the remark and avoided the stairs. Unfortunately, I lightly bumped my head on the canopy above. "You should have done what I told you. Now we are all having a laugh at you."

I was not about to respond and jogged towards the marina. I went to the ATM machine and got out $400 for the anticipated customs charge. (By design Bahamian dollars were worth one US dollar. Everyone in the Bahamas accepted both US and Bahamian cash.) I showered and changed into a different shirt and clean slacks. Then, I went out. I visited immigration again because I once again could not find the customs government building. Two new officers were in there. I asked for new forms because I thought I should not ask for Bimini Blue Water from its increasingly prickly ladies in the front office. After all, the lady on duty was the person who had introduced me to Tony.

I asked for 90 days in the Bahamas. I read that was the easiest time period to get. In addition, my request for 120 days several days before was frowned on my first visit to the office. Finally, my desire to stay a long time in the Bahamas had been dampened by some of the Bahamians I had met in Bimini. They stamped my passport, but they had forgot to advance the day on the stamp, and I had arrived the prior day, according to it.

Customs went well. He thought that I was missing one of four pieces of paper for the dog permit. I offered to go back to the boat and look for it, but the customs agent accepted the dog anyways. He was not concerned at all that twelve days had elapsed since Daly got his veterinarian certificate in the Marathon, Florida. The cruising guides were contradictory about whether or not my 31-foot sailboat was a small yacht that should pay $150, or it was a large yacht that should pay $300 for a cruising permit. He asked for $150.

I tried one more time to get a SIM card for my WIFI. This time BTC recommended that I go to a place up in Porgy Town because they had no SIM cards on this day, too. They did have phone books, and I asked to take the white and yellow pages and they said that was fine. I would later find how BTC would tout its store in Bimini in promotional videos as one of its generous investments in the outer islands. After over a mile's walk, I found the store that the BTC employee spoke of and got a SIM card, but since we were still in the process of unlocking the WIFI hotspot, we could not get it working. My iPhone was locked through AT&T, too and could not be used as a hotspot.

By the time I hoisted the Bahamian courtesy flag and dropped the quarantine flag, there were only four boats in the marina. I gave Daly his only walk since arriving, and started the engine. A three day weather window convinced everyone to head for the next stop for boats wanting to go to the popular Abacos or Exumas island chains.

The Bimini chain had only had a handful of settlements and anyone anchoring on the bank (the shallow enough water to anchor in) would be exposed to the eastern trade winds. The Berry Island chain had more settlements, but were mostly too shallow on the bank side and did not offer many good anchorages. The Abacos to the north

Linus Wilson

and the Exumas to the south were mostly on the eastern side of their respective banks. Thus, good anchorages in the lee of these islands abounded. From Bimini most boats would sail on the Great Bahama Bank go through the Northwest Channel and sail in the deep water until they came to Nassau harbor or another refuge on New Providence Island the island in which Nassau is located. For most sailboats, the trip to Nassau was a two day trip if you liked to sleep and stopped midway. I would take three days because I started late that day.

It seemed a simple matter to turn the nose of the boat and get out. Unfortunately, the boat did face a 10-knot wind in the direction I wanted to go, east. The nose of the boat was facing south. If I used the port bow line, I should be able to turn the nose east and towards the marina's exit. The entrance seemed wide and there were practically no boats to run into. What I did not realize at the time was that the four-inch rubber attachments on the pilings would pose a hazard. My little boat was so low, and made lower with the tide, that the rub rail was below the rubber attachments nailed to the pilings. Normally, the stern of the boat would turn on a piling against the rub rail. Unfortunately, with the rubber attachments above the rub rail, the turning boat's solar panel frame in the stern would get caught in the rubber bumpers.

As I turned to the east, port, the first time, I heard a terrible crunching noise, and all my momentum was stopped. The bow turned west not east. I had to quickly back into the slip before I lost all control. I did this twice before discovering the source of the crunching sound. The starboard side of the solar panel was no longer vertical and its mount was badly bent backwards. Nevertheless, it still stood.

A different approach to leaving was necessary as long as the tide was low enough that the rub rail was below the rubber bumpers. (I would find that most docks at marinas in the Bahamas were built for much higher-sided boats than Contango. Bimini Blue Water was one of the lower down docks that fit Contango better than most Marinas with fixed docks.) The method I used should have worked, and it had worked in 100 previous times that I had left marina slips. It just would not work at this dock at this tidal stage. Carina had vacated her slip right next to me to the east, and it looked like both the buddy boats Carina and Abby B had quit Bimini. I walked a bow line to Carina's old finger slip. Pulling in this bow line allowed me to turn Contango much more sharply towards the east exit without the engine than I could from my slip alone. Thus, there would be no problem of the stern rotating on a piling and its too high bumper.

Taking the bow line into the boat, I had plenty of time to put the boat in gear and motor out into Bimini harbor before the bow got turned around by the wind. Leaving the entrance channel, Contango and another sailboat were passed close by a 50-foot long or greater sport fishing boat. The boat was doing over 20-knots in the entrance channel, and put up a seven-foot breaking wake. I maneuvered mostly out of the way but the overtaken sailboat had crossed the Gulf Stream only to get a huge, unnecessary man-made wake break over its stern.

I followed my waypoints inside the bank to the Cat Cay. The shallow water route went down to 5.1 feet on the depth sounder. Thus, it posed no problems for Contango's four foot draft. North Cat Cay was one of the few other inhabited islands in the Bimini island chain. It is a private island, a large housing development, and it discourages extended visits. I had no desire to visit. Anchoring there shortened my trip of the next two days by a few hours. Most importantly, it was not Bimini.

I anchored just north of the airstrip. I put out 110 feet of chain and rode and the 22-pound claw anchor in 12 foot depths, letting out rode slowly until I felt it pull. I was over 300 feet from all hazards. The swell was noticeably less strong in the lee of the shallows where I was. I found the night with 5-to-10-knots of wind was too hard to sleep in the rolling v-berth in the bow. Daly and I moved to the port single berth, but returned to the v-berth when the wind died down. The bow never seemed to turn around. I had stupidly left the autopilot engaged all night. In the morning the wheel was turned all the way to starboard. That may have explained my trouble sleeping.

Linus Wilson

One time I woke in the night to look at the chart plotter and the lighted landmarks on shore to see if we dragged. We did not. Unfortunately, half a dozen "no-see-ums," biting bugs, attacked me. Contango and I had our bruises but we escaped our DH hell!

24. THE WILDERNESS

There is very little on the Great Bahama Bank. The middle of the bank where I was to be sailing on January 21, 2015, had water typically 9-to-15 feet deep. There is no land in the middle of the Great Bahama Bank. Instead, the islands of the Bimini Group, the Berry Islands, New Providence, Eluthera, Exumas, and Long Island lie on its edges. Being a day or two late for the mass migration, I would not have a lot of company.

I left before dawn as light filled in the sky. The distances are too great to reach the nearest port between North Cat Cay and Nassau, Chub Cay in the southern Berry Islands before dark. Thus, the guides recommend anchoring on the bank a few miles west of the Northwest Channel.

The Northwest Channel is the safest entrance to the deep water of the Tongue of Ocean, deep water that goes between the wilderness archipelago known as Andros Island on the west and New Providence and the Exumas chain on the east side of the bank. The quickest way to Nassau is to pass north of Andros Island and south of the southern Berry Islands into the Tongue of the Ocean and sail into the western entrance of Nassau harbor on the north side of New Providence Island.

There are no safe ports on Andros Island near this route on the west side of the archipelago. Andros is largely uninhabited. The west side is shallow and poorly charted. It is a sparsely settled wilderness similar in size to the Florida everglades. In both places, you'll find mosquitoes for company, but few people to help you if you get into trouble.

Thus, sailboats not transiting during night are encouraged to anchor in the unprotected shallows of the bank at least a few miles away from the frequented routes to the Northwest Channel. The Waterway Guide told some horror stories of transiting boats nearly colliding with anchored boats doing this. The only insurance against this would be to be well off the beaten path with your anchor and cabin lights on. I planned to anchor over two miles off the main routes to the northwest channel.

At North Cat Cay, I booked a flight to meet Janna while she was attending a conference in Dallas to hand over Sophie's passport in person. The flight left in three days on January 24. I found it was easier and cheaper to get the direct flight to Dallas than to fly into any airport in Louisiana. All the airports in Louisiana needed one more connections to reach Nassau.

I saw few boats in the morning. The weather looked squally but only shed a little bit of drizzle on Contango. I had a 60-watt bank of flexible, portable solar panels which had frequently required repairs to their plug. Its wires would come out almost every day at the flimsy marine plug fitting. This was the fifth and final time I repaired that bank's connection. The 200-watt panels despite their mounts mounting injuries had always put out a lot of reliable energy, peaking at over 10 amps during the day. In contrast, the flexible 60-watt bank of panels was just a nuisance.

I lost access to the BTC cell phone signals soon after leaving North Cat Cay, and I would be out of contact with the world until I got closer to another settlement with a cell phone tower. Passing south of Chub Cay would be the next most likely place to get a stray signal. I saw two large nurse sharks. While dolphins are common in the US, and I have never seen a shark while cruising US waters, sharks are the more common sights in the Bahamas.

The autopilot acted up for no apparent reason. I ended up locking the helm with a slight southward bias and this worked pretty well. The full keels of the Island Packets make them easier to abandon

Linus Wilson

the helm without the autopilot than the more popular and cheaper fin keel sailboats. My previous boat would not tolerate even five seconds with the tiller lashed. By the end of the day, the autopilot was working fine. It just needed a little rest.

In the endless expanse of light blue water, I installed a switch on the portable bladder tank's freshwater pump to keep it from sparking when I put on the alligator clips.

I was bracing for a rough night passage because I doubted that I could sleep in an unprotected anchorage. I dropped the hook fifteen miles north of the northwest tip of Andros Island. The zero-to-five-knot winds from the east that prevailed almost all day became a howling ten-to-fifteen knots of wind, by 10 PM. Welcome back to the trade winds! I had to wait until 12 AM to weigh anchor or else I risked arriving in Nassau in the darkness. I tolerated the rocking and rolling until 11:15 PM. It was a struggle getting up the anchor in the darkness so I did not leave too soon.

The transit of the Northwest Channel in darkness posed me with a dilemma. Do I believe the lights and follow them, or do I believe my GPS chart plotter and totally rely on it? I relied on the chart plotter. My experience in the Grenadines and the horror stories from the Lin and Larry Pardy's *Seraphin* series of books made me suspicious of charted lights. It turns out the lights were burned out and the lights that I saw were coming from Chub Cay or were anchor lights not the lights of the Northwest Channel. I felt the Northwest Channel from the swell. I certainly could not see it.

I raised the third reef before leaving the bank and exiting the Northwest Channel. I put up a 75 percent genoa, after turning towards Nassau, but I had to furl it because the wind shifted too much on the nose. I estimated that the east swells took half a knot of boat speed. There was light in the sky in front of me. It was not sunrise. It was the glow of civilization, Nassau. It got a little rougher as I left the lee of the Berry Islands. I could not see the sea. It was too dark.

I passed what I thought was a small freighter at 5 AM. I guessed that I would see very little ship traffic in this stretch of ocean since there are no deep water ports or large cities between Nassau and the Northwest Channel. I took 15 minute naps through most of the night, setting two alarms, which always woke me. To keep awake as I approached Nassau, I worked on my fold-up bike despite the awkwardness of this. I put on a new tube, which required taking off the chain and kickstand. The hardest part was slipping the new tube under the old tire as the old tire was also slipped onto the metal wheel frame.

25. THE SEARCH FOR SAFE HARBOR IN NASSAU

I did not see another boat until I was on top of Nassau. I mistook a hotel for a cruise ship as I approached, but, eventually, I realized my error when it did not move. The guides are very clear, warning boaters to not anchor in Nassau Harbor. They say the foul bottoms and strong currents make it unsafe.

Nassau harbor is made up Paradise Island to the north and Nassau and the north end of New Providence Island to the south. The ships can only enter the west side. Boats that can get their masts under the 65 foot twin Paradise Island bridges can go to the east side of the bridges, and exit onto the Great Bahamas bank on the east side of Nassau and New Providence Island. Paradise Island is made up of mostly gated communities and the huge Atlantis hotel, casino, and waterpark. Nassau has a reputation for having a crime problem, and the cruising guides recommend that you get to your boat before nightfall in Nassau. From my reading, the south east, Nassau side of the harbor sounded like more my speed. It seemed to have all the marine chandleries, the Yanmar diesel engine dealer, and a very good supermarket in Solomon's Fresh Market.

I planned to go to the cheapest marina, Nassau Yacht Haven, charging $2 per foot, and that was what I told the Nassau Harbor

Patrol when I did the mandatory VHF check in. When I entered the busy harbor, I measured a three-knot current as I approached it, passing under the Paradise Island bridges. I maneuvered around the huge ship marked "MAILBOAT" to pass under the 65-foot vertical clearance portion of the bridge. The guides said Nassau Yacht Haven was subject to strong currents. I had heard a horror story of how one couple cracked up their boat and other boats in a marina with a strong current running. I was not willing to chance it. It looked like all the south shore marinas lacked breakwaters and were at the mercy of these currents. I typically approached a slip at two knots. A three knot current would easily overwhelm any slow turns or approaches. I told the marina that I would approach only after slack water at low tide at 3:30 PM.

At 10:30 AM, I put out 5-to-1 scope, 60 feet of rode and chain, in nine feet of water with three feet of freeboard in an anchorage called the Cloisters. This was near Paradise Island just east of the bridges and on the north end of the harbor. Finally, I could sleep!

I set my alarm for 2 PM, and, by 3 PM, I had the anchor up. I noted that two other boats were in the Cloisters anchorage. It was pleasant except for the continual wakes that are unavoidable in Nassau harbor. At least, I was far from the ten-to-fifteen-story cruise ships that augmented the population of Nassau. Despite it being slack water, a 2.5 knot current was running at the approach to the Nassau Yacht Haven marina. I told the harbor master that I would not be coming. I had not come all this way to wreck the boat in Nassau. I figured that I could anchor another night before I needed to settle on a marina. My spot at the Cloisters was taken immediately by another sailboat. I saw an opening in the six foot depths between the popular and crowded southeast anchorage near all the marine supply stores on the north shore of Nassau.

I put out 7-to-1 scope, 65 feet. I deployed the dinghy in a 90-minute process and went ashore with Daly. I followed the advice of the cruising guide and omitted anything that might be stolen. I left the bellows pump for the inflatable dinghy on Contango. The outboard had a lock as did the dinghy itself. I searched for a long time for the dinghy dock. I first went past the anchorage and yacht club to a small fort on the far (east) side. I could have drug the dinghy on the beach, but securing it might have been problematic. Further, no other boater attempted this nor had it been recommended in anything that I had read. I turned back and asked another man on a sailboat in the anchorage where the dinghy dock was. He said it was by the gas station with an arc. This was the Rubis, not the Texaco, as the cruising guides said. Rubis was closed down, but it attracted many native Bahamian men, who like to lounge around it usually with a strong drink in hand.

I noted how slow the boat seemed to move when I turned west versus east. At first I thought this was an illusion, but then I realized I was fighting the current. I always found the current in Nassau Harbor ran strong from west to east. I never observed it to switch with the tides, but it may have slowed. I landed at the dinghy dock where four men hanging out who eyed the contents of my dinghy. I reassured myself that I have one of the least expensive dinghies and outboards at the dock. I left the paddle and extra gas in the dinghy but little else.

I found the big strip mall. First, I was tempted by my first Starbucks since Tallahassee, but since it was late I went to the very expensive Dairy Queen and bought their Peanut Buster Parfait. Daly alternated between his Sherpa bag and walking. I passed up the BTC store in favor of the Soloman's Fresh Market, which would rival any expensive grocery store in the States, such as Whole Foods, with the quality of its offerings. When the mall closed down, I went back to the dink.

I found both tubes of the dinghy especially the port side had been at least half deflated. This was odd since it held its air for months at a time and would not leak again until I sold it several months later. My conspiratorial mind sometimes thinks one of the loungers who saw me dock may have deflated it for nefarious purposes. I got in with the small load of groceries and Daly in his bag. It held our weight but there was limited freeboard, and the ride was precarious. Any wake had me bailing. We got back to the boat, and I pumped it up for the last time of the trip.

My spirits were not dampened, and I texted Janna that I would not leave this anchorage until she and Sophie left nine days later. That prediction would be proved wrong in the morning. In the morning, I got out my diesel jugs and dinghied back to Rubis. All the marina fuel docks looked way too high to fill jerry cans from. Six Bahamian men chose my landfall as an excuse to move their drinks and conversation to the dinghy dock from the parking lot. I realized that Rubis was not just closed for the evening. It was permanently closed. I found another gas station with diesel a quarter of a mile along the busy road to the west. After visiting the marine chandleries, I got eight gallons of diesel. To my surprise, the men had left and apparently ignored the contents of my dinghy while I was gone.

I faced two-to-four-foot waves on the dinghy ride back as the east wind of 10-to-15-knots opposed the east flowing current. I was barely able to bring aboard the jerry jugs with four gallons of diesel in each one as the stern bucked in the steep chop. It was too rough to use the boarding ladder. I had to move the dinghy to the side of the boat to break some of the waves. I was afraid I would be tossed in the water possibly injuring myself on the way in. I did not like my chances in such a swift current. I am a very confident swimmer, but I cannot overcome a three-knot current. What I found to be the most frightening was that the trades were on the weak side. It was not blowing 15-to-20 knots from the east as is the norm. Instead, it was blowing 10-to-15 knots. What would happen to my anchorage if the wind picked up above 20-knots?

I did not want to find out. I was convinced that the marinas on the Nassau side without breakwaters were unsafe. Therefore, I called the three marinas on the Paradise Island side. The cheapest was the Paradise Harbor Club Marina at $3.50 per foot. It looked like it should be well protected by geography and unlike most Nassau marinas it had a breakwater from the current. The harbor master said it had no current running through it, which I believe was true.

I was afraid of loading the outboard in those swells. It takes two hands and a dinghy well secured to the stern. I had neither. I should have tried anyway. I tied the dinghy to the bow with the transom stupidly facing forward. My aft line on the dinghy was shorter. So it was easier to tie that line to the bow and the painter to the beam.

My idea was that I could back in the slip only if the dinghy was in the bow. This was something that I had done with Janna before, but I had never single handed into a marina slip with the dinghy in tow. Further, I had never towed the dinghy with the outboard on. When I had been docking with Janna with the dingy in tow, I had held and guided the dinghy painter not just tied it off. Captain Ahab from my ASA 103 and 104 lessons told me to never tow a dinghy with the outboard on the back. Nevertheless, I had seen plenty of boats do it. Those boats had heavier inflatables than my rollup, and, on the other boats, the dinghy was towed front first from the stern. That day I was towing the dinghy and motor stern-first from the bow. The marina was 200 yards away from my starting place at anchor. What could go wrong? Plenty.

I first heard whistling from the sailboat that took my spot in the cloisters anchorage. "That was a rude way to gloat about snagging a better anchorage," I thought. Then I noticed the vertical dinghy with its stern holding the outboard submerged and the opened end facing Contango's bow. When I got enough sea room between me and the next passing boat, I pushed the dinghy's bow down with the autopilot on. This only helped in that the dinghy completely filled with water.

A passing ferry had about thirty people yelling "You're dinghy is sinking!" while I waved as if I was on the winning team in a Super Bowl parade. There was little else I could do. The marina was looming. I would have to go farther to find a spot to anchor and sort out the mess. It was already attached to Contango so even if it could sink by filling with water (it cannot when fully inflated) I could not bail it right that second.

Linus Wilson

I saw the dock master waiving me to slip 6 on the south side of the marina, which was clearly marked. I tried to comply as I motored into the east wind coming from the west. Unfortunately, as I tried to back in and turn around, I found my boat being blown into a 60 foot motor yacht on the north side of the marina poking out of the pilings. I felt I only had enough control to go forward into slip 13 just west of the huge boat before blowing into it. I threw the dock master who ran around to catch my line at this slip, and he was able to tie it off before I blew into the big boat.

"You know your dinghy is full of water," he said. I nodded. "You know this slip is taken," he said. There were dock lines all over this slip. "Are you new to boating?"

"No, I've owned big sailboats for over three years. I just went into here before I blew into the other slip. My full keel sailboat does not maneuver nearly as well as powerboats do. I think I can get a long line and use it to direct the stern into slip 6 after I bail out the dinghy," I replied.

I bailed the 3 inches of water out of the dinghy, and it did not sink with my bulk weighing it down further. I then attempted to use my longest line to stretch across the channel to slip 6 directly behind it. This was an abysmal failure. Without the outboard working, I could not stretch out the line before it snagged on the bottom or the coils and pushed the dinghy back, giving up all my progress from canoe paddling it. I tried this for over an hour before I finally gave up.

I put the dinghy to the side and backed up the boat while the dock master waited on slip 6 on the south pier to catch the stern line while backed out of the north pier. As I feared, this did not go well. Contango's bow immediately got blown by the wind and pointed west instead of north. The whole boat was drifting west with the east wind, but I managed to throw the port stern line to the dock master. Ideally, I could have thrown him the starboard stern line, but nothing was ideal that day. This stopped my progress towards the 60 foot boat on the southern pier just west of me. The friendly harbor master was able to pull me into slip 6. Contango had found safe harbor in Nassau at last, but only at great cost.

26. TROUBLES IN PARADISE ISLAND

You did not get much for $3.50 per foot. The laundry was taken up by the cleaners for the associated hotel until 4 PM. I was reusing my old clothes by this point. The showers were semiprivate and only had cold water. (Fortunately, I had little use for hot water in the Bahamas except at night. Moreover, there was hot water in the hot tub. It wasn't exactly camping out!) Clearly, the marina was very exposed to the wind. The docks were way too high and were designed for powerboats with 10 feet of freeboard. The restaurant on site was abandoned. It was a mile walk to the nearest restaurant or convenience store. On the plus side, the mats in front of the restrooms said "ENJOY YOUR VACATION IN PARADISE".

I met the fit retirement-aged couple Al and Mary on their 32-foot sailboat named Summer Semester. They said they anchored on the bank the same time that I did, but they found the motion OK and stayed until 3 AM. They also said they were close-hauled the whole way. It was not surprising their skinnier boat pointed higher than Contango. I worried that the motion that I found was unbearable on the bank was due to my mostly anchor rode. If the chain was not stranded by the Maxwell 800 windlass, I wonder if the all chain rode would make for a better night's sleep. Another thing Al said worried me. He had thrown out his back from anchoring.

I ordered a replacement windlass for Janna to bring to Nassau. This $3.50-per-foot not-so-great marina convinced me that a better anchoring set up would pay for itself. I wanted to use the all chain rode, but I worried it would be too hard on my back if I did not have an electric windlass. I bought a Maxwell HRC8 horizontal windlass

Linus Wilson

that handled the correct size of chain and rope rode and would fit on Contango's deck so that the chain could be fed and dropped properly.

I worked on trouble-shooting the marine air conditioner. I wanted Daly to be in climate controlled conditions when I left. Nevertheless, he could survive the 60-to-80 degrees Fahrenheit temperature range while I was gone. I conducted four tests. First, I blew water out the outtake with my garden hose attachments. On my first attempt, using the freshwater hose, the water went all through the cabin not in the outtake line, because I left the outtake seacock closed. On the second attempt, the outtake cleared a clog and water flowed freely. The second test had me clear out the sea strainer which was already clear. Thirdly, I redirected the hose leaving the pump to the sink. Only a trickle came out. Fourthly, I looked at the pump impeller and found it to be clear. I concluded from this that the pump was faulty, and a new one should be shipped to Janna at home. She could bring that too, when she and Sophie would come in just over a week. For some reason, I failed to test the intake line which also would explain the low water flow from the pump. These series of tests convinced me to ignore the air conditioner until Janna arrived.

I called the Honda outboard dealer in the Bahamas but the service contractor SOS Marine never returned my calls. The next day I tried servicing the outboard myself. I dumped the fuel, drained the carburetor, and changed the oil. I pulled the cord with the spark plug out, but no water came out. My father-in-law Tom had suggested this because of his experience with a submerged jet ski. When he pulled the cord with the spark plug out, a stream of water spurted up. Finally, I put in a new spark plug. The outboard started right up and ran for 30 minutes as recommended by the manual.

While packing for my flight, I discovered that when the ladies in Bimini washed my two pairs of Levi's jeans, they neglected to put them back with my laundry. I would have to make do in Dallas with my slacks. I actually gave Janna a lot of my winter clothes in Dallas, because winter was over on Contango, which was likely to be in the hot Bahamas until spring. To catch my flight, I took a $40 cab to the airport. I only had about 24 hours with Janna, and I would fly back the next day. I gave Janna our daughter's, Sophie's, passport in person. It was good to get a cappuccino, use our portable WIFI, and the unlimited internet on my phone in the States. I did not get to see Sophie because my mother-in-law had flown out from the suburbs of Chicago to Lafayette, Louisiana to take care of Sophie while Janna attended her conference in Dallas.

Janna gave me the instructions for unlocking our cellular WIFI hotspot. The international calling plan that Janna signed up for only gave us 800 megabytes of data per month for $120 per phone. With the WIFI unlocked and using the BTC service, we could get 2 gigabytes or 2,000 megabytes for $30. The AT&T roaming plan was 10 times more expensive for data than the BTC prepaid plan. Unfortunately, unlocking it would not be easy.

My plane was almost empty. Checking in through customs and immigration was easy. The immigration agent did not even look at my cruising permit, but she extended my stay another 90 days. An actor dressed up like a very enthusiastic and cheesy pirate greeted us as we got out passports and landing card. I had to get another $40 cab ride back to the marina. As far as I could find, there were no cheaper transport options.

I gave Daly a walk. He seemed to do fine with his day alone. Next, I deployed the dinghy. It was calm at the moment on Sunday, January 25, despite 20+ knot winds being forecast for Monday through Wednesday. Contango could use more fuel. It would be better to cross the harbor when it is calm with the fuel.

I motored off the dock so badly, the neighboring boat owner's four-year-old son, who spoke like Tiny Tim in a *Christmas Carole*, said "Where is he going, daddy?" as I bounced off of one piling after another. His father was diplomatic enough to ignore the voice of truth and innocence and did not respond. Perhaps, his father could not divine a direction from my zig-zag course. As soon as I got into a turning basin in the marina, I revved the motor but it did not move. A discarded plastic bag had wrapped around the propeller. I pulled the kill switch. At first I drenched my arm and could not clear it. On the second attempt, I tilted the 2 HP Honda and unwrapping the bag.

My plan was to go to the Hurricane Hole fuel dock on Paradise Island because I wanted to avoid crossing the harbor. I found that that marina was much farther west than I had anticipated, and I fumbled around until I finally found the fuel dock. The engine died several times. I found that starving the engine of air by choking it staved off the inevitable. I worried my service of it was insufficient. Once I topped off the fuel, it died no more times, and my confidence in it grew.

The fuel dock was deserted. I had called ahead and the marina said it was manned until 6 PM. At 4:30 PM, no-one could be found. It was just as well anyway. The dock was six feet over the water and there was no ladder. I could not imagine carrying jerry jugs over my head onto the dinghy. I crossed to the fuel docks on the Nassau side, which were also unmanned and very inaccessible by dinghy. I went back to the Rubis dinghy dock so that I could walk the jerry cans to the Esso gas station 100 yards away.

The eastern sky turned menacing. There was one other barely inflated dinghy at the dock. The owner smoked a cigarette over his auxiliary gas tank. What does that say about me if the only other dinghy skipper here is such a risk-taker? Some fellow tried to convince me to get a ride to the gas pump, which I declined. He followed me to the gas station, and while I was eating my ice cream bar next to my full diesel cans he offered his services to me again, which I declined again.

A cruiser with his miniature poodle was just coming to the dock. I asked him about groomers in Nassau as Daly was looking shaggy. The 30-to-40-something, dashing native of Quebec said he groomed his own dog. He said this was his sixth season in the Bahamas. He said he worked half the year and cruised the other half. I asked him if he liked the Abacos or Exumas better. He raved about the Exumas but was cool about the Abacos.

By the time I got back, Summer Semester was gone. I felt like I had missed an opportunity in the calm to leave this expensive marina, but I had little time to leave before darkness and no good alternative in mind. My thinking was that I wanted to be in a marina in New Providence before the 30 knot gusts forecast for Monday. I was not going to crack up the boat a few days before my most important crew members, my wife and daughter came aboard.

On Monday morning, I tried biking to the Dunkin Donuts by the bridges for breakfast. I got another flat. After my half hour of pumping left the tire flat, Daly and I walked the rest of the way. With sugar and caffeine in me, I walked the reluctant dog and bike back. I met some poodle owners and their dog, and they spoke of a mobile groomer. When I got back to the marina, I used their phone book to set up an appointment for the next day, Tuesday, January 27, 2015.

I had had it with the bike. I took the hotel's daily 11 AM shuttle which actually did not leave until 12:20 PM. The shuttle took most of the hotel guests to the downtown area just south of the cruise ship dock. The hotel guests were a rowdy bunch on one week holidays. They wanted to maximize their time in the sun. In contrast, I was more interested in boat repair. I got off the shuttle early much to the horror of the suburbanites on board. They were sure I would never emerge alive from the barbed wire jungle that is Nassau.

I soon found the Yanmar dealer. I bought two alternator belts for $24 apiece. The mechanic could not figure out how to use the credit card machine. I gave him a $50, and his buddy gave me $2 change. I got no receipt, but I did not complain. Where else was I going to get a Yanmar belt?

I shopped at the marine chandleries just east of the bridges on the waterfront for the huge wire and attachments that I needed for the windlass. The prices were typically 50 to 100 percent more than West Marine prices in the States.

I stopped at the touristy looking conch shacks under the bridges. I ordered the fried fish and chips at one stall. Forty minutes later the red snapper emerged—eyes, scales, tail, and all. It was either red snapper or barracuda. Both fish are on the list of likely sources of ciguatera poisoning. This snapper looked too small to be a big carrier of the toxin. After the wait, it tasted delicious!

I hiked over the bridge and started getting vertigo when I noticed a big RIB with a 25 horse power engine struggling in the three-foot waves. I was happy to be at the marina and walking instead of taking the dinghy that day. The steepness of the bridges between Nassau and Paradise Island meant that only a four-time Tour de France champion could climb them on a bike. Biking down them would be truly suicidal. After that work out, I found the towers of Atlantis beckoning, and I stopped for a fruity drink before returning to the marina.

The next day, I took the bike into Nassau. I walked it up and down the bridge. I got yet more wire and electrical supplies for the windlass, stopped at a bike shop, and found the biggest grocery store I would see in the Bahamas. I got a huge amount of groceries that my daughter Sophie likes and clearly needed a cab to get back. My bagger, who resembled the diminutive actor Gary Coleman, asked if I needed a taxi. I said, "Yes." He produced his buddy in an unmarked car. The driver told me $10 for the trip after I asked for a price, and I gave the Gary Coleman look alike $1. I held my breath and hoped that I would not get mugged. There was no problem, and he dropped me off at the marina.

I was expecting the mobile groomer at 1:30 PM. Unfortunately, she was a complete no show. I finally got a hold of her. She said she was robbed in her vehicle while she was waiting at the light before entering the bridge to Paradise Island right before Daly's appointment.

I did laundry until late in the hopes that I could leave the marina on the next day. However, when I awoke, the wind was still blowing strongly from the southwest. When I docked the first time, I thought it would be easy to get out because the east trade winds would help my turn on exit. A stiff west wind meant turning towards the exit would be tough. I was still shell shocked from my tough departure from Bimini Blue Water Marina and the tough time docking at this marina. I wanted to wait a day for the eastern trade winds to return before making my exit. Even, if I anchored for one day in the islands to the east of Nassau, I could save over $100 for my trouble while I waited for me wife and daughter to land in Nassau.

I tried biking for breakfast but got a flat. I ran into the skipper of a fast 33-foot racing catamaran at the marina, who I had met a few days before. I will call him Jacques for his privacy. Jacques said he was headed for Starbucks by Atlantis. I said I would join him after fixing my flat. Jacques' boat had a top speed of 22 miles per hour, and, like the Moth dinghy or the current America's Cup boats, his boat would fly above with only a small dagger touching the water.

This is view of the palms and the boats on the east side of the Paradise Island Bridge in Nassau. Daly's dog groomer said she was mugged 100 feet from where this photo was taken.

He lamented, "My wife does not like my boat," he said. She joined him on a one-day cruise to George Town, Exuma, over 100 miles away. Nevertheless, she would not sleep inside its coffin-sized berths. She instead took a hotel room in Paradise Island while she had visited a few days before. With no head, running water, *et cetra* his boat had exceptionally Spartan accommodations. It was basically an oversized Hobie Cat that sailed much more like a rocket ship.

"Your wife is very brave. I would not get on your boat for a day sail in Nassau Harbor. My wife would never have gone on a boat without a head or a shower," I said.

Like me, he was waiting for the trades to return. While I just wanted an easier time leaving the slip, Jacques wanted to sail his boat back to Key Largo, where he had a trailer and truck waiting. He planned to drive it back to the western coast of Canada where he lived. He was not going to wait for a day with a flat-calm Gulf Stream. Instead, he would likely go out in 10 foot waves, if that was what the weather forecast held, as long as the wind was blowing from the east. It was just a one-day trip on his boat.

Jacques said his wife was headed back to Panama to sell their flat there to pay for a cruising boat. He had his eye on a 52-foot brand new cat, but he would not consider buying anything smaller than 39-feet. He was convinced that she would only tolerate a huge boat, but I was skeptical since my wife subscribed to the Lin Pardey school of thought that says a smaller boat is more manageable for the women in cruising couples. My experience in the Bahamas would prove few cruising couples put the smaller-is-better motto into practice.

I tried to impress on him what a different experience he would have on a giant cruising cat versus his trailerable boat that had to be sailed with the care of a dinghy. I said, "I almost never hand steer. I spend most of my time fixing electrical, plumbing, or engine issues. I particularly like working on electrical projects. You have to enjoy fixing boats if you have a cruising boat." He looked at me with deep skepticism. His boat did not even have a 12-volt battery, and he was a minimalist with everything but the sailing.

"You have it pretty good right now. It seems like you can cruise anywhere you want on your current boat," I said. Nevertheless, it was clear he was taking the isolation of solo sailing worse than I was. My job was mostly writing and mathematical and statistical analysis performed while alone, which suited my personality. In most disciplines, writing a doctoral dissertation is a very lonely pursuit as it was in my case. My favorite pastime besides sailing, distance running, involves little team involvement. I doubted that Jacques' many years in the military and as a helicopter pilot prepared him as well for spending lots of time alone. Plus, he did not have a toy poodle with him!

I saw Jacques on the dock and asked if he wanted to get dinner. We went down to small place by the Hurricane Hole marina. I traded my US dollars for his Bahamian money since he would have trouble unloading it in the U.S. He planned to sail in the wee hours of the morning. It was clear that his catamaran that terrified me was a step down on the adrenaline level from his old job as chopper pilot who fought forest fires. After 35 years doing that and decades in the military, he seemed skeptical that sailboat cruising was what he wanted to do with his retirement, but that was where he seemed headed.

He told me that, when he got out his big money belt and roll off cash, he told me about how he was propositioned for drugs and prostitutes while wandering downtown near the cruise ships. I wished him fair winds, and he was gone in the morning. Mine was the last sailboat left in the marina.

I had awakened at 6 AM to string wires in the v-berth for the windlass. I wanted to finish this part of the project so that I could replace the contents of the v-berth closet which were sprawled out over the boat. The screwing in of cable ties proved to be the hardest part as there were many angles where the drill would not fit. Without the screws, the heavy wires would hang dangerously from the anchor locker.

After her 5th try with AT&T customer service, Janna got the WIFI hotspot unlocked for a fee of $94, more than the device retails for on Amazon.com. We still had to wait a day for the unlocking to "go through." By January 29, it was time for it to work, but my SIM card could not be activated without a Bahamian cell phone. There was no way around buying a Bahamian data-enabled cell phone so that I could activate the data package on the SIM card. Then, I would have to put the SIM in my WIFI hotspot. When I went to the BTC store in Nassau, I first bought the cheapest mobile phone, which was not data enabled. Luckily, I noticed my error quickly. I then had to exchange it for a data-enabled mobile phone for $60. That still did not work. The BTC representative had to change the APN address to direct it to the BTC network. Then, finally, we had access to cheap wireless data after weeks of work and much expense.

After crossing the bridges, I was blocked in my urgent mission. A herd of about 60 overheated, American tourists were panting from their extreme exertion of stepping out of their tour busses and were blocking the sidewalk. How dare they impede my progress to the Ben and Jerry's Ice Cream by Atlantis! My clown bike could not be slowed in its mission for $6.50 per scoop ice cream. After my sweet lunch, I could not get the tire to inflate, and I walked my unreliable bike back to the marina.

My rotund and snooty neighbors, with English accents, in the sixty-foot boat on the other side of the finger slip had been plugging into the electrical outlet by my boat for the last several days to use power tools all day long. The two middle-aged men that lived aboard had turned their much skinnier twenty-year-old "nephew" into a very noisy indentured servanthood. It seems that they had been using my electricity at a record rate on their energy-hog of a boat. The marina tried stick me with their electricity usage charging $130. My air conditioner did not work and my only electrical usage was a small battery charger on my already very energy-efficient boat. I refused to pay and complained to the owners of the complex based in North Carolina after the ladies at the office just demanded that I pay up for other people's electrical bills. The harbor master took $100 off my bill, but this would be my most expensive marina visit of the trip at about $900. I was also miffed about being charged for 4 percent for using my credit card. While this charge was common in the out islands, I thought it was stupid to encourage people to pay cash in Nassau and Paradise Island with such a crime problem.

It took an hour and a half to check out, while workmen were drilling into metal in the lobby at 100 decibels. The boat left the slip easily with the now-returned trades doing most of the work on the initial turn towards the exit. I motored to the uninhabited Athol Island which is just east of Paradise Island and Nassau harbor. I dropped the hook on the southeast side of the island letting out 120 feet of rode and chain in 13-foot depths. This time I tried securing a bridle with a rolling hitch to improve the motion. The weather was forecast to be very calm overnight. The 15-knot wind subsided to nothing in the wee hours of the morning, and I slept well. One of the great things about a cruising boat is that you can leave places like Paradise Harbor Club and Marina in your wake never to return.

27. THE LOVELY LADIES OF PALM CAY

On January 30, 2015, the marina called Palm Cay was next up. Its $1.75 per foot made it the least expensive transient berth on New Providence Island. (Despite its name, it was not on a separate Cay.) It was on the mental hospital and prison side of the island. I was hoping I would not have to be committed for going there.

I was somewhat apprehensive about the sail. The charts marked several coral reefs on this side of New Providence. Unfortunately, they never provided any depths for these reefs. Some routes seemed to go over similar reefs so I assumed that they were at the level of the charted depths. I would soon find out.

Before I departed, I called the marina one more time. A man who I would later find out to be JJ answered the phone with his South African accent, which I mistook for an Aussie accent. "You have a sailboat. You don't need power," he said.

I replied, "I don't need it, but I want it. At $0.65 per kilowatt hour I don't expect to be charged much for it."

"I want to save my slips with electricity for powerboats," he said.

"I'm not coming if I don't get a slip with power," I said. I was prepared to go to the good anchorage on the southwestern side of New Providence or Atlantis Marina if he held firm. I was sick of the customer service of Bahamian marinas already. He relented since it was unlikely that he was going to fill his marina. As long as I was staying less than a month, I could have a slip with power. I verified the previous quoted fee of $1.75 per foot, which JJ confirmed.

Marina managers in Florida and the Bahamas are often seduced by the 50+ foot-long-gas-guzzling mega yachts and sport fishing boats. Almost all the marinas with fuel docks in the Bahamas and most Florida marinas are geared to the thousands in profits they can reap from these boats that pump in hundreds of overpriced gallons of fuel at a time. My experience with Homestead Marina in Alabama and Gulfport Small Craft Harbor in Mississippi showed that the gas guzzler focus of marinas was not limited to just Florida and the Bahamas. This lesson would be driven home most times we tied up in the Bahamas. I could not wait to install the new windlass and free our 200 feet of chain. I no longer wished to patronize these places except via dinghy with my two diesel jerry cans.

Weighing anchor in the calm was easy. I just pulled the rode and it came aboard. The momentum of my pulling would get the boat ahead of the rode if I did not slowly bring in the slack. The highly touted Rose Island anchorage in the cruising guide was packed with five boats. I could not see the attraction as it offered no more protection than where I had dropped the hook that night. Moreover, it was surrounded by rocks and reefs. I stayed well off the Porgy Rocks and the Explorer chart waypoint because they looked so menacing. As JJ had suggested earlier in the week, I plotted a course that put me two miles off the eastern cape of New Providence Island. I would have the opportunity to see how shallow that cape actually was on a jog in a few days.

It was so calm that I forgot to take off the sail cover. This was the only time I had failed to do so. I did not even make an effort to unfurl the sail, and I had only done that when I had back problems, coming into Panama City. As I suspected, the red "+" marks for the coral on the charts did not mean the coral was anywhere near the surface. I would pass over these coral patches where there was supposed to be 15-feet of water and would see 17-feet on the depth sounder. I picked up the three markers, which were pilings with no day beacons. These markers did have red and green lights atop. I called the marina again, and JJ answered. He said look for the obvious channel, which was not on my chart. The channel seemed to have a black line marking the shallow water on the eastern side. Still, the brown color and evident shallowness on the west side made me favor the east over the west. I steered for the dark coral-looking patches not the sand. The turn into Palm Cay was marked in the water if not on the chart. It was exceptionally narrow, and I was glad no other boats were around.

When I came in slowly, JJ was waving me in to the first dock north of the fuel dock, pier 5. He was next to the "Hatteras" he mentioned earlier. It was a sport fishing boat on the southeast end of the first dock separated by water from the fuel dock. I approached from the east turned 90 degrees and backed in. At first, I had missed my mark and was lined up to back into the Hatteras' slip. In the calm, I just held my position 5 feet from the Hatteras' bowsprit at a full stop. When no drift was evident, I backed up a touch and used the boat hook to touch the Hatteras' bowsprit as a way to turn Contango towards its slip. Contango slid where it was supposed to go into slip 5-16. I tossed a line to JJ, and it was easy from there.

As it turned out, JJ used to work for the marina, but that day he had been filling in. He was now the skipper but not owner of the Hatteras. He had always answered the marina's phone when I called.

Linus Wilson

Despite our tangle in the morning, he soon won me over. He definitely would win the award for my favorite sport fishing boat skipper of the trip. However, the competition was not stiff. I spent the rest of the afternoon stringing wires from the quarter berth to the port aft locker where I planned to put the windlass' cockpit controls. JJ would mock Daly's barking while working into his case of beer with the occasional visitor while washing down the Hatteras. This would only send the little dog into an even more silly barking fit until I picked him up or scolded him.

On my first night in Palm Cay, I locked myself out. I had gone for a very expensive drink at the marina restaurant, the Billfish Grill. (If you have any doubt about the kind of boats the developers wanted to attract to the marina, you just have to look to the restaurant's name.) I am very forgetful, but, since we bought Contango, we had used a combination lock for the companionway. That night I cast around for the combination lock, and, not seeing it, I used one of the lazarette locks. The lazarette is a hatch in the cockpit seats. When I returned from my refreshment, I realized my pockets were devoid of keys. I had gotten used to not carrying keys and locking the boat keys into the boat, because I had been using the combination lock. My first instinct was to borrow a hacksaw. Upon further inspection, one small one foot square hatch was slightly open. It was locked in its middle half ajar setting. I could wedge my finger in but it was closed. I got a paddle out of the hatch whose lock I used on the companionway. It was worse at turning the handle than my finger. Finally, I found a huge hose clamp which did the trick.

There was no one on JJ's boat, but another neighbor came by this time. The owner of the boat next to me, whom I had never met, was strolling in at this time as I was breaking into my boat. I said hello, and he grunted. If this act of burglary bothered him, he never let on, and he proceeded inside and plopped in a James Bond film into his DVD player, which he watched on his big screen TV.

A screen which could only be opened from the inside separated me from free access to this small opening into my boat. I used the hose clamp to cut the screen. I had a lot of left over screen and would repair this vandalism the next day. The boat keys with their many floats and rings lay on the edge of the galley sink about seven feet from the opening. Daly was perched on a box intently watching my cat burglar antics. I carefully tried to lift the keys with the boat hook. After two dozen tries, I managed to snag them without knocking them further out of my reach. I owe this great dexterity to my being repulsed by the Billfish Grill's expensive drinks. I carefully balanced the key floats on the hook and slowly pulled the huge boat hook backwards. When it was close enough to reach the keys at the end of the hook, I reached out and grasped them while balancing the boat hook with another hand.

The next day I realized what an idiot I had been. The galley window was open. Only a screen, which can be easily removed without damage from outside the cabin, separated my arm from reaching in and picking up the keys. There had been no need for all the hatch picking, screen cutting, and key balancing.

The next two days were a bit dull. Sure, I busied myself, but I was mostly waiting. I removed the old windlass that refused to drop chain and sealed the hole with epoxy. I cleaned the cabin for Janna. This was not my first bit of waiting. I had been waiting in Nassau and Bimini before. The worries of the passport and DHL problems were in the past. The money problem of docking in Nassau was eased, and the search for supplies and provisions was done.

Palm Cay was a isolated and growing development. Palm Cay was beautiful, but it was not really near any shops or other developments. It was aimed people wanting second homes in the Bahamas who were not Bahamian. The weeks in New Providence lacked the beauty and charm of Bimini even if I was relieved of the passport stress. The seven-day tourism of the Nassau was not really what I was looking for in the Bahamas, and I thought that the city of Nassau lacked the charm of St. Johns in Antigua, for example. To me it was essentially suburban sprawl with some abandoned buildings by the waterfront. I thought it was a shame that there were so many beautiful Bahamian islands with and without settlements, but most visitors to the Bahamas only saw the relatively dirty water of Nassau. (That being said, the water in Nassau is much clearer than the water in of Florida!)

A birthday party invitation from one of Sophie's Pre-K3 classmates, had made Janna and Sophie fly out on Sunday instead of Saturday. My lovely ladies, Janna and Sophie, were due to arrive late on Super Bowl Sunday. Perhaps that was why their ticket was so affordable. I rarely care to watch the Super Bowl if there is not a team that I have an affinity for such as the New Orleans Saints in the game. Nevertheless, that night I went up with the expats who were mostly not Americans to watch the game. I found nothing compelling in it except the commercials involving Dads and their young children. (There were many of those!) They all made me fight back tears. I had lived apart from Janna for longer periods while we had been married, taking teaching jobs in other cities or countries. Nevertheless, I had not been away from Sophie, then age four, for such a stretch since her birth. I wanted my girls back!

Janna was weighed down by the 30-pound windlass, a part for the starboard sheet winch, and the air conditioner cooling pump. She got stopped in customs and paid duty on the parts. I had read there was no custom duty on boat parts, but that was clearly wrong. She paid the 10 percent duty and got to keep the parts thankfully. Unfortunately, this delay meant she got to the car rental counter at 8:15 PM or 15 minutes after it closed. She got a $70 cab instead. I met them in the parking lot, and we loaded the boat in the dark. The lovely ladies were in the Bahamas at last!

I had hoped that Janna's rental car could be used to take Daly to his grooming appointment 3.2 miles away. That plan was shot. I tried to beg for the marina's courtesy car from the marina office, but it was spoken for. I tried to bike Daly to his appointment with the new tube that I had put on while waiting for Janna and Sophie's arrival. I wound around the older subdivisions towards a more commercial road in my tiny bike with a four-pound dog in his bag. About 0.75 miles into the trip, the chain fell off, and I repaired it as a huge dog barked at

Daly in the distance. Daly returned the barks in his bag. When I looked up, a huge Siberian husky was barking behind a tiny fence, which well below his shoulders. I was not sure what was restraining the artic beast. Perhaps it was the Bahamian heat.

Daly and I eventually made it to the distant vet and grooming office after making more chain repairs along the way. I gave Daly a chance to "pee pee" before his appointment as his command goes. He had to poop. It was a mushy poop that would not get unstuck from his bottom hairs, which had grown way too long. I went into the drug store to get reinforcements because my old bank withdrawal slip was not up to the task. I bought a roll of paper towels and started the process of wiping his bottom from the mass of poop when a representative from the vet's office asked why I was taking so long to walk in. They had been watching me through the window. As there was no one else in that bombed out parking lot, I was hard to miss.

The groomer asked me a lot of questions about how I wanted him cut. I don't think we communicated perfectly. When I returned in the afternoon, he had more of a uniform buzz cut than a poodle cut. Pink patches of his skin were visible for the first time. I asked the groomer if any other boaters used their grooming salon since dogs on boats were common. The groomer replied, "No." Daly would look very strange for his trip to the out islands.

After dropping off Daly at 9:30 AM, I had the long ride back. My chain fell off again. I tried hailing a jitney, the tiny informal public busses in Nassau, but it stopped briefly and sped off as I tried to load on my miniature bike. A 6'3" 20-year-old local man, seeing my frustration, offered his services. "Give me that wrench. You are doing it wrong," he said.

"No thanks, I don't need any help." I replied. Besides my apprehension about handing my bike to a guy that hangs out in front of a liquor store at 10 AM, I was absolutely certain that I had more experience fixing the chain than he did. Only after three further refusals did he return to his stoop across the street.

Linus Wilson

I pedaled on sweating with Daly's empty bag and my backpack. At a gas station ½ a mile up, a man asked "Are you from Palm Cay?" I replied "yes" and Gary the salesman gave me a ride back. I stood out with my floppy hat, huge orange cell phone around my neck, and my clown bike.

I decided to leave my bike at home for the second half of the half marathon when I picked up Daly in the afternoon. I thought the jitneys would be much quicker since I saw five of them pass me on the way up to the groomer in the morning. That still meant I had a mile of subdivision jogging to get to Prince Charles Avenue where the 15 and 15a jitneys ran. I caught a jitney once I hit that street and hopped in. I was asked to hand over $1.25 as the dingy bus rambled on. I did not have exact change, but the young driver made change. A girl, perhaps his girlfriend, was managing some music program playing modern hip hop tunes at high volume in the seat behind the driver. I hopped off a little early and picked up Daly.

My attempts to catch a jitney back were much less successful. There were no obvious bus stops on this side so I jogged slowly looking over my shoulder with Daly bobbing patiently in his bag. I made it to the end of the jitney route with no busses stopping. I stopped at the grocery store and the drug store there. I picked up some Mardi Gras beads and a shovel and pail for Sophie, who wanted to use them on Palm Cay's well-manicured beaches. About ¾ of mile from the boat, I saw Gary again going the other way. I begged off his offer of a ride this time.

Janna and Sophie's beach time was marred by their difficulty washing off afterwards. The beach shower was only partially done. Since my parents visited every beach on the Florida peninsula, in my youth, I could recognize a properly constructed one. Really, it is common sense. You don't want to wash of the sand and salt from your feet until you are out of the sand, for instance, when you are on a raised wooden walkway. Unfortunately, the foot shower at Palm Cay was in the middle of the sand. If you washed off a foot, it would get immediately covered in sand. Janna and Sophie would swear off the beach several more times before the trip was done. I mostly avoided beaches, too, to avoid the sand mess. Also, I went to great lengths to avoid sun exposure, but a perma-tan was inevitable. Sitting on a sunny beach seemed less preferable to sitting in the shade of a Bimini in the cockpit.

In the afternoon, I installed the new pump in place of the old one, but the water pressure was low and the HPF error persisted. I took apart the hose in the evening with Tom's encouragement. The outtake line was spurting out seawater with the outtake seacock open, but the intake would not let out water when its seacock was open, and the outtake seacock was closed. I found a plastic bag blocking an elbow. I removed the plastic bag and elbow and put together the simpler system of hoses. This still did not solve the problem, and I was up until midnight opening up hose before the air conditioner could run without the HPF error. I believed that the pump had to be primed before it would work.

With the AC pumping out cold air, I turned to the windlass installation. I wired the solenoid and fuses in the battery compartment first. As daylight was fading, I put in the windlass on the only spot that it would fit and work on the foredeck. Surprisingly, it plopped into place almost perfectly. The cheeky manufacturer, Maxwell, put the warranty card on the same page as the windlass cut out, which was used to drill the holes. If you did not copy the template page, you would lose the warranty as the drills shredded it. I bet very few buyers sent in their warranty cards.

I was wiring the anchor locker connections until after Sophie went to bed. Janna was very patient with the mess that I was making with my eight open toolboxes and the salon cushions askew almost all the day. I had hoped to depart Wednesday, February 4, 2015, but I was not done with the windlass installation. I did not want to leave New Providence until I was sure that I did not need more parts.

We decided on cruising down the Exuma chain. I had heard more enthusiastic endorsements of that chain than of the Abacos from people that I met. Moreover, it was easier to get to the Exumas from

Linus Wilson

where we were. To get to the Abacos we had a long sail to Spanish Wells in Eleuthera and a 55-mile sail in the deep water between the Great and Little Bahama Banks. In contrast, it was less than 30 miles to Highbourne Cay in the Exumas. From there we could do short day hops on the shallow waters of the bank in the lee of the Exuma Islands. That would allow us to meander to the cruiser's mecca of George Town in Great Exuma.

Our weather window would close if I did not complete the windlass install on February 4. 20+ knot winds were forecast for February 6. I installed the cockpit up and down switch, made a backing plate for the screws attached to the windlass, and tidied up the wires in the chain locker on February 4. Because of a design flaw, the cockpit up and down switch was too skinny to pass through its plastic cover and a thin layer of fiberglass. I had to drill the plastic cover down to make the switch work.

It was time to turn it on. The windlass was dead as a doornail. The foot switches and the cockpit switch did nothing. My first hunch was that the three amp breaker button was not reset so I circumvented that breaker. That did nothing. I reread the wiring diagram, and I saw how I could have interpreted the placement of the negative control wire differently. This reinterpretation worked, and the windlass came to life with each tap of the cockpit and foot switches. With Janna's help, we threaded the chain through bottom of the windlass and onto the bowsprit. We switched the anchor on the all chain side from the 17-pound Danforth to the 33-pound Shark plow anchor which resembles the more popular Delta brand anchor. The Danforth was moved to the tertiary anchor roller attached to six feet of 3/8-inch chain which is shackled to the deck with no further rode.

We had dinner at the restaurant that night. It was deserted at 6PM, but the expats came in after we were seated. When we went back to the boat, JJ and a Palm Cay resident were drinking beers on the Hatteras and stringing lures for the big fishing trip the next morning. The other resident said he was from Sydney, Australia and it took four flights to reach Nassau from Sydney, Australia, 15,000 miles away. I told him it also took four flights to reach Nassau from my home in

Lafayette, Louisiana. My home was less than 1,000 miles away as the plane flies.

I set the alarm for 5:20 AM to leave at dawn. JJ warned me the previous night that the marina office does not open until 8 AM, but my experience was that it was only manned at random hours of the day. When I walked Daly and threw out the trash, a big chain closed off the entrance and exit to the marina. I saw a man milling around with a Palm Cay shirt and asked him if he could let out the chain. He said, "Yes." I asked if he could take my water key, the hoses locked at each terminal so no one could steal water from his neighbors. Further, I asked if he could take my payment for the slip fees.

"No, you have to wait until the dock master comes around 8 or 9. After you pay, I can open the gate for you," he replied. I was trapped.

This was a first for me. I had never been at a marina that locked its entrance. JJ checked me in and always answered the phone before I arrived. He did not take payment because he did not work there. JJ, the man from Sydney, and the Hatteras owner were all preparing the Hatteras to go. They were planning this offshore trip all week despite my warnings of squalls that day to the northeast where they were headed. We were headed southeast to the nearest marina in the Exuma chain at Highbourne Cay, and would likely miss them if we left soon. 3 PM was my weather forecast's best guess of when the squalls would hit Highbourne Cay.

I wished JJ goodbye and good fishing. I watched the Hatteras go out. The man that I had spoken with earlier unlocked the chain and opened the channel so they could pass. He kept it unlocked and left. I left a message on the voicemail for the dock master to call me to take my payment. I slipped the water key under the marina office door. We started up our engines and slipped off the lines.

I was at the helm because of the tricky channel, and Janna pulled in the port bow line last to help us turn out of the slip towards the exit channel. The southwest breeze aided the turn and we headed for the exit. We glided past where the chain had been strung and met with no resistance. We had to sneak out of Palm Cay, but the family's cruise of the Bahamas had begun!

28. HIGH TIMES AT HIGHBOURNE CAY

I was expecting a motor through calms and shifty winds, which would be mostly behind us. Instead, we were motoring into the two-foot seas and 10-knot sustained breezes. We left the dock at 7:30 AM but by 8:20 AM Janna was complaining of sea sickness and emerged from the cabin. Soon after Sophie, who had been on a sailboat since she was six weeks old, came down with the second bout of seasickness of her life. One minute she was carefully coloring a page in her *My Little Pony* coloring book. The next she was puking and only quick movements kept the log book and her coloring book from being ruined. I scrambled to clean up the mess with water and hid the smelly paper towels in a trash bag under the dinghy in the bow. This was not exactly the gentle introduction to the cruise that I had hoped for!

I was not able to get hold of our destination marina at Highbourne Cay over the cell phone before we were out of range. I did successfully hail it over VHF channel 71 from about 20 miles away. The operator asked me to call back when I got closer since she had more trouble hearing me than I had hearing her.

By noon both Janna and Sophie felt well enough after avoiding the cabin to start eating. Janna benefited from the Scopalamine patch, but the seasickness medicines were not dosed or recommended for kids and the resident pediatrician, Janna, thought it best to not give her anything. I thought the conditions were mild and took nothing. We put up the second reef and unfurled the genoa to 75% of the fore-triangle, but the wind angles sometimes necessitated that we furl it.

My five previous attempts to call the dock master failed, but Janna showed me his card. She got it when he let us use the courtesy car.

Slow Boat to the Bahamas

My e-mail went through and our long stay at Palm Cay ended up costing less than half of what I had paid to Paradise Harbor Club. The dockmaster called me at 6:30 PM to take my credit card details.

As we approached Highbourne, we looked at it through the binoculars, and I snapped an adorable picture of Sophie in her pink baseball cap, raincoat, and life jacket. In the picture, she peered intently through the binoculars or "spyglasses" as she liked to call them off to the stern but Highbourne lay off the bow.

Sophie is looking for Highborne Cay through the binoculars.

Highbourne Cay was buzzing with activity as we approached. A sailing cat passed us on the way in. That allowed Janna at the helm

Linus Wilson

to divine the correct approach among the narrow channels and visible rocks around the marina. The cat made a 90 degree turn north to go west of the western rock, which had a white and red marker on it.

Janna navigated through the rocks into the marina. She needed to keep giving the throttle a few seconds of forward to straighten out her bow. Fortunately, the wind was mostly blowing us into the slip so the docking was relatively easy with Janna putting the wheel hard to starboard in opposition to the wind while putting the gear mostly in neutral or reverse.

Highbourne Cay was my first exposure to the increasingly common Bahamian private islands. While most of the Bahamas are without any settlements on its hundreds of islands, many islands are the property of one family or a corporation. Many are turned into marinas while others do not accept outside visitors and are the fifth home of some rich man. Cat Cay, where I anchored but did not go ashore, was the home to a development sold to many well-to-do foreigners. Most Bahamian private islands are owned by foreigners. I much preferred outer islands with actual settlements of Bahamians such as those on the islands of North and South Bimini, Staniel Cay, Little Farmers Cay, Great Guana Cay, and Great Exuma. The private islands ranged from Disney-sweet, Highbourne Cay, to underdeveloped and creepy Cave Cay, in my opinion. We embraced civilization whenever we found it in the Exumas whether that was a private island or an older settlement.

At Highbourne Cay everything had a price. Each timed shower cost $4. Janna and I wondered if they were timed or based on water flow. We never settled the question, but my money is on the water being on a simple timer. WIFI was $15 per day. We declined that. $30 per day for 30 amp electrical service. We paid for that. We only spent $30 in our six days at Palm Cay, but they were hooked up to the Nassau grid. I'm sure electrical generation was expensive in Highbourne. It was not the highest charge for that service we would see, but it was the highest we would pay for a multiday stay. The golf carts and Hobie Catamarans were extra charges. The bikes and kayaks were no additional charge, thankfully. More importantly, trash disposal was free for marina guests. Hooray!

Slow Boat to the Bahamas

As we checked in at the marina office, the ladies at the counter were explaining the weather reports to a couple who planned to depart. They convinced them to stay a day or two more. The boats were coming in fast and the marina was full before dark. We docked at 2 PM, and I gave Daly a walk in the oppressive heat around 3 PM. He got less than 100 yards before he threw in the towel, and I had to carry him. By 4 PM, the 30-knot winds of the predicted squall line came in, and I felt the first sustained rain of the trip. I reveled in the storm opening our water catchment tanks, which quickly filled since we had used little since leaving New Providence that morning with full water tanks. I adjusted lines and fenders, leisurely enjoying the cool, free, fresh water, but a neighbor who did not understand my rain lust commented, "You got here just in time."

Next morning, I tried to get my money's worth after picking up a $9 half gallon of milk at the store which I had bought for $4.50 in Nassau the week before. (The same milk would cost $2.50 in New Orleans.) I took a "free" bike around the island. I discovered what was referred to as the "gym" on a hilltop. Two concrete slabs with grass in the middle formed a golf cart track up to the top. This grass gap in the track road was OK for golf carts but hard for a bike swaying as its rider struggled up hill. I had a three-inch ledge for the tires to fall down if strayed off one of the narrow concrete slabs. I walked the bike up, and all I found in the gym was jump rope, bosu balls, and yoga mats. I would have to do pushups if I wanted to do strength training that day. I did discover an outdoor shower that did not require a $4 token. It was completely private as long as no one chose to occupy the hill when you were washing. I would end up using this, wearing a pair of swimming trunks, later in the week. I had no visitors.

I peddled down the road marked "Explorers' Way." There were many bungalows for rent named "Columbus," "DaGamma," and similar names. I found the bus stop that the marina staff referred to with a smirk as I checked us in. There was a sign marked "BUS STOP, a bench, and a skeleton waiting for the next bus to come by. I was glad that I had a bike!

Linus Wilson

After that, I turned into the village where the people who worked on the island lived. After passing the very tidy chicken coop, I went past the University of Miami reef exploration program. (What a tough academic assignment!) Then I went down a sand road that probably led to the trash burning site. I backtracked and came upon the bonfire beach where Hobie cats and kayaks were laid out. The big Hobie cats looked like too much boat for me. I was tempted by the Optimists at Palm Cay, but not by the huge fast Hobies.

My ten minute bike ride had already stretched more than an hour, but the kayaks and paddles proved too tempting. I hid my wallet in the gazebo under some cushions because they certainly would get carried away if I capsized and started swimming. I tried launching the kayak like I had been taught in the still waters of Lafayette, Louisiana. You lay it parallel to the water line and get in and push off with your paddle. That did not really work with the two-to-four foot ocean swells breaking on this Atlantic-facing beach. I got beat up and the boat pinned sideways against me as we were punished by the sea on my beam.

Another tactic was necessary. I waded out to my hips and climbed into the middle of the boat one leg at a time and paddled quickly before I was knocked onto the beach. Once a few dozen feet out I could paddle more leisurely and slowly inch out to sea. I was tempted to go out to the far point of the bay and get a better look at the boats anchored by what I believed to be iguana refuge of Allans Cay. Nevertheless, I thought better of it and tried to stay closer to the other rocky bank on the east. Despite my efforts, I was pushed towards the outer point on the west. By the time I turned around, I still was not close to either side of the horseshoe shaped cove. Once I was turned around, the kayak was quickly back on shore. The breeze and swell propelled me onto the beach more than my oars.

When I got back, I saw Rod and Deb the Texas couple from *Si Bella* for the first time since we met at the Clearwater Beach Marina. I figured with their bigger boat and since they were probably not going through my passport problems or waiting for crew that they would be far south east of me on their way to their South American hurricane season haven. Nevertheless, here they were. I said hello and asked if they were delayed by breakdowns; but, if they were, Rod never said they were. I admired his Hawaiian sling spear gun.

"Why don't you shoot that fish?" I said, pointing to an 18-inch Barracuda just by us under the dock. He pointed out that if he shot his spear without a rope he would lose it. That was a pretty good reason!

It was so cool that I went and bought a spear and sling from the gift shop.

I began to realize that the nurse shark that I had observed swimming around was not just one shark but many different sharks. I counted 18 sharks under the fish cleaning station when no fish had been cleaned all afternoon. Occasionally, one would wander by, and I would get all excited with the Hawaiian sling and then I would realize that I glimpsed the end of a 200 pound shark not a 15-pound fish.

Sophie was getting antsy so I offered to take her and Daly to see the sharks at the fish cleaning station. This time there was Banana Bread Man who accosted us at the store selling his fresh banana bread. He had a 20-pound fish that he was cleaning.

"What kind of fish is that?" I asked.

"It's a grouper, man."

I saw many fish down there and not just sharks. I was tempted to abandon Sophie and Daly for my spear gun. Nevertheless, I was deterred by the NO FISHING sign and the knowledge that, if on the off chance my spear struck anything but a shark, the fish would be devoured immediately and my steel spear would be lost.

I asked what the yellow and black striped fish were. Banana Bread Man leaned close to Sophie and pointing and jabbing in the direction of the fish with his blade, "Dem are sailors' delights. And dose sharks are reef sharks. Dat one's a bull. Come closer now," he said beckoning with the 18-inch wickedly curved blade. "We not going to throw you in."

Linus Wilson

"That's OK my daughter is scared of sharks and does not want to get too close," I replied.

"The worthless, lazy sharks sittin' in da sand are dem nurse sharks. They won't bother you. But that reef shark or that bull shark will tear you up so get out da water if you see dem," Banana Bread Man warned.

To me, all the sharks looked the same. I was worried that Sophie was not up to the feeding frenzy that would follow as she was hugging me tightly on our approach to the fish cleaning station. So we retired to Contango after Banana Bread Man halted his lesson on fish identification.

Little birds were populating our pier all day. I brought out our plastic owl and placed him on deck in order to scare them. I was unsure if it would be effective and said, "Fly away little birds. We have an owl which of course you don't recognize because you have never seen an owl. GRRRR!"

For the next five minutes, Sophie was taunting the little birds saying, "GRRRR, I'm and owl."

Janna discovered a couple using a complicated net to catch those funny little birds, which they identified as ruddy turnstones. I found them so tame that they almost landed on my hand when I got out the clothes pin bag which probably sounded like a bread bag to them. The ornithologist told Janna, "Those little birds are very hard to catch even though they look slow."

The next morning the two scientists were tagging their great catch of ruddy turnstone birds. They traveled in a small sailboat boat named Plover. The plover is another type of small wading birds. I had gotten 1/3 of the way through the novel named *Plover* about a sailboat named Plover, and asked if they had read it. It is the story of a crazy old man who went out in the north Pacific with no destination. The book had some deep philosophical meaning that could not hold my interest and that I could not fathom. Unfortunately, the owners of the sailboat Plover had never heard of the book *Plover*.

Slow Boat to the Bahamas

The man and women sat under one of the tiki huts with six cotton bags of birds. The sixty year old lady was drawing blood samples from their captives and the seventy year old man was talking to his audience while tagging it or reading it for his partner's blood sample. They said the ruddy turnstones ranged from the artic to more tropical locations like the Bahamas. For some reason these winged travelers were not afraid of growling plastic owls. The scientists wanted to test the blood samples for the effects of oil spills.

Having sat on university research committees, I know that the hard sciences research projects are often driven by the government or private sector honey pots. The Deepwater Horizon oil spill in 2010 was the catalyst for many oil spill grants. Even if the ornithologists were not terribly interested in oil spills effects on the ruddy turnstone, tying their research to oil spills would likely make financial sense.

I saw Rod and Deb going for a walk and invited Rod to join me for a snorkel with our new spear guns. He said he could join me after he got back from his long walk. I assured him that it took me forever to load the dinghy. By the time he was ready to go, I was still gathering gear. I put in the look bucket with the clear bottom, our portable VHF, dry bag, marina map of reefs, fish identification chart, paddles, dinghy anchor, rubber bands and cloths for spear tips, bellows pump, bailer, two knives, outboard servicing kit, gas can, auxiliary gas tank, and auxiliary tank pump and attachment.

Of course, when I pulled the cord with an audience, the Honda 2 HP outboard would not start. I put more oil and gas in since it looked low on both counts and it started. Rod offered to use his dinghy instead, but I declined. I said this one was already loaded. No doubt Rod's dingy would be bigger and faster than mine.

About halfway out to the reef a mile away we realized one of the paddles had fallen off. We searched for about 10 minutes but saw nothing. The wind was blowing from the east, and we were on the lee side of the island. That meant the paddle would not wash ashore until it hit Andros Island about 50 miles way. Ironically, that would be where we would drift if our outboard died and our tiny anchor could not bite. At our reef, on the northwest side of Highbourne Cay the waves picked up to three feet instead of one-to-two feet on the approach. Rod jumped out first while I idled the engine. I had a bad feeling about stopping it in such an exposed location so far from the anchored boats. He declined to try to spear anything.

"There is no reef by the rocks. There are some pretty tiny tropical fish and a little coral. I don't want to get out my spear. There are no fish here. You can take a look," he said. I plopped in and saw he was right. I kept on getting water in the snorkel, which we shared. I struggled to get back into the dink. Rod gave me an awkward high five and said lets go. I thought that was a braver way of expressing the sentiment, "This is crazy. Let's get out of here before we both drown!" At Contango's next stop, the outboard engine would start dying for no apparent reason. In retrospect, we were very lucky the Honda 2 horsepower (HP) that was submerged in Nassau did not die on that long excursion to an exposed reef. Neither Rod nor I fancied a drift to Andros Island in an eight-foot rubber boat.

Back at the marina, I was taunted by the barracudas that were so still in the water. Once one of the dock helpers threw an apple core at one, and it hardly flinched. He then proceeded to mock the patient barracuda, or my shooting, saying it would be his for dinner when it got two feet longer. I was not willing to wait. I took several shots before leaving, but the water refracts light so that a 45 degree angle might really be 65 degrees, and I always missed. The only thing that I hit was the sandy bottom, and one time the spear stuck. Only by carefully pulling my 50 pound line and by using the boat hook to trip it did I get the spear free and back in the boat. I would catch no fish here, and tomorrow we would sail into a fish preserve where I would have to leave my sling and spear in the hatch. Which, in my case, never hurts my odds of catching a fish.

29. PARKED

Slow Boat to the Bahamas

Sophie was sprawled out on the starboard cockpit seat as we attempted to leave the dock. I grumbled a little about this. This made it harder for me to make the quick movements that are sometimes necessary. The night before I had loaded the outboard on the stern. I kept the dinghy in the water near the bow and was moving it and the lines as necessary. We left the dock easily with Janna at the helm, and there was no need for Sophie to move into the cabin.

Rod had explained the selection procedures for the moorings at the headquarters of the Exuma Land and Sea Park. You listen in on the 9 AM VHF broadcast and ask to be put on the wait list for moorings by the headquarters in Warderick Wells. I called in while we were just underway and asked to be considered for some "moorings in the north of the park." I thought that meant we were interested in moorings in Shroud or Hawksbill Cays in the north end of the park that encompasses the islands south of Wax Cay and north of Compass Cay. The operator 30 miles away thought we wanted a mooring at the north mooring field near the middle of the nature preserve in Warderick Wells. By the end of the VHF broadcast, we had been awarded mooring ball 20 at the north mooring field of Warderick Wells. This was dumb luck since this was one of the few good 360-degree protected moorings in the Exumas.

The bad luck was in that we now had a tough 30-mile slog against wind and sea instead of the 10-to-15 mile motor that I had promised Janna. The forecast for light and variable winds did not materialize that day. Instead we had 15-to-20 knot winds from the southeast mostly in the direction we were heading. Three-to-four foot waves made the going tough.

"We have 20 miles to go to. We can divert to Shroud or Hawksbill Cay and look for a mooring ball there," I shouted over the pounding.

"No, let's keep going," Janna replied. Janna looked at the wind indicator atop the mast which was pointing 40 degrees off the wind and said, "I want to try unfurling the genoa."

Linus Wilson

"We are too close to the wind. We need to be 60 degrees off for the genoa to not luff. We would have to change course," I objected.

"Let's try it." We tried it. For only 8 of those 30 miles could we fly the genoa because the wind angle was too close for the Island Packet 31. I probably should have bit my tongue more, and let her experiment without comment.

At the very end, as we entered the cut to the sound, which was the approach to the north mooring field, a few five-foot waves slowed our five-knot progress to just two-knots. As soon as we turned south to the moorings, a calm descended on the water. I had probably decided to leave a day too soon, but had we waited a day we would not have gotten a mooring at this oasis of calm.

Sophie was fascinated by what looked like a dinosaur skeleton on the beach across from our mooring ball. We took the outboard and rubber dinghy to it. I unwisely declined to tie up to the dinghy dock because I did not realize it had stairs for Sophie to climb. Instead, I landed on the beach. Our dinosaur bones actually came from a 52-foot sperm whale that had washed up on the beach decades ago. We tried to walk around the trail but got lost in the moon rocks, limestone in a tidal pool that had big holes worn into it from the tidal flows. Sophie did not like the careful stepping and insisted that I carry her back to the beach.

I could not get the outboard engine restarted. The problem with a beach is that you can tend to drift out to sea if you don't start your engine quickly. The east wind was blowing us off the beach towards Contango's mooring. I declined the first offer of a tow when a promising pull made me think that I was soon to start the Honda up. This was false hope, and I started canoe paddling in the bow.

"Why are you paddling, Dada?" Sophie asked.

"The engine won't start," I replied.

Eventually we were rescued by a couple in a 10 foot dinghy as I was running aground in the sand bar that separates whale beach and the park headquarters from Contango's mooring ball. They, too, got stuck in the sand bar as I missed the line when it was tossed to me the first time. We eventually got off, and he said, "Where are you going?"

"We are on the sailboat Contango on 'ball 20 next to the big white boat,'" I said, repeating the phrase that the park operator had uttered.

Sophie is unsure of her footing in the moon rocks on Warderick Wells on the breezy afternoon.

The woman responded, "We know. We are on the 'big white boat.'" We all fell in a sullen silence after that. Needless to say, we did not hit it off with these neighbors.

The park office was open the next day, Monday, February 9, 2015. Andrew, the voice behind the VHF was a volunteer who had a small sailboat which he had sailed from Connecticut. He loved interacting with Sophie. Janna was interested in the book exchange. Sophie and Janna would use the kayak to bring three of Sophie's books to exchange later that day.

Linus Wilson

Warderick Wells has no mobile phone signals. The nearest towers in Highbourne Cay and Staniel Cay are too far away. If you want to download the occasional text e-mail, such as the daily weather report from Chris Parker, you need to pay for their satellite WIFI. I got two days for $15 per day. You are limited to a puny 100 MB, so streaming movies or even web surfing is out because of the slow speeds of their satellite internet.

I would not be able to download e-mails from the park office with my iPhone. I found that if I sat in our dinghy just east by the docks where the wardens kept their boats, I could download a few e-mails or update my Windfinder app very slowly. I opted to have Chris Parker send me evening updates. I took the dinghy out and idled and bounced around nearby the Warden's Dock in the dark. I was bouncing between shallows, anchored boats, moored boats, and the dock in that tiny cove. A security officer came out and warned me not to land. I eventually gave up without getting my weather e-mail. By the last day, when we left, I found that if I hiked west on the path near the closed access building with the antenna, I could get enough bars of the satellite WIFI to download a few e-mails on my iPhone.

We had initially planned to press on before another bout of high winds hit as early as Tuesday. I could not get a hold of the marinas at Sampson Cay or Staniel Cay with the VHF. Janna and I agreed we should keep our $20 per night mooring ball here because this seemed as secure as any marina berth with such an amazingly well protected harbor.

Janna and Sophie had planned to play in the sand on Whale Beach. Janna attached the paddle by the safety cord but not the paddle holder on the side of her green kayak. The kayak was tied to the stern of Contango. While Sophie and I looked on from above the boarding ladder, the paddle had drifted six feet away down current by the time Janna had climbed into the kayak. The safety strap broke and Janna jumped into the water to retrieve it wearing her half-zipped life jacket. That action spilled the contents of her beach gear. Sophie's mask, snorkel, and bucket fell into the water. I was worried that I would have to rescue Janna from the inflatable dinghy, and clipped

Slow Boat to the Bahamas

Sophie's harness to the boat's port jackline in anticipation of going after Janna. Fortunately, Janna managed to retrieve the paddle, bucket, and shovel, and get back to the kayak. The water bottle and mask were driven north towards the nearest Atlantic Ocean cut with the strong outgoing ebb tide. Sophie's mask and snorkel were slowly sinking. I spent 20 minutes looking for it in the inflatable dinghy, but I never found it.

I dropped Janna and Sophie off on Whale Beach with the inflatable and promised to retrieve them in a half hour or so. I had my eye on some dinghy moorings by a snorkel site. I decided that I had better only attempt the reef snorkel at slack water at 5 PM that day. I used my bucket with the clear plastic bottom, the look bucket, to inspect the reef from the dinghy. It was very colorful and seemed worth a snorkel later in the day. I noticed that one solo snorkeler did not use the dinghy mooring. Instead, he held the painter of the dinghy while drifting or paddling above the reef. That is what I ended up doing at slack water. I admired the plentiful orange and purple coral formations and schools of small fish until I spotted a three-foot-long shark and scrambled back into the rubber dinghy.

The greatest asset that the wife in a cruising couple can have is a poor sense of smell. In the wilderness, such as Warderick Wells, trash is the first thing that will drive you to depart. There is no trash disposal at Exuma park. Flushing toilet paper is a recipe for stinky hose replacements or worse cleanings in remote locations. Thus, the toilet paper must go in the trash bag. Three days on a ball or anchor without shore side trash disposal or toilet facilities as was the case here means the trash, and thus the cabin reeks of poop. If this was bothering Janna, she did not let on, and I was the first to exile the offending bag tied to the foredeck.

The next day was the big blow with 20-to-30 knots coming from the west. This was the day when everyone was grateful to be moored at Warderick Wells and the wait list swelled. Warderick Wells' north mooring fields is one of the few moorings or anchorages in the

Linus Wilson

Exumas with protection from the west wind. You generally can't anchor on the east side of the chain's islands because of the Atlantic swell and the great depths on the east side of the islands.

I dinghied out to the park office dock very carefully. On my approach, I tried to hit the west end of the dinghy dock. The visitors tie up on the north side of that dock and the wardens tie up on the south side. The east side attaches to the land and the west end is narrower than a dinghy. I figured that if I let the wind blow me onto the west end and pin the dinghy, I could use my hands to move the dinghy to the north side where I could tie up. Alternatively, if I went directly to the north side, the dinghy would probably bounce off and the wind and swell would push me into the rocky shore and disable my propeller in the shallows. The former plan worked perfectly. I landed on the west side and turned the boat to the north side with my hands.

Some other cruisers from the New Orleans area, Mandeville on the north shore of Lake Pontchartrain in the sailboat Lagniappe raved about the Boo Boo Hill hike. Once in the park office, I asked Andrew for a map and more advice on how not to stray off the "trail." The trail, he said, was marked by yellow spray paint on various rocks and cairns. This helped. Still, I did not do well reading the trail map and hiked to some western beaches instead. The closest way to Boo Boo Hill was going back to the park office and Whale Beach. Janna and Sophie had sworn off the horrors of sand the day before after their beach outing. Thus, this intrepid adventurer abandoned the 0.2 mile trek because he was afraid of getting sand in his shoe.

I was also careful on my departure of the dinghy dock. I once again moved the dinghy with my hands to the west end of the dock so it was pinned against it. This prevented me from getting off the dock unless the outboard was firing on its only cylinder. This time I was motoring against the wind and swell, which was a wetter and slower proposition. Once I rounded the sandbar, I motored beam on to the waves and got soaked sitting on the windward port side.

On my approach to Contango, I figured that if I approached upwind I would drift in if the motor died. I forgot that the dinghy can't turn under power without the propeller turning as the outboard acts as both propulsion and a means of steering. I had to rev the engine to turn into Contango. I ended up grasping Contango's stern cleat going six miles an hour. I nearly knocked myself off the dinghy with this maneuver. I let go of the cleat and chose to tumble into the center of the dinghy rather than trying to hang onto the stern of Contango without the dinghy. After I recovered from nearly dislocating my shoulder and losing our most reliable way of getting on and off the boat, I sensibly approached Contango from the stern. Janna saw these antics and decided that leaving the boat that day was unwise.

I had big plans for further snorkeling but the wind and cold had sapped my resolve. I barely mustered the courage to program waypoints for Staniel Cay into the chart plotter on the chilly deck. Sophie played inside, creating a tent out of a sheet and the quarter berth cushion, which I removed to take a kink out of the auxiliary water tank's hose. I was successful in downloading Chris Parker's e-mail from Contango, and he forecast 15 knot north to northeast winds to Staniel Cay the next day. That was a fair breeze, and we planned our departure.

30. ADRIFT IN A RUBBER DINGY

While Warderick Wells and the rest of the Exuma Land and Sea Park make a beautiful nature preserve which we loved to visit, they did test our self-sufficiency. We had laundry to do, trash to get rid of, and groceries to buy. Janna was leaning towards staying an extra day, but she was willing to leave. No one else chose to go before us as we pulled in our mooring lines and motored out. When we heard the morning VHF net a little later, we found actually 6 of the 20 boats in the north mooring field decided to depart that day.

Linus Wilson

The wind was indeed fair. Janna gybed us most of the day to avoid sailing dead downwind. The Staniel Cay Yacht Club would not let boats tie up because it was unsafe in the west wind. They gave me the name and number of Solomon, who ran the mooring balls. Unlike what was marked on the chart, Solomon said there were only four mooring balls just south of the island of Big Majors Spot and east of the rock called the Thunderball Grotto. The charts said there were four more just west of Staniel Cay by Club Thuderball, a building with that huge sign. Solomon was right and the charts were wrong.

We found all the balls filled when we arrived at 1:00 PM. Instead, we anchored just south of the mooring balls and east of Thunderball Grotto in seven-foot depths with the aid of the new windlass. The Thuderball Grotto was a rock formation that opened to the sky. It was only accessible by swimming underwater at high tide. Under the cathedral-like opening was a coral reef with many fish. Tourists were encouraged to feed the fish, but no fishing was allowed. Where we anchored had about 360-degree protection with Staniel Cay to the east, north, and south. Big Majors Spot was on the west, and three large rocks, which included Thunderball Grotto on the west.

Janna and Sophie stayed aboard for the first run with the trash, laundry, and water bladder. A full water bladder was too heavy to transport all three of us in the 600-pound capacity dinghy. Thirty-two gallons of water weighs about 270 pounds. The outboard, a little extra gas, paddles, and I probably weigh 230 pounds. That leaves only 100 pounds for Janna and Sophie, which is too little. Besides, there was a foul brown liquid in the dinghy after it had been storing the trash bags on passage. The ladies would wait until I bailed it out without the trash bags.

The dinghy beach was at the Staniel Cay Yacht club about half a mile away. This breakwater was made up of three 3 by 3 feet by 2 feet-sandstones stacked on one another. The northwest wind rolled me in through the entrance and onto the beach. It took a long time to get anyone's attention as the Staniel Cay Yacht club is the headquarters of the continual party for the foreign boat owners who anchor near there or the tourists who rent bungalows nearby. I paid to dispose of the trash and arranged to get the laundry done, calling the lady suggested by the bartender, who took my trash money. (It was $3.50 each for our three small bags. Large bags cost $7 per bag.) I asked to buy water, and I was introduced to a one-armed man who showed me a hose on a pier outside the dinghy beach.

I motored into the swell. I approached the high dock from the side. A heavy swell was crashing into the rocks behind the pier to which the one armed man had directed me. If I approached directly from the east side of the pier, where the ladder and hose access was, I risked a poor approach would pin the dinghy on the rocks. However, landing on the sided of the pier, I had room to motor on if I did not grab it well the first time. I hand walked the dinghy to the east side to the ladder and put in 24 gallons before getting nervous of overfilling the bladder. A nurse shark swam below waiting for me to fall off the boat. I never asked the one-armed man how he lost it. (Did I need to?) After paying for my $0.50 per gallon water, I hand walked the dinghy to the end of the pier a few feet away and easily motored off. About half-way to the boat, the outboard motor started dying. After failed attempts to restart it, I accepted my first tow in Staniel Cay. It would not be my last.

Janna and Sophie wanted to go ashore next. Unfortunately, our Honda outboard was not prepared to take us there. It died half-way to the dinghy beach at the Staniel Cay Yacht Club. Janna paddled us to a nearby private dock with a ladder which she and Sophie climbed up. We were a boat in distress after all! The homeowners waved, and Janna suggested I stay with the boat and sort it out after I passed up Sophie's tether. She planned to cure our toilet paper crisis while I fumbled with the outboard. I promised to meet her at the legal landing at the yacht club.

The outboard started, and then it died just as quickly. I frantically paddled back to the dock. I changed the spark plug, but it would not start. After I drained the carburetor, it started. I motored all the way to the fuel dock at the yacht club. Then it died as I was rounding the 120-foot supply ship that was refueling there. From there I canoe paddled the dinghy into the tight entrance to the breakwater for the dinghy beach. Having made it to the dinghy beach for the second time that day, I set out to find Janna and Sophie at the Burke's Blue Store, but got lost and ended up at Isla's General Store on the south side of the island.

I met up with Janna and Sophie at the yacht club, where we had dinner. Janna's Dad had several suggestions, which he texted to me and I tried to follow; but, I was confounded by the sandy beach. You can't keep the motor upright without holding the dinghy in deeper water. Sand and salt water threatens to contaminate an already suspect engine. Did I mention that I saw sharks nearby?

A lady stopped me and said, "We saw you adrift. We were going to offer you a tow, but we thought you would get it restarted."

"I did, too," I said.

"You really need to do something about that!" she warned.

"I'm trying to fix it now," I said. I showed her my empty Coruna bottle, which I intended to drain out some oil into. She did not seem convinced of my ultimate success.

When Janna came and loaded up the dinghy with the groceries, we got the motor started for all of ten seconds before it died just as we exited the dinghy beach breakwater. We quickly used hands and oars to reenter the breakwater. After that, we did not have the confidence to motor out into the dark bay where the chances of getting a tow at this hour were slim. We got a tow back to Contango a few minutes later.

The next morning the anchor drag alarm went off. I went through the tedious procedure of pressing the foot button for 15 feet of chain. Then I ran down to the v-berth and cleared the chain pile. Next I ran up and used the windlass button to pull up 15 more feet of chain, I repeated this until all the chain was up. Our bow lacked access to the chain locker. The only chain locker access was from inside the cabin at the head of the v-berth. We picked up an empty mooring next to Thunderball Grotto.

I redid the sunken motor service procedure that I performed in Nassau. I dumped the gas and changed the oil and the spark plug. I ran the outboard for 30 minutes continually and had complete faith in it. There was a good chance that the outboard took some water in the tank in the rough conditions when it bobbed behind Contango on its mooring in Warderick Wells. However, that was not an insight I had at the time.

We loaded up the dink and with two more trash bags and landed on Club Thuderball's dock. We climbed up the ladder, and the only clear way to the road led straight through the club. There were two middle aged men playing chess on the porch of the club which was 40 feet above the dock. I asked, "We picked up a mooring ball. Is Solomon around, or do I pay someone in the club?"

"Naah, you gots to see Solomon, but he's in Nassau today," one replied.

The benefit of landing at Club Thunderball, which was little more than a half-abandoned building except for the men that hung around in odd places, was that it was near the dump. If you take your trash bags to the dump, you don't have to pay the yacht club rates. It is free. A large mass off flies and the smoke rising above the brush served as our guideposts along the hot dirt road.

After our stinky mission was completed, Janna and Sophie opted to ride the dinghy into town rather than hoof it in the heat and swirling dirt. The dinghy did great, and we landed on the dinghy beach.

We got laundry and learned the about the out island exchange rates since the laundromat doubles as a liquor store. Inflation in the prices of food and drink in the Bahamas is best reflected in the beer prices. You'll pay $8.99 for a 6 pack of Corona bottles in Miami at a random convenience store. In Nassau, the six pack will cost $14.40. In the Exuma settlements of Staniel Cay, Little Farmers Cay, or Black

Linus Wilson

Point Settlement it will cost you $24.00. If you make it to George Town, you will find Nassau prices of $14.40 for a six pack. You can make money just buying things at the Nassau retailers and selling them in the small settlements as little as 30 miles away.

Consider the equivalent in the United States. Only a madman would go into our great cities of New York or Washington DC and buy foodstuffs in the local retailers and sell them in rural Arkansas and hope to make a profit. Such a madman would lose all his capital in the first week. In the Bahamian out islands, this is probably the best business one can be in. Forget about learning to code and building the next great app. Buy stuff in Nassau and charge an 80 percent markup on a small island, and you will be on the road to riches.

We were gouged terribly in Staniel Cay but never complained, and we would come to regret that we did not buy more groceries while we were there. I had laughed at Herb Payson's account in *Blown Away* of his wife's dozen trips to the grocery store. They packed every available air space in the boat full of non-perishable foodstuffs. We were not crossing oceans as Mr. Payson had been. Ironically, we were visiting populated islands less than 200 miles from Miami. I operated on the principal that if you visit islands with people, there will be places to buy food. I would soon find this was not the case. Further, this means you may pay exorbitant out island prices for low quality food stuffs as we often did.

We also realized by Staniel Cay that we did not carry enough cash. We were nearly wiped out of cash by that time. There were no banks or cash machines between Nassau and Great Exuma. If there was someone who accepted a credit card, you would have to pay four percent over the sticker price for the credit card fee. Most places would not accept a credit card. The laundromat did not have a credit card machine, but the proprietor accepted a credit card if you paid her relative at the Blue Store by credit card.

I got out the plastic as Isla's General Store for some 4-stroke motor oil and small propane canisters for the grill. Looking back, I should have sprung for a new gas can at Isla's too. The odds were that a large part of my outboard troubles were caused by watery gas from a five gallon gas can filled with 3.5 gallons in Alabama in December. Since that chilly day in December, I had had a lot of water splashing over the bow where that plastic can was stored. As the contents of that can got lower it was harder to pour in the gas without pouring in the water from the bottom. I can't know for sure, because at this time I did not examine the gas in clear plastic Glad Slider bags as I did by the end of the trip.

I dropped off Janna and Sophie on the boat with the motor running great. In my haste to load on the bladder tank and diesel jugs, and unload our laundry and gear, I unloaded the paddles. I refilled the small one-gallon gas can with my large one, and used it to fill the dinghy tank. I also must have knocked one of the inflation inlets because the boat quickly lost air. I had to reinflate it before departing. Thus, I went out in a leaky rubber dinghy with an unreliable outboard and no paddle. What could go wrong?

Well, nothing went wrong! I filled up the diesel cans and water with the motor performing fine. I topped up the Honda's tank with my one-gallon gas can. However, soon after I departed for Contango, I noticed it lacked power. Then it just sounded weak, but I throttled up. That killed it. It restarted with some choke but died when I let the air in. I drifted to the west shores of Staniel Cay while I checked everything. I put more oil in, checked the spark plug, and drained the carb for the last time. (The carburetor drain screw would seize up after this and would be impossible to open. This is one reason I had trouble easily testing the watery gas theory.) I had drifted onto a rocky part of Staniel Cay's west shore north of the dock where Janna and Sophie had been dropped when the engine died the day before. I waded in the deep water to keep the outboard in deep enough water. By some miracle, it started, and I hopped in.

I got 200 yards before it died. Choking gave me 20 more yards but no more. This time I was out of ideas. I got out the bailer and started paddling straight for Contango. My bailer paddle made slow progress. The current was setting me north towards the Atlantic Ocean cut. Contango was northwest about one-third of a mile. No other boats were close. If I made my westing, I would hit Contango before drifting out to sea. A man passed fast in a fishing skiff, ignoring my bailing of the ocean. A white-haired man witnessed it all and left his sailboat to rescue me. He was one of the few cruisers with a dinghy smaller than mine. I asked for help, but then he hesitated as if having second thoughts about his rescue mission.

"I can help you, but I have to check my fuel first," he said.

"I have plenty of fuel," I offered, showing my almost-full gallon gas can.

"I have a two stroke," he objected. That probably saved us since my fuel probably would have stuffed both our engines. Two stokes need an oil-gas mixture so, even if my fuel was not watery, it was not going to work on his outboard without oil.

He said he had enough and threw me a rope. I pointed out Contango, but he was towing me 90 degrees from that target. "My boat is that way," I repeated.

"I know. My boat will have to zig-zag to get there," he said. He had a super light mercury 2 HP, 2-stroke.

We thanked him profusely at the boarding ladder but could not convince him to stay and chat. Janna had seen my distress, but was not sure what to do with the green kayak and Sophie. I'm glad that she stayed aboard. "If we have a weather window, we need to go back to Nassau and get a new outboard," I said.

31. A NEW OUTBOARD

When you think of the failures that can end a trip, your dinghy's outboard motor does not come to mind, but it is a key piece of gear. A rigging failure, an engine, or propeller problem are worse. Nevertheless, without a dinghy that can get you to shore, you have to marina-hop and marina-hopping in remote places is limiting and may not be possible. We had lost one of its oars, and it was never easy to row, even with both oars clicked in. In most anchorages or moorings, rowing that dinghy would be a gamble with one's life. A three-quarter mile row to the dinghy dock as we had in Staniel Cay was out of the question in our rubber dinghy.

I still liked Honda's smallest outboard—the new 2.3 HP model—over other brands because it was so lightweight. Unfortunately, the next day I found that the only Honda outboard dealer in the Bahamas did not carry the 2.3 HP.

On a whim, I called Watermaker's Air which had direct flights to Ft. Lauderdale from Staniel Cay. I had met a woman who got a ticket on it for $150 booking months in advance yesterday, but I could fly right away for $700. Given that I expected a 50 percent Nassau markup off of U.S. outboard prices, this flight might pay for itself.

We also faced a pee pad crisis. Without pee pads for our dog Daly, our boat trip would become a smelly ordeal. He peed primarily on the square absorbent pee pads. I had not seen any since landing, and the prospects for shipping them appeared awful.

I found a Honda dealer with a new outboard in stock who would sell it for less than $900. They would be open Saturday, February 14. Thus, if I flew out that afternoon on Friday, February 13, I could be back by Sunday, and we would be on our way with the outboard and new pee pads and other less urgent supplies in my opinion (My Little Pony toys) and on our way.

Since this was likely our last day next to the Thunderball Grotto, I wanted to use the green kayak to paddle the 200 yards to this marvelous snorkel. However, my tide predictions were less than perfect. At supposed slack water 6 AM, I tied a line to the stern cleat and tried to swim back to the boat without pulling on it. I could make no progress without grabbing the trailing line. After repeating this I found I could swim by 8 AM, and I paddled out. There were two

Linus Wilson

dozen people there, and about one-third were less than 10 years old. I hopped off in the three foot deep water and lifted the kayak and paddle on a low rock shelf. (Janna and Sophie stayed on Contango.) I swam to the easiest entrance, which was not submerged at high tide as the cruising guide warned. The most dangerous part was avoiding your fellow swimmers who might push you onto a sharp part of the sandstone walls. 15 feet into this rock cave we emerged in the sunlight-filled grotto. I fed the many dozens of fish the soggy crackers from my pocket. If I held the crackers in my hand, I would get suction-like kisses. Finding that level of intimacy with the fishes disturbing, I preferred to scatter the crumbs and watch the fish and observe the coral formations ten feet below.

After I paddled back, we found that the Staniel Cay Yacht Club was allowing boats to tie up at the marina that day. Logistically, this was the only thing that made senses since we really could not use the dinghy. We docked along the long pier as directed. No pilings held us off the dock. However, the weather was forecast for 5 to 15 knots from the north for the next three days. I felt confident in leaving Janna and Sophie with Contango tied to the dock for two days, and they were excited to be able to walk off the boat. You actually checked into the flights at the yacht club. I got a free golf cart ride to the flight on the 8-seat propeller driven plane. We waited in an open-air shelter looking out on the strip of dusty asphalt, which passed for a runway. Our plane was large only in comparison to the other planes that had landed before it.

Janna, Sophie, and I had seen the pictures of swimming pigs everywhere and read about them in the cruising guide. Sophie had only approved of going forward with the trip based on the promise of swimming pigs. However, I was very uncertain where they were until the plane flew over their beach. You could make out the pigs on the beach and swimming on the west side of Big Majors Spot. For every boat anchored by Staniel Cay, there were at least four anchored off Big Majors Spot.

Actually, the plane retraced my entire trip through the Bahamas going over the north mooring field in Warderick Wells where every boat could be pointed out. It passed Highbourne Cay, New Providence, Chub Cay, and Bimini and then crossed the ocean to Port Everglades in Ft. Lauderdale that clear afternoon.

The Watermakers Air plane above was actually large compared to most planes that flew between the Bahamian settlements outside of Nassau.

Huge container ships and cruise ships raced into and out of Port Everglades. I had originally thought that I would cross to the Bahamas from Port Everglades the sea access from Ft. Lauderdale until I abandoned the idea of taking the Okeechobee Canals. I was glad that I did not depart from such a busy shipping port. I got to see too many great ships close up on my Gulf Stream crossing from the remote Angelfish Creek!

We flew into the executive airport in Ft. Lauderdale and taxied to the customs and immigration hangar. We were hustled outside and stood next to a huge private jet the size of a 737, which insisted on firing its engines not 30 feet from us. I was knocked over by the wind blast of smog and had to retreat around the corner of the building until we were allowed in to meet with the representatives of our government. Everyone from the plane waited for all others to be checked in because the only way out was to get back in the plane. We finally taxied to hangar 19, where Watermaker's Air flew out of. The English engineer, who had earlier offered me a ride, bowed out and recommended I get an Uber to my rental car, which was at the far away international airport.

The airline offered to call me a town car or a cab. I opted for the cab, but downloaded the Uber app for the first time just in case. Uber is app that matches private drivers with passengers and is usually cheaper and quicker than calling a cab.

The car rental and international airport was next to the "mothership" West Marine store, which is the largest West Marine store in the country. I, of course, dropped several hundred dollars on my first visit there, getting among other things, the paddle I had lost in Highbourne Cay. The pee pad crisis was solved by stopping at the first grocery store I saw before I went to bed. My Dad had to work miracles to find me a $100 per night Motel 6 on a weekend where budget motels were renting rooms for $250 per night.

When I picked up the new Honda 2.3 HP outboard, I told the parts guy about the problems that I was having with the four-year-old Honda 2 HP. He said he thought it was a carburetor issue. Clearly since the drain screw could not be opened, a new carb could not hurt. However, he said he had no spare carbs in stock, and it would take three business days to order them. I called about ten other Honda Marine dealers within driving distance, and none stocked the carb I needed. I packed the new Honda 2.3 HP outboard with its propeller removed in my large travel bag. Its box was too unwieldy to transport. Plus shipping it in the box ensured a customs duty and possibly delays clearing. I used pee pads for padding sprinkled with over a dozen My Little Pony toys to keep morale on the good ship Contango high.

Janna texted me on Saturday night, "You would not believe the motion of the boat. We are at the yacht club to get dinner and respite." Janna is a very sound sleeper (unlike me), and she never calls or texts after 10 PM. She gets plenty of emergency texts as a physician while on call, and thus would never want one from me unless there were a true emergency. However, at 3 AM she texted, "One of the cleats broke last night. V hard to get on and off the boat with Sophie. Gas and diesel spilled." When I asked which cleat broke one she texted, "Wooden one on the port side behind the winch." Dean had predicted the demise of that teak cleat. He must have a voodoo Contango doll! "There will be more damage. Can't modify the motion of the boat anymore," she finished.

I encouraged her to use the dock lines and fenders to better protect the boat. It made no sense for her to depart alone, which I don't believe she has ever done, when I had no means of boarding the boat. However, I said, if she could get another sailor to help her leave, she could do it if she felt it was necessary for the safety of the boat or her and Sophie. In all, the cleat broke, a dock line snapped, the upper support of the solar panel snapped, and the port beam rub rail was badly bent.

It was extraordinary because we have stored this boat in New Orleans for weeks on end without being able to adjust its dock lines and it never has sustained had any damage. This boat rode out Hurricane Katrina in the Municipal Marina, by all accounts the graveyard of many sailboats. Unbelievably, I left the boat tied up in a marina for two days with an experienced sailor on board, who has American Sailing Associations (ASA) 101, 103, 104, 105, and 106 certifications, and the boat sustains structural damage. The weather was mild, supposedly with north winds of 5-to-15 knots forecast. That is much less than the 15-knot average wind speed. How could this have happened!

I had trouble sleeping and was dropping off the minivan at the car rental counter at 5 AM. I paid half as much for the Uber car as the cab two nights before ($15 versus $30) to get back to Watermakers Air's hangar 19. The problem was that no one checks in early for executive jets. I arrived at 5:05 AM for a 7 AM flight. The pilot did

Linus Wilson

not show up until 6 AM. I had no warm clothes and it was very cold that morning in Ft. Lauderdale. Instead of calling another Uber to take me somewhere warm, I decided to use some of Bear Gryll's cold weather survival tactics. Exercise until you start to sweat and then stop until you get cold. (Sweat induces hypothermia, and makes you stink!) Then repeat. My 50 yard jogs worked well and released nervous tension. In an hour, I was inside and did not need to go to the gym.

We cleared customs and immigration in Andros Island. It was a landing strip cut out of a huge forest. I wondered if there was any town near this remote outpost. I was not asked the value of my bags, and I cleared without having to pay more duty. Janna refused to rent a golf cart to pick me up texting, "I won't be able to pick you up. We cannot get off the boat." I hitched a ride on one of the marina carts after collecting my bags in Staniel Cay.

Contango was scarily close, just four feet from the stern of a trawler in front of us. It was three feet below the dock on average because of the tide bobbing in the one-to-two foot swells. The north wind was blowing Contango off the dock, which would have normally been good. However, it made it very hard to get on and off the boat. With Janna's help, I used a line to get the boat close enough to the dock so I could board it. Then, I winched the line closer to the dock. Because the angle was wrong, it kept getting jammed with the wraps on the drum overlapping. Janna helped keep it from tangling. When the line was winched close enough, I loaded the luggage and thus the new outboard on board. Then we started the long process of having the winch to move the boat further away from the white trawler.

Janna said the trawler owners told her that they were waiting for us to leave so they could have an easier time exiting. One of the trawler's dock lines caught on their 50 HP dinghy outboard and was lifting the dinghy and outboard into the air. That cut our four-foot clearance to one foot at the closest wave cycle. I warned the trawler owner about this, and he secured his line so that it did not completely knock his outboard off his boat.

I read the marina the riot act about how unsafe their dock was. However, they maintained they had never heard of boats being cracked up. Janna had spoken to owners of other boats being damaged while we were there. She had seen other owners retying their dock lines and fenders throughout the night. In one case, workers from the Staniel Cay Yacht Club brought out a huge fender for one of the large power yachts. I asked, "Why did you close the dock when we first arrived in Staniel Cay four days earlier if it was so safe?" They did not have a satisfactory answer. I refused to pay the full price and asked for the manager. The owner, an American-accented, middle-aged man came around and only relented when I said I would do a lot more than sue the marina if I had to pay full price for the two nights. "Don't test me! I will 'take you to the mattresses'," quoting the line from the Godfather. He waived the two nights of transient fees.

I would have rather had the boat without the damage, but that was better than nothing. From now on, we would to be very careful to see if places posing as marinas have basic protections such as a breakwater or land on all sides and pilings or a floating dock so that the dock does not become a lee shore. Staniel Cay Yacht Club disabused us of the notion that being tied up in a marina was safer than anchoring.

After pulling Contango far back from the white trawler, our only hazard was to swing too wide into the shallows to the south. We were on the south side of the long dock with no boats to the west and the trawler to the east nearer to the shore. The north wind would blow us off the dock and turn the bow away from the dock towards open water. That is what happened, and we left without further incident.

32. WHEN PIGS SWIM

We anchored on the south side of Big Majors Spot west of the Thunderball Grotto rock. We had plenty of room and this provided protection from the north winds. Our hope was to dinghy out to the see the swimming pigs.

After adapting a new outboard motor mount for the starboard stern rail over several hours, I put the new outboard's propeller on I filled it with oil and gas. The engine would only run at full throttle. If I attempted to run it at idle, it would die. This was a disappointing revelation for a brand new engine. Until I could fix the idling issue, I did not want to attempt long dinghy rides to the Pig Beach a mile away. I called and e-mailed the dealer and awaited some advice.

My father-in-law suggested that we may have had bad gas. This was really unfortunate timing since we just moved over a mile from the fuel dock when we had been tied up 100 feet from it for three days. We could have gotten fuel easily before, now we had to visit the fuel dock in Contango or by kayak. Neither option seemed appealing. The gas that I had in the big jug, which I was using, had no ethanol, but it was bought in mid-December at the Alabama fuel dock. The gas in the auxiliary tank was bought in late December in Carrabelle and had not been used but was also ethanol free.

I tried the jug gas in the generator and it would not start. It was a one-half gas and one-half water mixture in the generator's carb. I dumped all that gas back into the big jerry jug. Then I tried the gas in the auxiliary tank from Carrabelle, the generator started right up. I surmised the amidships-stored auxiliary tank got less green water than the five-gallon jug gas stored at the bow. I dumped all old gas out of the outboards into the big jug and emptied the one-gallon gas cans contents there also. I used the newer gas from Carrabelle in the two outboards and the generator. The old 2 HP outboard died after 17 minutes. It still seemed unreliable. The new 2.3 HP outboard ran forever, but it could not idle.

Only months later would I inspect the inline fuel filter on the 2 HP and see that it was badly worn and had probably failed. These filters are not even as fat as a pencil and are only a couple of inches long. They are definitely a weak link in these engines. The filter's failure was likely responsible for the intermittent stalling of our Honda

2 HP. However, bad gas likely also played a role. Compression and spark plug tests performed by me months later indicated the engine had a perfect compression, and the ignition system was working. That indicates a fuel system problem plagued this engine. I had no access to parts to fix it in the middle of the Exuma chain, and U.S. Honda Marine dealers do not stock most essential parts for the 2 HP and 2.3 HP engines.

Just-in-time inventories might make sense for Honda dealers in the U.S. with reliable overnight delivery. But for a cruising boat with no fixed address working with shipping companies that are completely unreliable outside of Nassau or the U.S., the just-in-time model does not work at all. A cruising boat must carry a large inventory of spares. Because I lacked the spares, I never attempted to use the old 2 HP Honda outboard on our dinghy until we reached the U.S. and received these essential parts.

I might have been able to diagnose the fuel filter problem had I studied the Seloc manual for 2002-2008 Honda outboards more carefully, but, besides being outdated, 95 percent of its discussion did not pertain to the 2 HP outboard since it discussed up to 225 HP models. It was not until I obtained a copy of the 2 HP and 2.3 HP shop manual that all these issues became clear, and I had the detailed diagrams and discussions of procedures to find the fuel filter and the various ways to adjust the idle. Our internet was slow and often non-existent due to distant signals or cell phone service going down for a few hours. YouTube videos of Honda owners fixing their engines or detailed searches of chat room advice were time consuming, expensive, or impossible in the Exumas. Thus, having the relevant shop manuals for the boat's engines is the most practical solution for extended cruising outside the U.S.

Finding a mechanic on one of these islands becomes very far-fetched proposition when you visit them. If food is so hard to get, how much harder will it be to find a Honda outboard mechanic! The out islands don't have enough people to expect that kind of specialization. A mechanic needs access to parts, and there is little of that in an out island. The Honda mechanics in Nassau were so busy that they would not return my calls. I could have asked for help from fellow cruisers, but in Staniel Cay there was not a regular cruisers net. In George Town, I could have gotten a lot of advice, but I'm not sure how many would hear or respond to a plea in Staniel Cay. I should have tried, but it did not occur to me at the time.

We wanted to see the pigs before seeking shelter in the very protected marina at Cave Cay. A blow of over 20 knots was forecast for the next several days. So we tried plan B, given that the new outboard had the idling problem, and the old one was still dying at inopportune moments. We would anchor close to pig beach, and Janna and Sophie would land on the beach with the green kayak.

There were over 30 boats in this anchorage radiating back from pig beach. It was clear that to get within kayaking distance, one-third a mile or less, and preferably less, we would have to anchor in front of people. This is a dodgy and un-neighborly practice called "backing down." If you anchor upwind of a boat, you have no idea where their anchor is and are guessing their rode or chain length and their arc of swing. In contrast, if you drop the hook downwind a boat behind their stern and there are no boats downwind of you, then it is highly unlikely that you will swing into one another unless the boat in front drags. This latter procedure is the safest and friendliest way to anchor.

After I saw the situation, I suggested that we treat this as a lunch hook and I would stand watch with the motor running the whole time Janna and Sophie paddle out and back to the beach. I kept on telling Janna, "closer," until we were between the first and second line of boats. The sailing catamarans ahead appeared to be in too-shallow water and probably had shallower draft than Contango. Many boats had looked over our anchoring spot as we approached, and they decided that it was too dicey. It was like a boat parade coming into pig beach. We dropped the hook between a 60 foot trawler and a cat. On our first attempt we backed down right onto the big trawler. I hauled the chain quickly on deck as we prepared to reset.

Slow Boat to the Bahamas

I found to my surprise that I was strong enough to haul up the 33-pound plow and chain without the windlass. Using the windlass was very time-consuming because after every 15 feet pulled up I would have to go back to the cockpit companionway, descend, get into the v-berth, and open the anchor locker to pull the chain pile to the back of the locker. We lacked anchor locker access on deck so piles had to be cleared inside. A windlass will not work and will jam if the chain pile gets anywhere near its drop hole.

We reset a little to the side of the cat and the trawler, but we let out so little chain we were in danger of dragging. Janna paddled with Sophie the one-quarter mile to the beach and were swarmed by pigs so quickly that I was afraid that the pigs would trample them. However, another boater distracted the swine so Janna and Sophie could get to their feet after sitting on the kayak. They followed around the pigs and petted the little ones. I intentionally did not give Sophie and Janna food for the pigs because I did not want aggressive and hungry pigs capsizing their kayak. The little pigs don't swim much, but the big pigs are hungry. The big pigs focused on the large dinghies approaching or anchored.

While I was waiting, the parts guy at the Honda dealer called back despite it being President's Day in the U.S. He said the idling either is from bad gas or the idle adjustment screw. I had confused a set screw that cannot be easily turned for the idle screw. He told me where it was and added, "Only use little 1/8 turns when adjusting." I adjusted it while the ladies met the pigs. Three 1/8 turns got it so I could turn the throttle to full idle, and it would no longer die. By this time, visual cues were indicating that we were dragging. We started a boat length in front of the trawler to the south and cat to the north. Now we were parallel with them. I texted Janna about departing, and, after 5 minutes, she got the message and started paddling back. When they boarded, I hauled up the chain on deck by hand to save time.

Now it was painfully obvious that we needed new gas to run the outboard, but Janna did not want to dock Contango at the fuel dock at Staniel Cay. I said I could dinghy out. However, we could not find anyplace close to anchor that late in the day. We inspected the one boat anchorage just south of the Yacht club that had three boats in it. The small rocks that circled it were right on top of us before we backed down. The mooring balls were full. The winds were shifting to the east 15 to 20 knots. We found some deep water by driving between Thunderball Grotto's rock and the big rock just to the south. At 4:30 PM we dropped the anchor. However, the fuel dock closed at 5 PM. I was 0.8 miles away, and the dinghy was tied to the foredeck. It would take at least that long to load the outboard and hoist the dinghy on deck. I got up at 4 AM in Ft. Lauderdale this day, and I was exhausted. I was running myself ragged and needed to rest. In other words, there was no way I could get fuel before they closed.

Going to the Staniel Cay fuel dock in the morning posed problems. Bad weather was coming. We had 24 miles to reach Cave Cay, and waiting until after the fuel dock opened meant we could not depart until an hour afterword. Besides, our next destination Cave Cay had gas and diesel, according to the cruising guides.

Still, I had work to do that night before we could go to sea in the morning. I wanted to better secure the solar panel. Instead of popping out as it did on the way to Clearwater the fore top crossbeam had cracked two feet from its port end. I had bought a piece of 18-inch stainless steel rub rail attachment at West Marine in Ft. Lauderdale for the rub rail damage, but actually this 18 inch piece would be better used to support the solar panel mounts. I used a latex glove and an odd round fastener to tie the "splint" as Janna called it to the cracked cross beam. I made dinner as I always was the primary cook at home and on the boat. Finally, I entered all the waypoints for the trip ahead.

What a long day! In the same day, I had flow from Ft. Lauderdale; we extracted Contango from a dangerous dock; we anchored to install a new outboard motor mount; we moved and dragged anchor next to the swimming pig beach; I serviced the new outboard; we anchored for a third time of the day near Staniel Cay; and I fixed the broken solar panel mount. Most of this activity was an attempt to compensate for the fact that we had no reliably working outboards. At the end of the day, we had hardly any gas to run the new outboard, which was belatedly working well.

33. THE LIFE OF CAVE CAY MEN

We woke to a 5:30 AM alarm, but the dawn departure was delayed. Janna found the autopilot was not working. I took everything out of the sail locker in the starboard lazerette. None of the electrical connections seemed loose. However, I found motor oil leaking from the buttons of the autopilot display. When I had worked on the generator the other day, I spilled a lot of lube oil on it and the cockpit cushions. When I took off the face plate and button overlay and wiped the motor oil out, it still would not work. The unit appeared waterproof, but it was not motor oil proof. Finally, I found two fuses hooked up to the unit and replaced them. The autopilot turned on.

Next, the windlass conked out. (It's wiring was nowhere near the autopilot where oil had spilled.) There was no movement. It was just dead. I hauled up the chain by hand and looked to make repairs under way. Janna was driving us out by 7;45 AM. I could not find loose connections. I bypassed the fuse for the controller. Nothing worked. Since the chain was spread out on deck, I used some old paint to mark the 30 foot and 60 foot lengths as my permanent marker marks were no longer visible.

Cave Cay's aptly named Safe Harbor Marina was getting calls right and left on the VHF. I hailed them 40 minutes out, and the operator said, "We should have room for you. It's first come first serve." Despite the 5 to 10 knot winds we saw that day, the winds were forecast to exceed 20 knots for the next several days. After the debacle at Staniel Cay Yacht Club, we liked Cave Cay because the marina sat in a cove with only one narrow entrance. In other words it had 360-degree protection. However, we could have made for the well-protected Emerald Bay Marina in Great Exuma if Cave Cay were full.

I promised to call when I had a visual on the entrance channel. By noon, I could make out one green and no red markers when the chart said there were three green and three red markers. On the VHF, they said we were too close to the south wall of the opening. Unless the residents had the ability to see through rock, I couldn't fathom how they could know that since the view from the marina was blocked by 30-foot high stone walls.

The operator told us to come and share a slip occupied by the 40 foot Beneteau named Pelican. That was clearly a dumb idea since $40 + 31 = 71$ and Cave Cay's docks were 60 feet long. Besides, they had plenty of free slips, and the marina was going to charge me a 35-foot minimum fee. If I was going to pay big boat prices, I wanted my own slip. "No way are we going to take a double slip" I yelled across the water. "Janna, we don't need to take crap from bullies. Don't go into that slip."

This confusion just rattled Janna at the helm. Next, they signaled for us to take the first free slip. However, as Janna started her turn, they changed their mind again and had us take the closest slip to the rocky east shore of the lagoon by the bridge. By this time, the dock committee had swelled from five to two dozen all yelling different, idiotic directions, all shouted with great resolve. As we would learn, Cave Cay is one of the most boring places on earth, and the sensory-deprived retirees were desperate for this entertainment. I have never had a marina change their slip assignment so many times, let alone in a two-minute interval while we were backing in.

I tossed the stern line to one of the mob of power boaters, who likely had bow and stern thrusters on their 60-foot behemoths. Predictably, the bow was being blown towards the bridge with the southwest wind. I ran the bow line outside the starboard spreaders to the stern where I could toss it to one of our many smug saviors. After the second line was tied on the floating dock, I said to one of the more vocal grumpy old men, "Blue shirt, you were really out of line." That cemented our pariah status with the other boaters.

Drawing by Sophie Wilson: Sophie helped me deal with PTSD, Pet Traumatic Stress Syndrome, by drawing a picture of the battle between Daly (4 pounds) and the sadistic German shepherd (90 pounds). She wrote "BIG DOGS," "DADA," and "DALY" to label the picture above.

    I took Daly for a quick walk as soon as we landed. He was quickly being stalked. The owner of Cave Cay had something like three German shepherds. They would ride in or chase behind bulky man's off-road golf cart. Evidently, there were no leash laws on Cave Cay in force for the dogs of the island's owner, who resembled an aging Marlon Brando in his all-white uniform. "The horror" was that one of the attack dogs took a shine to Daly. In particular, that dog thought Daly was a rabbit and charged him on sight. The first time she saw the toy poodle, she charged growling and barring her teeth ready to throw her 90-pounds fully into ripping the four-pound dog into two. I quickly scooped Daly up and exposed my neck to her vicious maw. The beast was only distracted from her task when a mixed breed collie began to mount and hump her from behind.

From then on that attack dog would charge and attempt to climb onto Contango if Daly was there. We had to keep Daly in the cabin when unattended. The great white hunter did not find it in his heart of darkness to even scold his pooch for these homicidal attempts. Moreover, he never said anything to us let alone apologize for his dog. I began to suffer from PTSD, Pet Traumatic Stress Syndrome. I was hypersensitive to the approach of any four-by-four golf cart and its canine entourage, fearing it would soon turn into the next poodle apocalypse.

Sophie helped me deal with the PTSD. We drew a picture of Daly's battle with the German shepherd on our second day on the island. By the end of our stay, the sadistic German shepherd was locked up on the second floor balcony of the dockmaster's house, which loomed over Contango a few feet from our finger slip. The dog's owner had flown off in an airplane, and the dog could only look on helplessly as Daly paced the deck or went for a walk with me unmolested.

Shark, the dock attendant, was as nice as the owner of Cave Cay was creepy. Shark was a tall lanky Bahamian, who could always be found in baseball cap and sunglasses, sporting a big smile. Unlike the water guy at Staniel Cay, Shark had both arms. "We got tomatoes you can pick. And if you ever want ice, call me. It's free," he offered after we settled in after a few minutes and the crowd dispersed.

In my aborted attempt to walk Daly, I was turned back at the top of the bridge by the first of many NO TRESSPASING signs posted around the island. However, Shark informed me that marina guests could ignore those signs and indeed the showers and free washing machines were in the small house just over the bridge. However, he was also the bearer of bad news, too. "The gas and diesel pumps are closed. Der is a dispute with our supplier," and the "store" mentioned in the cruising guide did not exist. Our outboards would not be running until after the storm. We had about three-quarters of a gallon of non-watery gas between the two outboards and the generator. It also seemed likely we would be dipping into our canned food stores before the winds abated. I was already regretting that we had not pressed onto Emerald Bay.

We had a lot of laundry that needed to be air-dried in Cave Cay.

We made the mistake of washing all of our dirty clothes at once on the first evening. While there were three free washing machines, there were no dryers. Most of the big boats that were there did not seem to use them since they probably had the ultimate in cruising excess, the inboard washer and dryer. So, we seized the chance to wash our clothes, but we did not think about what we would do with the wet clothes when the washers stopped. Janna strung thin 550-pound paracord all over the boat's decks and interior. However, still we had two wet loads in the washers. It took Janna two days to dry these loads. In the meantime, we had reinforced our image as the Cave Cay hillbillies to Janna's mortification. She was still smarting from the dock committee, but I had gotten over it. I was used to humiliating myself in public while docking.

Linus Wilson

On the first full day there, I shirked boat work in favor of a long rambling jog/exploration of the tiny island. I climbed the hill past the houses and got a few glimpses of the angry Atlantic Ocean over the scrubs and rocks. There was an abandoned road that led to the southern side of the island and small cove with a little beach and high hills. I paid for my exploration getting my shoes and socks covered in burrs. I would take ten steps back to the boat and a burr would penetrate to my ankle, and I would stop to remove it. I tried high stepping to minimize the number of burrs captured with each step, but my progress was always interrupted soon with another spike in my ankle.

On the way back, I found an access point to the lagoon beach, which was visible from the marina. Janna and Sophie were up for some beach time and instead of marching through the burrs we all kayaked out to the beach. Janna and Sophie shared the green sit-on-top kayak, and I took the blue sit-in kayak.

This was the first time that I had got out the blue kayak, and I had a good time exploring the lagoon while Sophie made sandcastles on the beach with Janna looking on. On the first part of my paddle, I found a floating coconut on the west side of the lagoon still full of milk. I kept it for later. I found an indent that I thought may be the "cave" of Cave Cay. Then I paddled to the back side of the marina and met a nice English couple in their late 60's who told me about how their crippled boat, which had crossed several oceans before visiting the Bahamas, came to Cave Cay.

The couple had been anchored when a squall came through with 30-to-40 knot winds. They tried to lift the anchor and reset, but before they could do so, their propeller hit a rock and sheared off. They ended up pinned to the rock with a huge hole punched into the bow. They were far out of range from Sea Tow or Tow Boat US. Local boats tried and failed to tow the huge boat off the cliff face. Their savior was another cruising sailboat boat named Amazing Grace. Now a piece of plywood fastened down the crudely patched the hole. Their insurance company planned to tow the boat to south Florida to get it fixed. It is notable that the insurance company would rather tow the boat hundreds of extra miles and across the Gulf Stream rather than have the work done by Bahamian yards. The couple was emptying and drying out the contents of their soaked boat, and there appeared little hope that any electrical gear would have survived the ordeal.

Carving coconuts was one way to ward off starvation in Cave Cay.

With my water shoes to protect my feet from the jagged sandstone, I explored the "cave." The broken boulders opened to the entrance channel of the lagoon. I went up to 10 feet from the top of the rocks where the west end of the island was covered in thick brush. While this was an "easy" chimney climb, that I had seen climbers on TV do without gear, I was no climber and was loath to be walking around that part of the island where marina guests were not welcome. (A chimney climb is when a climber can stretch her legs far enough on one rock face that her back or arms can reach another rock face. The friction between those points of contact allow the climber to ascend without really using their upper body muscles or relying on difficult hand grips, which are the tools of more technically difficult rock climbs.)

I drilled my coconut in two places and got out the coconut milk for some pleasant drinking. I cut out the meat after using a hacksaw to cut it in half. Sophie and Janna tried some. I found the coconut pieces addictive if not filling. I would cut up three coconuts before we left.

The next day I explored the north side of the island by way of the long landing strip, which was free for marina guests to use. Too bad that I forgot to bring my private plane! There was strip of beach that joined the Exuma bank to the Atlantic Ocean by way of a lagoon. At low tide, this beach was dry all the way to the northernmost point of the island, but, at high tide, part of the beach was submerged.

We met one of the more or less permanent residents of the island. He was an American Indian who had wrestled alligators in the Everglades and had lived in New Orleans. He had a big black dog, which had one ear pointing down and one ear pointing up. This dog only responded to commands in a language that I had never heard before. Unlike the vicious German shepherd, this dog was friendly, and sniffed Daly's nose respectfully. This dog would love to play fetch with an old coconut and would encourage me to pull it from its teeth, something I could not pull off.

It was not long before our stores started running out. First, wine was gone, much to Janna's despair. (I somehow managed to stretch the beers out by rationing and constant re-provisioning.) Then, our chips were eaten. Next, the last pizza was baked. The bacon and sausage lasted a couple more days. I started eyeing the foot-long lizards that populated the island. I only spared them because I figured their tails had less than a hot dog's worth of meat, and we still had hot dogs. My attempts at fishing ended with an empty spear. Our boat neighbor, Jim of the powerboat No Regrets, a white-haired man with a stately Southern accent, started by giving Sophie gifts of food. First, he gave her a little ice cream treat, then he gave us pecans, and finally he gave us a bag of potatoes. Famine may have broken out without the potatoes! I started frying green tomatoes from the Cave Cay garden breaded with what remained of our instant pancake batter. Janna declared that after the Exumas that she wanted nothing to do with the Abacos. She wanted to go back to Miami and cruise Florida where food, fuel, and Tow Boat US was not in short supply. She was tired of huge cell phone bills and wanted to spend more time with Sophie's grandma and grandpa.

Janna had a bad day with Sophie on the second day in Cave Cay and hit a low for the trip. Unlike me, she interacts with a lot of people every day in her busy medical practice. Sophie has been in daycare and most recently pre-school since she was two months old. Thus, the transition to full time care-giver and pre-school teacher was a big change for Janna. I started taking Sophie for walks with Daly on the air strip to burn off Sophie's pent up energy, and this seemed to work for the rest of our too-long five-day stay.

I combatted the boredom by trying to resolve the windlass problem, by calling Maxwell-Vetus' technical support. I would hike up the hill near the showers to get a signal. At $0.35 per minute their technical support person would give me a series of tests rearranging wires, using the multi-meter, testing the battery under load. After many hours of testing, and several hours on the phone we tried rewiring the solenoid and the 30-pound lump of metal came back to life.

I hoped to revive my faith in the Honda by getting a new carburetor. I purchased one from a Ft. Lauderdale dealer and tried to have FedEx pick it up from the Honda dealer and ship it to Watermaker's Air in Ft. Lauderdale. I figured that FedEx could handle a cross-town delivery in the U.S.A. I would be proven wrong in the coming days.

34. THE HARVEST AT LITTLE FARMERS

I was somewhat surprised by the speed of our progress down the chain. We left Cave Cay early on Sunday, February 22, 2015. I had wanted to make it to the last few days of the George Town Annual Cruising Regatta, which was to taking place between February 19, and February 28, 2015. However, I did not want to rush to get there. I had imagined we would slowly wander down the chain, snorkeling and visiting remote beaches and anchorages. I could not interest Janna in snorkeling, and she was not crazy about cleaning up Sophie and the boat after visiting the beach. More importantly, the desire to avoid doing laundry in a bucket, the outboard problems, and to a lesser extent food, water, and fuel dictated we gravitate towards the few settlements of Staniel Cay, Little Farms Cay, Black Point Settlement, and George Town. So far we had only called at Staniel Cay, but George Town lay ahead.

To get to George Town in Great Exuma, most cruising boats must enter the Atlantic Ocean, the Exuma sound, near Cave Cay or some point north. Going further south on the shallow waters of the Exuma Bank means being trapped behind shallows that dominate the southern part of the Exuma chain. However, while the winds were back to normal after five days in Cave Cay, the waves on the Atlantic side were still pretty big. Waiting a day would let the seas subside. My idea was to visit Little Farmers Cay about five miles to the North, which had an anchorage on the west side of the island or moorings on the east side. The anchorage was in the lee of Little Farmers Cay and the moorings were in the lee of the south end of Great Guana Cay. Emerald Cay said that there were no stores nearby, but the fuel dock was working. Thus, despite its tiny population the nearest settlement at Little Farmers was the surest way to get a few more provisions before making the jump to George Town.

Right before we left, Jim from No Regrets had one more gift. He told me of another hurricane hole in a private island, Rudder Cut Cay. It had a six-foot approach and good depths once we entered the 360-degree protected lagoon. He said three boats had holed up there while we were at Cave Cay. "It is up for sale. It used to have a chain blocking the entrance, but the chain is no longer up and anyone can go in," he said.

Janna had no trouble motoring straight out. As we exited the lagoon and turned north, I saw the cave on the west side of the island, just under the buildings used by the marina staff, which were off-limits to marina guests. It was just around the corner from the fissure in the rock I had explored. A small beach led to the cave.

We picked up the farthest north mooring ball near the beach on Great Guana Cay. It had the name "Little Jeff" written on it. The guide was clear that all moorings in Little Farmers should be snorkeled before settling on that spot. In Staniel Cay I used a trailing line and hung off the stern ladder to look at the mooring line descending over 20 feet down. In that crystal clear water the Staniel Cay moorings lines went deep into the sand. Thus the screw or the concrete to which they were attached seemed very well buried. In contrast, the "Little Jeff" marked mooring line was attached to a grapnel anchor which only had one fluke out of four buried. Worse, this anchor was smaller than Contango's smallest anchor. The second Little Jeff mooring was a Herreshoff, or traditional anchor. This is the shape of anchor that most land lubbers think of when they think of an anchor. Herreshoff anchors are rarely used since they have a poor holding to weight ratio. Since all anchors need five-to-one scope minimum and both of these anchors had a one-to-one scope, these Little Jeff moorings were clearly unsafe.

In *It's Your Boat Too: A Woman's Guide to Greater Enjoyment on the Water* by Suzanne Giesemann, which Janna read after we returned to the States, the author speaks of how her boat drug its mooring at Little Farmers Cay. This was not surprising based on what I had seen. Ms. Giesemann does not mention if she or her husband had snorkeled the mooring before going to bed. Janna and I picked up the mooring labeled "Ocean Cabin," as in Staniel Cay the line went to the sand and the screw or the concrete slab was well buried. We would not drag that night, but Contango would not leave the mooring field unscathed either. We called Ocean Cabin, which requested that we come by to pay, and they assured us that they could sell us some food from their store, even though it was Sunday.

We landed on the Farmer Cay Yacht Club, which was deserted. Some fishermen that we met later said the proprietor had been attending a wedding in the States. (Everyone we met in Little Farmers knows everyone else and all were exceedingly friendly.) We had ruled out that dock as unprotected with no break water and lacking an

Linus Wilson

excellent natural harbor. For the dinghy, it was the closest landing, allowing us to conserve our precious gas.

The runway at Little Farmers Cay in the Bahamas has some great views.

This also meant a long walk in the hot sun down the island's airstrip before coming to town. After we climbed the ladder and tied up the dinghy, we snaked around the back of the Yacht Club by the 20-foot-long gas and diesel canisters. We were told that Cave Cay had put the Little Farmer's fuel dock out of business, and, when we visited, neither were working. The Yacht Club lies on the northeast tip of the island. The north side of Little Farmers is made up of the airstrip and mangrove swamp. Sophie started complaining of the walk before we were done with the airstrip. Ty's Sunset Grill lay just south of the airstrip on the western beach. That oasis drew us in, and we enjoyed their air conditioning and drinks. I asked the bartender if I could get a half a gallon of gas somewhere and he gave me half a gallon from his own stock. This meant that I walked up and back on the airstrip four times before the new fuel was deposited in the dinghy, and I met Janna and Sophie back at Ty's Sunset Grill.

Slow Boat to the Bahamas

At Ocean Cabin we paid for our mooring and bought more food from the owner's store. It was a long walk back with groceries, and Janna had to use all her powers of persuasion to get Sophie back to Ty's Sunset Grill. We ate an early dinner there since I told he their rib dinner was less expensive at their restaurant than what I could make buying the ingredients at the out island prices.

We found the dinghy four feet lower than we had left it. We struggled to drag it to the ladder. It had slipped to the other side of the dock and was not really floating, but dangling a couple inches off the water in the bow. I went down first and picked up Sophie as she climbed down the last rungs of the ladder. Janna passed the groceries down and took off the dock line after I started the engine, and we were off. The new outboard did great.

As the sun was setting, the fishermen Don and Carlo an uncle and nephew team came by and offered to sell us some conch. I bought four for $10. We should have paid more in retrospect, and convinced Don to shell them for us. He took a long time, but did a great job and we enjoyed Carlo's stories while we waited.

Don's careful removal also gave us the opportunity to watch how a conch is removed from it shell. The back side of a hammer is used to separate the conch from the shell by hammering near its second or third fluke. Then Don used a butter knife to push the conch out of its shell. All the brown or black pieces were cut off leaving the pink and white meat. He cut off the sharp foot and eyes but was careful to leave the delicious pink lip which tastes like lobster.

The conch muscle has a pink lip and white body muscle. The big white muscle is very tough but is good eating if cooked in small pieces and tenderized. While a mature conch looks about the size of chicken breast, one conch is as filling as four chicken breasts. None of us could bite through its dense white muscle, which is similar in taste and texture to squid or calamari. In the Bahamas, tiny shavings find their way into fritters, fried dough balls, or in conch salad raw doused with lemon, lime, and other fruit juices. We would enjoy that cooked conch for two months.

35. SHIPWRECK

Overnight the mooring buoy banged against the hull. We planned on exiting the Little Farmer's Cay cut at dawn. I awoke at 5:20 AM, and Janna was up soon after. Since Janna was nervous about helming through the ocean cuts, I took the helm this morning. Ideally, you will go through an ocean cut with good light and slack water. Crossing ocean cuts are some of the most dangerous times for a boater. Tides race in and out of ocean cuts. Large ocean swells can break in the shallows of the cuts, and if the wind opposes the current, the waves are more likely to stand up and break. If the current is too strong, the boat can actually be pushed backward in a cut. In our case, a six knot current coming from the east would stop our progress out of the cut. Ocean Cabin said that low was at 5:11 AM and high tide was at 11:11 AM. That meant the tide would be coming in as we left the cut opposing our progress. However, the tide would be headed east until 11:11 AM in the same direction as the 10-knot wind. Thus, the waves should be small.

When we slipped off the mooring lines, Sophie insisted that Janna help her use the potty, leaving me alone at the helm. Sophie uses the potty at pre-school on her own, and I am not sure why at this age she required our assistance when she was with us. She always seems to require that we help her use the potty right before we docked and as we are leaving. Sophie needed to use the step stool on the boat and at home, which is something she does not need to do at the miniature restrooms at school or day care. That may justify why we had to help her use the head at this age.

It was clear from the GPS tracks that Janna had floated over charted four foot depths at high tide. Religiously following her high tide tracks at what was now low tide was risky. Stupidly, I did not examine the tracks carefully before having Janna toss off the lines.

Janna never mentioned to me that she passed over the shallows accidentally on the way in. As I increased the speed from 2 to 3.5 knots in anticipation of the tidal rush, the GPS plotter appeared to lag the landmarks. The exit channel was a good deal less than 100 feet wide and unmarked. Further, I had no one to look at the water from the bow. I was worried that I was getting too close to Great Guana, but I was not close enough to the rocks at the tip of Great Guana Cay. In actuality, being 50 feet west of these visible rocks was too close the shallows on the east, but still not as far east as Janna's track. Then, at 6:45 AM disaster struck! The keel hit rock, and I hit neutral. The bow turned sharply to starboard as we skimmed the east end of the shallow patch. If I had examined the chart more carefully, I might have chosen to avoid the narrow channel by the tip of Great Guana Cay and instead gone north of the shallow patch, heading west until I hit the deep water channel east of Little Farmers instead of going south. Ultimately, I was at the helm, and it was my fault for not being better prepared to exit the mooring field without Janna's help.

We checked the bilges, and saw no water coming in. There were mooring balls in the deep channel east of Little Farmers and west of our previous mooring. We picked up one of these moorings. I got a trailing line and swam with my mask to examine the damage. I could see a white bit where the back end of the keel is attached to a metal piece that is attached to the rudder. The keel should have had maroon anti-fouling paint unless some was rubbed off. I was not able to swim that far forward because of the strong current, but it seemed we had avoided anything worse than losing some paint.

By this time, I was much more risk-averse about traversing a narrow channel, which was the Little Farmers's Cut. The cut was more or less east to west. Thus, in the morning the light was shimmering on the water making reading the depths impossible by sight. Ideally, you want the sun overhead or at your back to read the depth colors. Little Farmer's cut was only 180 feet wide. That meant little margin for error and a stronger current than a wider cut. The Galliot Cut north of Cave Cay was about four miles south. The Galliot Cut was over 500 feet wide, but our delay meant that we would be transiting it closer to full flood. The delay also meant that the sun would be higher in the sky which would improve visibility. Further, Galliot Cut ran northeast to southwest. Thus, we would not have the sun in the east directly in our face but on our beam.

When we approached the Galliot Cut, the light was good, and the water looked deep blue. The waves were small. Thus, I decided to plunge on through and not attempt to anchor and wait for slack water and better light. At 2300 RPMs, the highest throttle setting we would attempt to sustain throughout the trip, our speed was 6.5 knots over the water, according to the paddlewheel knotmeter. However, our speed over the ground in knots showed 4.7, 4.2, 3.6, 3.0, 2.4, and 2.0 as we plunged deeper into the center of the cut. Then, it finally climbed as the land widened out and the eastern ends of Cave Cay to the south and High Cay to the north fell away. The course was 40 degrees through the cut, but I had to steer about 50 degrees to compensate for the current pushing us west.

36. CRUISERS' MECCA

I raised the third reef to stop us from bobbing in the four-foot swells. However, our 140 degree course towards Emerald Bay was too close to the due east, 90 degree wind, to keep the genoa unfurled. This frustrated Janna, who wanted to sail, and, for most of the trip down, we struggled to unfurl the genoa due to contrary winds. She also did not like that I said that all attempts to sail close hauled would fail. The southeast swell slowed our pace, and the best we could make in the deep water was 4.5 to 5 knots, running the engine at 2200 RPMs. When we came up to Emerald Bay's channel, there were breaking waves on either side of the well-marked entrance.

I got gas and diesel while Janna took Sophie with her and battled to get into the washing machines, which were full. It was really hot, and my feet were swelling until I changed into sandals. I saw tons of fish in the water and aimed my spear at a 2.5-foot barracuda. It got away and my spear's retrieval line came undone. With my spear lost, the gruff dock attendant warned there was no fishing on the piers. I agreed, without a spear, there would be no more fishing that night.

While getting the 16 gallons of diesel, I met some cruisers who told me that most people were staying in $.50 per foot slips. We were paying $2.25 per foot! I had never imagined such prices were possible. It was a new marina, and Emerald Bay was pretty empty otherwise. It was not close to much except the Sandals resort that owned it. That $.50 price was cheaper than the cheapest mooring ball. That being said, the experience seemed pretty much like being in America, and we went to the Bahamas to experience the culture. I'm pretty sure this would have been a better place to stay for a blow than Cave Cay, but with good weather making the last leg easy, we wanted to experience George Town rather than stay at another "safe" marina.

I saw the "happy hour" sign upstairs. It was not really advertising happy hour. It was advertising free food and drink! Therefore, I got my fill of chicken, cheese, and fruit and brought a plate down to Janna who was not going to leave the laundry line. I took her place so that she was free to go up. This was definitely the first and last time that we found free food and drink on the entire trip.

We would get started late since Janna wanted a second shower and Sophie wanted to visit the playground. I was not in a rush to leave since we were only 12 miles away from George Town. After we left, I spent the next several hours calling ahead for a mooring and trying to figure out what was going on with the new carburetor. There were some moorings in Stocking Island north of George Town. One might become available in a day or two, but we would have to anchor tonight. I scheduled a second pickup after the first one failed because the Honda dealer misspelled my name and could not find my part when the FedEx guy came. I did not bother to raise sail while doing this, while Janna gave Sophie a pre-school lesson in the cabin.

When we started entering the entrance to Elizabeth Harbor, and I invited Janna and Sophie to take a look. Elizabeth Harbor is a

Linus Wilson

huge roadstead made up of the very long Stocking Island on the northeast and Great Exuma and the city of George Town to the southwest. In some ways, the harbor resembles Nassau Harbor where Paradise Island plays the role of Stocking Island and New Providence and Nassau plays the role of Great Exuma and George Town. Cruisers enter George Town by way of Lake Victoria. Most cruising boats anchor a mile or so north of George Town along Stocking Island because it offers the best protection from the easterly trade winds. On that day, there were over 200 boats anchored in Elizabeth Harbor. Janna said, "I have never seen so many boats at anchor!"

Because we were having a temporary weather system with light south winds forecast, I suggested that we drop the hook as close to the entrance of Lake Victoria and George Town as possible. Janna showed me how to turn the useless windlass, which was not responding to the foot or cockpit controls, into freefall mode so I could let out the chain. We dropped the hook a half a mile from Lake Victoria and the free dinghy dock at the Exuma Markets grocery store.

Wendell, the owner of the moorings called back to say we could have a mooring after high tide tomorrow afternoon in "Basin 2 in front of St. Francis Resort on Stocking island next to the sailing catamaran Gryffin." These strange directions were analyzed endlessly for the next 24 hours.

We deployed the dinghy and new motor and tied up at the huge Exuma markets dinghy dock with 40 or more dinghies packing its sides. Exuma Markets was small by U.S. standards. However, it had its own dinghy dock, and it was the only grocery store that I saw in the Bahamas outside of New Providence. Moreover, a bank, gas and diesel pumps, a liquor store, and a hardware store and chandlery were all less than 100 yards away from the dinghy dock. We stocked up on everything. Right away, we got a replacement for our broken deck cleat. We even had time to have a drink at the Two Turtles Bar, which had a statue of three turtles. When we dinghied out, there were hardly any waves, and we slept soundly. George Town seemed to solve all our problems almost immediately.

37. ON THE ROCKS

At the cruisers net on VHF channel 72, the next morning, I introduced Contango and its crew under the new boats section. "Sophie is four, and she would love to meet other children her age."

The skipper of Mojo called after the net on the hailing channel, VHF 68. VHF 68 was always a scrum of many boats, hailing right after the net. Most callers would respond something 15 and down or 71 and up. The former meant that the callers would switch to 15 and only speak when you found a free line below 15. The latter meant that the callers would switch to 71 and only would hail one another on a free channel above 71.

When we found a free channel, he said that his daughter, who was also four-years-old, would be going to the "Kids' Day" festivities. This was part of the 35th Annual George Town Cruisers' Regatta. Kid's Day activities were taking place from 1 PM to 3:30 PM that day.

"We have to move the boat at high tide at 1 PM today, but that sounds fun. We'll try to get her there," I said.

We decided to not ask for advice about entering the mooring field because, with about 300 boats in the harbor, and one free mooring ball we thought some boat may get the $18 per day ball instead of us if we advertised it by asking for advice on the VHF. It had taken several calls and a referral to obtain this mooring ball. We had a broken windlass and little experience anchoring. Moreover, all the anchorages looked very exposed when the wind picked up from the wrong direction. In contrast, basin 2, also known as "Hole 2", had 360-degree protection and was easy rowing distance to Stocking Island. In retrospect, I should have scouted the area by dinghy in advance instead of getting one of our propane tanks refilled in the morning, but hindsight is 20/20. Besides scouting the exit to John Pennekamp State Park in January, I had never scouted another mooring or marina by dinghy before.

Linus Wilson

When we left for the mooring ball, we knew where St. Francis Resort was, but we were still fuzzy about the location of Hole 2. Janna was at the helm, and I hauled up the chain by hand since the windlass would not work. There were orange cones in Stocking Island's Gaviota Bay that led to the St. Francis Resort. On the south side of this small bay, was volleyball beach. In the middle, several dozen cruising boats were crammed in at anchor. We went to the east of the orange cones, leaving them on the port, thinking that if no boats were there it probably was shallow. Right before we left George Town, we learned that we should have left those to starboard. The orange cones were supposed to be viewed as red channel markers, and boats would follow the red right returning rules. (In Alabama, I had used an orange barrel as a green channel marker. So the orange equals red interpretation was not universal.) Of course, none of these obscure markers or what followed was charted or mentioned in any cruising guide that we owned.

We were using walkie talkies. As we wound around the anchorage we came upon moored boats right before our turn into what was called Hole 2. The chart seemed to indicate that you should hug the visible rock that is the last visible barrier to the northeast entrance to Hole 2. I was at the bow, and Janna was helming at the stern. A small, derelict sailing catamaran, Shamrock, was anchored right by that entrance in the orange cone area. On the rock that we wanted to hug there was a homemade green square marker number 1. Markers on the land are not terribly helpful, but this seemed to support our interpretation that the channel was from that rock to the uncharted red ball marked with a 2. I pointed out both markers to Janna. Things were happening fast despite our two knot speed, as I spied the closer red and white ball. I asked, "Is that a mid-channel marker? Over."

"I'll keep that marker to port," Janna said.

That would not have been my call if I was at the helm since it was red. Keeping to starboard would be consistent with red right returning. I should have said that. I instead said, "If you are going to keep it to port, you want to hit the middle marker."

Slow Boat to the Bahamas

Then, we hit the rock. "Neutral, reverse," I yelled over the walkie-talkie. We stopped.

I did a poor job of reading the water. Perhaps I was using the binoculars too much and not scanning the colors. All the depths looked shallow. At low tide, this shallow rock would have been clearer than at high tide. We had enough depth to clear the six foot channel at low tide. We were waiting for a deeper draft vessel to exit at high tide and vacate the mooring. Many obscure uncharted markers are put exactly on rocks so had we swerved to either side we might have missed it, but I think in this case keeping it to starboard, staying to the south of the red and white marker, would have avoided the hazard.

Ten seconds too late a cruiser in a dinghy came by and said we were on the wrong side of the middle marker. "There is a rock there."

Janna called, "Where do we go?"

I pointed backwards towards the rock with the green 1 on it.

We seemed to be free. Next we passed between the unnumbered green and red balls further into the Hole 2 towards our mooring. We found the sailing catamaran Gryffin. Wendell told us to take us the mooring ball by that catamaran. There were two free balls. I directed Janna to one and the owner of the powerboat Winterlude came by in his large center-cockpit rigid inflatable dinghy.

"Who is renting you the ball?" he asked.

"Wendell," I replied.

"Wendell's mooring is the other one," he said. He held our bow while his dinghy towed us to the other one. Then, he took our port and starboard lines and looped them through the ball's pendant. We thanked him for his help. He said he kept his boat in Florida, and he had crossed the Gulf Stream to the Bahamas over two dozen times.

We saw no evidence of water in the bilges, and the pump was not running. I dived under the boat and saw that there was a scrape on the leading edge of the keel where the maroon antifouling paint was removed. There were no signs of cracks or structural damage. Wendell's mooring had a chain that descended to the sand, and a big metal piece consistent with being attached to a concrete slab, screw, or rock.

The water was flat in the Hole 2, and Janna and Sophie went to the Kids' Day at Volleyball Beach at about 3 PM in the green kayak. I joined them later after putting the new outboard back on the dinghy. I tied up the painter to the mooring line that ran along the beach. Daly and I found Sophie and Janna covered in face paint and surrounded by little girls. Daly earned many a liver treat as the little girls doted on him. After sampling the offerings at the Chat N' Chill hut, Daly and I pushed off. As I was topping off the dinghy's gas tank in the deeper water, a big collie on a dinghy started barking at the dog in the bag. Then, then the bag started barking. The owner of the collie was completely confused as Daly and I motored off. Both munchkins, Sophie and Daly, were making friends on volleyball beach.

38. TEN FEET SHORT OF THE MEAN

In George Town, we for the first time encountered boats with other kids on them since Janna and Sophie came aboard. Most cruisers are retired couples with no kids. Indeed, kids' boats made up only six percent of cruisers in George Town based on my study. I found a list entitled the 2015 Cruisers List, which included many boats and crew that I recognized from our ten days in George Town. This list underestimates the numbers of boats that were anchored, moored, or at a marina berth in George Town during the 2015 Cruisers' Regatta; because, for example our boat, Contango, did not find its way on to the list. However, it still gives us an idea of the characteristics of cruising boats at the regatta. There were 191 boats on the list. Eleven boats were kids' boats. I defined "kids' boats" as boats that had more than two people sharing the same last name or where the last name was not listed.

Sixteen boats had a solo sailor or about eight percent of the sample. There was one boat where there were two couples traveling together. The rest were two-person boats. Over 83 percent of the two person boats had couples sharing the same last name. Seventeen percent of couples did not share the same last name. Thus, 85 percent of the boats had married or unmarried couples without children.

Most of the boats on the list were sailing vessels (89 percent). Twelve percent of boats were catamarans. Of the 110 boats that listed their length, the average or median boat was 40 feet long. The smallest boat was 20.5 feet long and the largest was 65 feet long. If our boat was in the sample, Contango's 31-foot length on deck (LOD) would have put it at the 97th percentile with the 20.5-foot boat at the 99th percentile. The 65-foot boat would be in the 1st percentile of length on deck. The kids' boats in the sample ranged in size from 35 feet to 60 feet with an average length of 43.6 feet. If our boat, Contango, had been in the sample, it would have been the smallest kids' boat. The couples' boats (with two crew listed) ranged in size from 20.5 to 65 feet with 40.0 feet being the average length. Solo sailors had boats that were on average 40.5 feet long or about the same size as couples' boats. On average, the kids' boats had over three extra feet in length compared to couples' or solo sailors' boats. However, I found the difference between the average size of kids' boats versus couple-sailed or solo-sailed boats was not statistically significant. It is safe to say that we had a really small boat in comparison to other cruisers at the 2015 George Town Cruisers' Regatta and an unusually large crew of three people instead of the norm of two.

The crew makeup or the distance the boat came from its home port really did not explain boat size. The only factor that affected boat size with any statistical significance was if the boat was from Canada or the U.S. On average, Canadian boats were four feet shorter than U.S. boats. Canadians were travelling farther distances in smaller boats. This may explain why a country about one-tenth the size of the U.S. had one-third as many boats as the U.S. in George Town instead of one-tenth. Canadians were setting sail earlier and not waiting to earn enough to fund a 40-foot boat. Another factor, affecting the size of Canadian boats could be that the U.S. has a higher GDP per capita than Canada. Thus, some Canadian sailors perhaps could not afford boats as big.

This is one more factor to underscore how weird we were. We were Americans with a kid in a tiny boat. Janna is a devotee of Lin and Larry's Pardey's smaller-is-better mantra, "Go small" *et cetra et cetra*. I like things small, a case in point is our four pound dog. In Lafayette, Louisiana, our home town, a GMC Yukon XL SUV is considered a compact car. Pickup trucks in our town have four doors. However, I do boat repairs out of the only car I have ever owned, a Mini Cooper. (The name gives away that it is small.)

Once a hardware store attendant admired my car, saying, "I like your car. I want to drag it behind my 40-foot RV." It was not clear how he wanted to consummate the proposed transfer of ownership. Perhaps he thought it was too small to be anything but free.

I used *distancecalculator.com* to calculate the distances that the boats were from their home port. One hundred and thirty-six boats reported their home port. The average and median boat in the sample had a home port of about 1,200 statute miles away. However, the minimum sea route was probably double that. New Orleans was just less than 1,000 statute miles as the crow flies, but we were about in the 60th percentile or in the middle of the distribution by that measure. Nevertheless, the round trip from New Orleans to George Town was about 2,400 nautical miles or over 2,600 statute miles. Thus, most boats had to travel over 1,000 miles from their home port to reach George Town.

There was a great diversity of boat makers represented. The number one boat make represented was Beneteau which represented about nine percent of the fleet sampled, or 110 boats, reporting the boat manufacturer. The Morgan sailboats were well represented with eight percent share despite having gone out of business in 1992. Thus, not all boats were "new" by any standard. This was the only manufacturer that was out of business that placed in the top five brands. Catalina accounted for seven percent. Hunter and Island Packet (both with six percent) rounded out the top five manufacturers. The top twelve makes, with three or more representative boats in the sample, only accounted for 56 percent of the boats reporting their make at the 2015 regatta. There seems to be little consensus about the ideal cruising boat manufacturer at the George Town Regatta based on the boats owned by the participants.

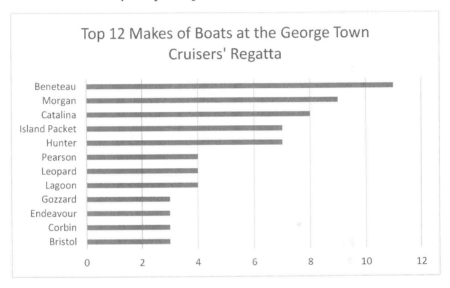

We were typical in that we were an American boat. Only 136 boats reported their home port. Ninety-eight percent of boats came from either the U.S.A. or Canada. The U.S. represented 75 percent of boats, and Canadian boats amounted to about 23 percent of boats. The George Town Regatta was not well represented by boats outside those two countries. The Bahamas may be more a North American destination for cruisers than a draw for boats from around the world. There were no European boats. Sailing to George Town from Europe, for example, would put a boat upwind of the popular Lesser Antilles in the Caribbean.

Roughly three-quarters of the U.S. flagged boats came from Florida or the East Coast. Twenty-nine percent of U.S. boats came from Florida. George Town is at least a three-day overnight sail from Miami, but it certainly easier to reach from Florida than any other state. The closest U.S. boat was 330 miles as the crow flies from George Town from Islamorada in the Florida Keys. Moreover, Florida accounts for a large percent of the coastline and boating activity in the United States. Green Cove Springs, Florida with inexpensive moorings and a do-it-yourself boat yard was the most popular reported home port. This town on the St. John's River near Jacksonville, Florida was home for 14 of the 136 boats reporting their home port. The second most popular home port Hampton, Virginia only had three boats. I define the Gulf Coast here as Texas, Louisiana, Mississippi, and Alabama. These states only make up six percent of the boats in the sample with two of those coming from my home port of New Orleans. I defined the Great Lakes region as the states that touch the Great Lakes but not the Atlantic Coast. Those states are Minnesota, Wisconsin, Illinois, Indiana, and Ohio. Only seven percent of boats come from that region. The eastern region would be all the states east of the Mississippi River not including the Florida, the Gulf Coast, and Great Lakes. Nearly half the U.S. boats come from this region or 48 percent of the 103 boats that came from the U.S. The West is defined as all boats from states west of the Mississippi not in the Gulf Coast or Great Lakes regions. Ten percent of U.S. boats in the sample came from the west. Our neighbor Winterlude was classified as coming from the west because the owners put Oregon as the home port on that on the survey. However, Art the skipper of Winterlude said they kept their boat in Florida not Oregon. Thus, farther locations may represent the owner's perceived home rather than where the boat originally sailed from.

39. BUY-SELL-TRADE

We spent about 10 days on the mooring ball, in Stocking Island, from February 25, to March 7, 2015. I snorkeled the blue hole, which was 50 yards from our mooring. Its huge depths spewed cold water and many fish. Spear fishing is prohibited in George Town and that hole in particular was a no fishing zone. Sophie and Janna would visit Volleyball Beach almost daily. Often Sophie would play with the 4-year-old daughter of a woman who worked at the Chat N' Chill or other children from the "kids' boats" on the beach.

Janna and Sophie would sit in the front of our roll up dinghy and often get soaked on the way to George Town, Great Exuma from our mooring ball

I would make almost daily trips for water, food, supplies, fuel, and laundry into George Town. While our mooring was always floating in calm waters, the waves could be as high as four feet in Elizabeth Harbor and Janna and Sophie in particular would often get soaked in the bow on the 20-to-30-minute trips each way. Our new Honda 2.3 HP was slow, but the real problem was that our flat bottom, roll-up dinghy did not have a very high bow. Thus, we coveted the rigid inflatable boats (RIBs) with their high bows and v-shaped hulls.

In George Town, my 32-gallon water bladder really came in handy since we showered on the boat. We thought our mooring was not private enough, and the water was not clean enough to do "Caribbean showers" as we called them. In a Caribbean shower, Janna or I would lather up over the stern in our bathing suits, using sea water. We would do a seawater rinse while swimming. Then, once aboard, Janna or I would use the cockpit shower to rinse off the saltwater. (We never showered at the same time!) Without this fresh water conservation measure, we used about 10 gallons of water per day, showering inside the boat.

Janna got interested in buying a rowing and sailing dinghy. The green kayak was a little unstable and could not carry much. We look at one offered for sale on the cruisers net's Buy- Sell-Trade segment by the skipper of Von Dutch, Igor. When we saw it on the beach, it seemed too heavy. I told Janna that she should not compromise on weight. What she really wanted was a Walker Bay 8. Those dinghies were great to row and came with optional sail kits and were light, 71 pounds. Best of all they were very common, and many boats had them. Given how unreliable our outboard was proving to be, a rowing dinghy would be a great backup. Walker Bay 8's were typically an auxiliary dinghy because cruisers usually would want an inflatable dinghy that required an outboard. Inflatable dinghies have very large carrying capacities, and the Walker Bay 8's 425-pound capacity was at least half the carrying capacity of the typical cruiser's dinghy. While it is more stable than a kayak, any hard-sided dinghy will be much less stable than an inflatable dinghy.

We asked the net if anyone wanted to sell a Walker Bay 8, and Mojo's skipper Jeff Goff responded. While Sophie played with their 4-year-old daughter—Lilly, Janna and I checked out the dinghy. Janna had chatted with the mom Abby on volleyball beach before. Their Bahamas trip was the least of their adventures under sail.

Jeff was a rigger from St. Augustine, Florida who had built their sailing catamaran. He had done a great job rigging and improving the Walker Bay 8 with makeshift parts. It had non-standard wooden oars with a fiberglassed horseshoe oar lock fittings, and two sets of oar locks. He used an optimist sail and a non-standard sprit and mast. Gray boat plumbing hose was secured with a tight weave of small line to create a rub rail so it would not hurt the mother ship when it inevitably bumped against it. In the hands of most people, such improvements would fall flat, but everything Jeff did to that boat worked elegantly.

Slow Boat to the Bahamas

After 45 minutes, Sophie put an end to our chat, saying "Are we going home now?" The play date for parents and daughter were over. Janna loved rowing the dinghy. We would learn it was a great boat to row or sail. That being said, the puny Honda 2.3 HP, and our roll up dinghy could easily double the speed of Janna or I rowing. We never attempted a crossing of Elizabeth Harbor in it. Jeff said he had crossed under sail, but it involved a lot of bailing. Janna used it to ply the shores of Stocking Island.

We were entertained by card games of UNO with Sophie at night, and the cruiser's net on VHF by day. The skipper of the sailing vessel Paisley, offered his children during the Buy-Sell-Trade section of the net. "We have three children to go to a good home. They have their shots, and they come with the associated clothes and toys, but they are noisy and don't pick up after themselves," he said.

The next day on Buy-Sell-Trade a scratchy throated man named Can E. Ball responded. "I'll give you $20 for the kids."

The father responded, "Can E. Ball, I've spoken to my wife. We have decided that they can go to any home not just a good home."

Another day, I was disappointed that the master trader Igor of Von Dutch beat me to the pumpkin-flavored beer being given away, "Die can't believe you don't like pumpkin beer! Zat tis my favorite," he said.

The skipper of Skylark responded, "I tried to drink the stuff for months. It's just sitting in the bottom of my fridge."

"I vust trade vu sumting fur yit. Do you vant sum peanut butter? I've got ein eextra large jar, vich I vill leave it on zie port side of my boat," Igor said. "My boat tiz zie traditional keyetch wit de bikini clad ladies on zit." That was how I was limited to lager and stout in George Town. Igor's peanut butter beat me.

I met Igor on Volleyball Beach. The early-middle-aged skipper had long blond locks like a 1980's heavy metal star. He was looking for fair winds to blow him and his bikini-clad crew to the eastern Caribbean.

40. OFF THE GRID

I wanted to get rid of the 30-pound lump of metal off the bow soon after arriving in George Town. If we ever left, the lifeless electrical windlass would be an impediment. Further, George Town, as the biggest town in the Exuma chain, had the promise of being a good place to ship it back to the States. After many more tests, including one that had me moving the 50-pound battery to put more loads on it from the house bank, their tech finally gave me a returned merchandise number (RMA) and promised that Maxwell-Vetus would reimburse me for the shipping costs.

I held no hope that I would use the windlass again in the Bahamas. I did not want to wait in a port for a hunk of metal that I did not need. If I shipped it to Maxwell-Vetus, I would ask for the new one to be delivered in Venice, Florida, where my parents were collecting my mail. However, when I visited the shipping agent in George Town with my heavy package, he wrapped the windlass and solenoid in a flimsy box with a hundred plastic bags as padding. It would cost $250 to arrive in Rhode Island in about four days by means of UPS. That seemed crazy, and I did not ship it. I planned to wait until I got back to the U.S.

In more adventures with international shipping, I learned in George Town that FedEx shipped the old Honda outboard's replacement carburetor not to Watermakers' Air across town, but to my house in Lafayette, Louisiana. Janna's medical assistant from her practice picked it up from our front door where it was left. Then, we had FedEx overnight it from Lafayette, LA back to Ft. Lauderdale, FL. Janna's medical assistant Kerri got the package to Watermakers' Air, who would ship the package to Staniel Cay.

As it turns out, if you schedule a pickup from a third party with FedEx, FedEx will ignore the delivery address specified by the person paying for the shipping. FedEx relies on the person at the third party pickup location to specify the shipping address. The Honda dealer, on the fifth pickup attempt, had FedEx ship the package to my home, not the delivery address I that I had given to FedEx.

Contango really had not left shore power for more than three consecutive days. On the trip up, I had run the Honda 2000-watt generator at anchor, which ran the battery charger. The 200 watts of solar panels were keeping up with the battery for the refrigerator. However, we only ran the refrigerator during daylight hours. The rest of our electronics and the engine starter were run by batteries 1 and 2 which had about 190-amp hours of capacity. For these, we ran the engine as much as four hours a day. However, their voltage slowly dipped down from 12.8 to 12.1 volts as if the alternator was not charging. More distressingly, the voltage did not spike when the engine was running, regardless of the RPMs.

Lee Haefele from the 38-foot sailing catamaran Alesto 2 gave a seminar on solar panels. I attended because I wanted to get to the bottom of the charging mystery. He said you should think about your boat's electrical system as amps (amperage) in and amps out. Amps are a measure of electrical current. A typical cruising sailboat boat with a refrigerator will have a 300 amp hour bank. (Contango had about 360 amp hours spread over 4 batteries, but most of the work was done by the 190-amp hour bank of batteries 1 and 2.) A common problem that he saw on other boats was alternators charging at too low voltages. This could be caused by bad alternators, loose connections, or wires that were too small. If the voltage does not get near 14 volts while charging, there is a good chance that the batteries will all die he warned. He said he saw a 1,000 amp hour battery bank of expensive AGM batteries totally depleted and ruined. The best that owner could do was to buy a few cheap lead acid batteries at three times what such batteries cost in the U.S.A.

I had batteries three and four isolated to avoid such a complete catastrophe. Right now I was convinced that the Honda 2000 was keeping the batteries one and two on life support. I asked him why my Honda 2000 generator was not running the 20-amp battery charger at higher voltages. He thought cruisers had excessive faith in the Honda EU2000i's. They only produce 1,600 continuous watts if working well, and can only put out 13 amps at 120 volts. Thus, it was not surprising it could not run my 20 amp charger at full capacity. The Honda EU2000i could only fully charge a pretty full battery bank. Weak charging proved better than no charging, and our house batteries would have probably died without that little Honda generator.

I got out Don Casey's *Sailboat Electronics Simplified* that Tom had given me several years back. I tested the alternator terminals which were putting out a good 14.4 volts when the engine was running in neutral at 1,800 RPM. That meant the alternator was working. However, there was a 1.3 volt drop between the alternator and the batteries 1 and 2's negative terminals. Casey argued that any drop of over half a volt meant the wires should be replaced. I eventually hailed Lee from Alesto 2, and he agreed with the diagnosis.

Boats were fleeing the harbor by this time. Less than half of the 300 boats that we saw when we motored in remained. The light southeast winds seemed an easy ticket up the Exuma chain. While southeast winds had stymied our attempts to sail down to George Town, if they held, we would have a glorious downwind sail back to Nassau. The waves were forecast to go down in the part of the Atlantic known as the Exuma Sound the next day, Saturday, March 7. Our engine maintenance was up-to-date with our oil and fuel filters changed.

Over the last couple of days, I had started feeling like a commuter. The long dinghy rides were no longer fun. The community that made George Town great was slipping away.

I lacked the big black wire necessary to fix the alternator problem. I arrived 15 minutes too late at Top-to-Bottom the only retailer of boat wire in George Town. On a soggy ride back with fuel and last minute provisions, Rod from Si Bella invited me for a beer. Si Bella was anchored right in my path to George Town from Stocking Island. I had seen Rod and his wife Deb in George Town and on Volleyball Beach.

Rod said they still had plans to reach South America before the start of hurricane season. They planned to wait for better weather to island-hop east against the trade winds. This route through the Bahamas to the eastern Caribbean against the trade winds is often referred to as the "thorny path." They passed on participating in the departed Long Island, Bahamas rally, which would get them to the next stop towards the Caribbean. Feeling like a drowned rat with many tasks to do before we could haul up our mooring lines, I declined. Our paths would cross no more this season. Contango was headed northwest and Si Bella was headed southeast. A boat tracking website that relies on AIS signals showed them moving down the eastern Caribbean islands towards South America in late May and June of 2015.

41. GOING DOWN THE MOUNTAIN

An oft-quoted bit of mountaineering wisdom is that most climbers that perish die on their way down the mountain. Having reached the farthest south and east point we wanted to reach for the cruise, we planned to leave this morning before high tide at 9 AM. However, we did not want to repeat the mistakes that we had made on the way in. We decided against one more run for cash and supplies in George Town. My ATM card had expired at the end of February, and Janna was the only one who could get cash. Instead, we focused on leaving on a rising tide and seeking out help on the strange navigational markers that confused us on entering.

It was unclear at this point what the orange cones in Gaviotta Bay next to us meant. Some sailboats treated them like a channel, staying to their north side, and others avoided them like the plague, staying on their south side. Unlike what the charts indicated, the sailboats on the northwest side of these cones did not seem to run aground. Wind Dancer was a boat parked right by the channel to Hole 2, and Sue McDonald on that boat was the cruisers' net moderator while we were there. I hailed the boat, believing she would know what the strange markers meant. Despite being 200 feet from our boat, Sue said she could not hear us. The frustrated rally organizer who was listening in on our exchange interjected angrily, "The cones are red!"

"You mean to say the orange cones should be interpreted as red channel markers, which I should keep to port when exiting the hole, over," I said.

"They are red!" he repeated. If the regatta says orange is red, it is red. The laws of physics be damned! I had clearly violated some cruising regatta pecking order with my insolent questions. You're not allowed to ask questions until after your twelfth regatta. I'm sure that is in the bylaws.

Not everyone felt that way, thankfully. Winterlude's owner Art, who had heard the exchange, took me for a ride in his deluxe dinghy to carefully walk me through the channel. We should be half way between the number 2 red ball and the outermost rock marking the entrance to Gaviotta Bay. He recommended staying 20 feet off that rock. Next, instead of being between the semi-abandoned sailing catamaran Shamrock and the marker for the rock we hit on the way in, he recommended steering northwest of the cat closer to hole 2's barrier rocks. Then we should keep the cones 30 feet to port on exiting with the barrier rocks about 60 feet to starboard. His dinghy had a depth sounder and he pointed out the lowest point of the channel right next to the cat Shamrock at 5.8 feet.

Basically, the Explorer and Navionics charts for Gaviotta Bay and the Hurricane Hole by St. Francis were garbage. Instead, of being three-to-four feet the coned-off area carried six-to- seven feet. The rock we hit carried one foot at low water, not the six feet on our charts. He chatted about how he used to own an Irwin sailboat before

Winterlude. I asked him about the Rudder Cut. "It's a piece of cake," he said.

We motored off easily following Art's directions. There was a big line of boats leaving Elizabeth Harbor. All the boats eventually passed us. Even the deep water of the Sound was crowded. We had a nice downwind sail with a 10-knot southeast breeze and a three foot swell.

I tried to inquire about the moorings at Musha Cay on the west side of the island on the Explorer charts. However, the posh-sounding staff assured me that those moorings did not exist. "We only have some jet ski moorings next to the beach," the Musha Cay representative warned. The best prospects were to anchor near Rudder Cut Cay soon after passing though the cut.

Rudder Cut was calm at slack water. We went through at 3 PM. When we emerged into shallow waters of the bank, we saw many boats anchored near the reefs and caves. Janna had no interest in snorkeling; so we decided against adding to their number. At the second anchorage, the Garmin depths were four feet. That was too close for comfort. I encouraged Janna to try the hurricane hole inside Rudder Cut Cay recommended by Jim from No Regrets.

The narrow entrance and shallows especially on the east side seemed foreboding, but we easily passed in. We anchored in seven foot depths. We had 500 feet to swing around and no boats joined us that night, but several boats took note of our exit the next morning. We took Caribbean showers (with our swimming suits on) and enjoyed the seclusion.

That night we played Chutes and Ladders and UNO with Sophie. We got a Chutes and Ladders game in George Town, and it soon was Sophie's favorite. (She did seem to win 80 percent of the time. I'll leave it to the mathematicians to prove why the youngest player, who goes first, is more likely to win.) However, by this time Janna and I were calling it "Shoot Myself and Ladders" because we

Linus Wilson

would rather commit suicide than play it again. Unlike UNO, there was absolutely no strategy in Chutes and Ladders. There was only one direction to go once you spun the wheel. UNO was random, but you had some choices about what cards you threw down. A little bit of choice makes all the difference.

You don't need to use Google Maps to find your way around Black Point Settlement in Great Guana Cay.

We left late to wait for high tide and better light since it is shallow around Rudder Cut Cay and we did not have far to make Black Point Settlement. We lost an hour due to daylight savings time and left the anchorage at 10:30 AM. The cruising guide emphasized that you should use visual piloting rules here (VPR). However, Janna at the helm got annoyed with my communication from the bow. I could not see the depth sounder. I only had my Navionics chart app. Eventually, we abandoned this water reading when we cleared the shallower bits, which were plenty deep for Contango. Unlike our trip into Rudder Cut

Cay, we never got low depth readings as we headed north along Rudder Cut Cay, Musha Cay, and Cave Cay.

Janna and Sophie are walking back to the dinghy in the fading light at Black Point Settlement.

The surrounding scenery was gorgeous. I regretted not dallying. The turquoise water, the swaying palms, and the lagoon filled with bikini clad women, made me want to stop. Janna was not so impressed and opposed my attempts to drop the anchor. The sirens were lounging on Musha Cay, the magician David Copperfield's private island that could be rented for $60,000 per night. We still had some money in the cruising kitty, right? Not really.

We had a glorious beam reach, which became close-hauled against the east wind of 15 knots. Black Point was very crowded by the time we arrived at 2:30 PM. We dropped the hook in the back of the wide bay with protection from the eastern trades. Janna, Sophie, and I went into town enjoying the free trash disposal. Since it was Sunday, we could not take advantage of the token laundry and showers. We did get some free WIFI and inexpensive drinks in town while reading their many "cruiser friendly" signs. If you want a reputation, just say what you want to be. Black Point wanted to be known as "cruiser friendly" and it was. That being said, the rainbows that we saw as we strolled down the main street also helped. I don't think the tourist board had a hand in those.

42. UNFINISHED BUSINESS IN STANIEL CAY

The winds were forecast to pick up to around 20 knots, and Janna preferred the Staniel Cay mooring balls to this or another anchorage. At breakfast on anchor near Black Point Settlement, a small squall blew in with not enough water to catch in our tanks, but it left another rainbow. I chided Sophie in the morning for her excessive napkin use at breakfast, "Napkins don't come in on the tide, but they do come from trees." We picked up the chain just before 10 AM and had a wonderful downwind sail of 4 to 5.5 knots to the west of Harvey Cay with 18 knots of breeze and only 75 percent of the genoa up and a second reef in. We took down sail as we turned northeast for the final approach to Staniel Cay.

Our good fortune did not extend to picking up the mooring. On the third attempt, I picked it up amidships. The current even more than the wind was making picking it up difficult. Unfortunately, I threw the new heavy-duty boat hook onto the deck with a clatter and did not follow its progress. I had my hands full looping in the first mooring line. It fell overboard. After looping the second line and cleating it off, I discovered its absence. I clung to the ladder and looked in the water for 20 minutes. The outgoing tide was strong. The water was deep and clear. It probably was in the Sound, because I could not see it on the ocean floor anywhere nearby. While I drifted I could see tiny fish feeding on the sandy bottom, but my good boat hook was gone.

Slow Boat to the Bahamas

As we dinghied out to the Staniel Cay Yacht Club in the inflatable with the new Honda 2.3 HP outboard, the engine started sputtering. Janna and I were reliving the horrors of our last visit to Staniel Cay when I realized I had forgot to open the air vent on the outboard. The outboard did not cause any trouble after that.

Watermakers' Air had assured me that they had flown out the carburetor a couple days before. It was waiting for me in a small plastic shed at the Staniel Cay Yacht Club. Hooray for Watermakers' Air! It cost $125 for the FedEx shipping and the Watermakers' rush delivery. We paid about $10 in customs duty for the $76 carburetor. This was a successful parts delivery. We did not have to wait in port for this part although FedEx and the parts dealer messed up this delivery for over a week of repeated incompetence. Coupled with the experience with DHL in Bimini, I had been convinced of the need for a boat cruising outside the U.S. to carry extensive spares. International shipping can triple the part's cost and lead to weeks of frustration.

Janna was taking care of the laundry with Sophie, and I went grocery shopping. I bought an ice cream bar for Sophie. Unfortunately, by the time I finished the 10 minute walk in the noonday sun, it was soft. Sophie was excited by the pink ice cream in the Neopolitan bar, but refused to bite taking little licks until it dripped everywhere. I yelled for help, but Janna could not hear me to bail me out because she was inside folding laundry. A kind cruiser saw me holding the dripping mess that was an ice cream bar and got me a napkin from the bathroom inside.

Around sunset at slack water Janna wanted to go swimming. "You should swim to the Thunderball Grotto it is only 100 yards away," I said.

"There won't be anyone to take care of Sophie," Janna objected.

"I can take care of Sophie," I said.

"I just want to swim near the boat," she said.

Linus Wilson

"I told you there were six-year olds doing it. Not snorkeling the Grotto when you are so close is like visiting the Grand Canyon with a blind fold on," I said. "You don't even have to paddle out. Sophie and I can take you in the dinghy."

She finally relented.

"Oh, the ground feels disgusting here," she said. After getting into the dinghy I let her out in the three foot deep water by the shelf where I set the kayak.

"It is soft. It is deep enough that you can swim," I said as I held the dinghy still by standing near her. I was wearing my water shoes, but Janna was in bare feet. Sophie was enjoying the show from the dinghy. As usual she was clipped in with her life jacket on.

Janna went into the rocks that formed the entrance for a few minutes.

"There's momma," Sophie said pointing.

"Wasn't it gorgeous?" I asked as Janna got in.

"Well yes, but I got nervous about the fish and other wildlife attacking and the snorkel not working," she said. The only fish that I had seen were no bigger than 18 inches long, and they would give you little kisses in exchange for food.

That was the only time Janna snorkeled in the Bahamas.

I wanted to get the alternator rewiring done since we had several days more off the grid with limited access to gasoline for the generator until we got to Highbourne Cay. I had visited Isla's General Store on our first day in Staniel Cay. Their stock of boat cable was disappointing. The only large black wire they had was 00. (Wire sizes rise the lower their number. 00 is bigger than 0, and 0 is bigger than 1). That was too big for my connections. Moreover, it looked used.

I had an extra number 2 red wire on the boat. I used black tape and labeled it carefully and used it to attach to the batteries. The voltage drop on black was no more than 0.12 volts at 1800 RPMs.

More importantly, the battery voltage spiked to 13.3 volts right away with the engine on. It continued to climb slowly.

We ate dinner at the Staniel Cay Yacht Club that night. As we dinghied out, the engine died. Oh no! Had the Staniel Cay curse struck again? No, I just needed to put more gas in the tank. I put more in and took a shortcut between the two big rocks south of the Thunderball Grotto's rock. The tide was coming in at full flood, and I realized why this was a poor short cut. Our little boat was virtually standing still. We inched between the 20-to-30 feet high rocks. I adjusted our course so we were dead center trying to avoid swifter streams flowing fast around the edges. Eventually we emerged from out between them and tied up behind Contango.

After that display of the power of the current, Janna took a Caribbean shower swimming behind the boat. I opted for an inside shower. My motto is "life preservation takes precedence over water conservation."

After two rolly nights on the balls at Staniel Cay, we slipped off the mooring lines at 9:30 AM on March 11, 2015. I wanted to visit the swimming pigs, because I was on anchor watch last time. We soon dropped the hook behind the stern of the last line of boats. As we did, we observed a huge mega yacht, which had a huge and growing slick of yellow fouling the turquoise waters. They were emptying their 1,000 gallon holding tank in a crowded anchorage. The law is that you have to be at least three miles off shore before throwing human waste overboard. That certainly would have only taken 10 minutes for this boat. Failing that, a more responsible action would have been to empty their holding tank as they were travelling on the uninhabited Bank. That would not have delayed their fast progress at all as they were picking up anchor. The captain on that boat should lose his license, and the boat owner should be fined. Unfortunately, I could not make out its name of it as it sped out, leaving the yellow plague drifting towards Contango, the other boaters, and the swimming pigs.

Linus Wilson

In search of more solid waste, Sophie and I dingied out towards the pig beach of Big Majors Spot, which was strewn with pig droppings. This time Sophie and I brought the burnt bottom of the pink velvet cake we had made the previous day. A speckled midsized sow greeted us on our landing. I threw her some burnt pieces. We walked towards a litter of baby pigs down the beach. The midsized sow was having none of it. The pink cake was hers. She nudged Sophie correctly sensing that her aggression towards the little one would sway me more than nudging me. I guess she had learned that going after the children was the best way to get your way. The pink mobster was right. I gave her all the pink cake I had, and she piggishly ate it all. I got all the rest from the dinghy, and she gobbled that up, too. She never bothered us again, concerning herself with more promising marks.

Sophie petted the wild but gentle pigs at the beach on Big Majors Spot. The bigger pigs swam out to meet boats and beg for their supper.

We petted the pigs, which were mostly gentle. We watched the bigger ones swim out to meet the bigger boats. Thankfully, none swam out to meet our eight-foot boat. I started getting impatient to leave, tired of dodging pig poop. It was a good thing I did! I had dragged the dinghy up on the beach without anchoring it or tying it off. It had started floating with the incoming tide and would have gone to sea in five minutes.

43. NUDITY, SHARK ATTACK, AND POOP, OH MY! ADVENTURES AT EMERALD ROCK

We picked up anchor, and I was thankful to be free of the windlass. Anchoring with the haws pipe and pawl was so much easier than using the electric windlass even when the lump of metal worked. (The pawl stops the chain from going out so the person at the bow can rest. Janna convinced me to install the pawl before leaving New Orleans based on an article in *Good Old Boat* magazine, and I'm glad she did.)

I intended to go to Cambridge Cay. Our pig visit that morning meant we would be approaching the south entrance to the mooring field as the tide was going out at 1:30 PM. High tide had passed at 12:30 PM. The current was opposing the east southeast wind of about 17 knots. We had a nice sail until we rolled up the genoa to turn east into the wind and swell leading to the Conch Cut south of Cambridge Cay. It only took a few seconds before things in the cabin and on deck started crashing and the motion became awful. The three-to-four foot waves became five-to-six feet tall and our speed was being staggered back to under three knots.

I was just about to say "turn around" when the kayaks crashed off the deck and were lying in the lifelines. "Turn around," I yelled. Janna had turned white and seemed frozen in position. "Can I take the helm?" I asked. We switched places, and I did a 180-degree turn. Suddenly, the motion was fine, and all was well. We would not get a mooring at Cambridge Cay this day. Having not studied the chart, Janna did not fully appreciate what was going on, but I did.

Linus Wilson

I had a backup plan. My backup plan was to get a mooring at the large Emerald Rock mooring field in Warderick Wells. This mooring field was a disaster in the west winds of 20-to-30 knots on our way down. However, the east trade winds had made these moorings well protected on this day. Moreover, it was a much easier approach than the North Mooring field where we stayed at on the way down. The North Mooring field approach would mean steering towards an unprotected ocean cut with tide opposing current similar to what we faced in the Conch Cut. Emerald Rock was in the middle of the Warderick Wells Cay so we would not have to worry about swell from the Exuma sound.

Sophie entertained herself on deck on the way by combining the red and white slab reefing lines. Janna asked, "Why are you tangling those lines together?"

"I'm trying to mix red and white to make them pink, momma," Sophie replied.

We picked up a free mooring behind a smaller 35-foot sport fishing boat, named Sylvia. That itself was interesting at the headquarters of a fish preserve. However, I soon saw that man on board wore no clothes. Janna got out the sextant for the first time of the entire trip. I forgot to ask her if she got any moon sites from the Sylvia. (Actually, she worked very hard to avoid seeing the naked man.) I had never opened the sextant on the whole trip. A sextant is used make celestial measurements that can be used to fix a boat's location when it is out of sight of land. Most boaters favor the more accurate and easier GPS for fixing location offshore.

The next day, Thursday March 12, we paid for our mooring and heard that gusts up to 30-knots were forecast for Friday, March 13. Thus, if we wanted to get farther north, we needed to move that day. I wanted to get to Shroud Cay's mooring field before the blow because I wanted to stay some place new if we would not be travelling on Friday.

I asked about the snorkeling in Emerald Rock and the volunteer in the office pointed out the snorkeling buoys in Emerald Rock. He said they were not really affected by current so I could snorkel them about any time. After I dropped off Janna and Sophie on Contango, I decided that since I was already soaked from the dinghy ride, now was a great time to snorkel. I saw only one of the three buoys and tied the dinghy to it and took the plunge. I saw little tropical fish ranging from 3-to-10 inches and various types of coral. I saw the other two buoys and went to the second. After jumping in, my eyes focused, and I saw the three-foot-long reef shark in the middle of the coral head. I found super human strength and speed that propelled me into the dinghy. My snorkeling expedition was over. We had better make haste to the moorings at Shroud Cay.

As we got ready to drop the mooring, three boats came into the mooring field. We paused to see what they would do, not wanting to run into them. The two sailboats dropped anchor just short of the field. The third was a 55-foot powerboat, which picked up a mooring. Then the powerboat released a yellow cloud in the crystal blue water as they evidently emptied their huge holding tanks with their macerator pump.

For the second time in two days, I had witnessed this boorish behavior by large powerboats. This current environmental devastation was, in some ways, more stupid than the first. On the previous day, the mega yacht dumped its poop on the anchorage and got out as fast as they could. On the current day, these fools were dropping poop and pee around the mooring ball where they would spend the night. The sewer they made was where they would swim and board their dinghy. We called the Exuma Park office to report the yellow cloud before slipping our moorings right before noon.

44. SHROUDED IN MYSTERY

We had a nice downwind sail powered by the 10-to-20 knot east southeast breeze that eventually became closer hauled as the Exuma chain turned more northward. We had three-to-four-foot

Linus Wilson

waves in the Sound, but it was an easy sleigh ride. I picked up a vacant ball with my old bent boat hook and Janna at the helm without any problem at 3:30 PM.

Since I had read that most of the creeks were no-motor zones, I got out my blue 8-foot sit-in kayak. Solomon the mooring ball guy from Staniel Cay had said this was his favorite place in the Exumas, and I wanted to see why. From our ball, I paddled close to the 5-foot high sandstone barrier to stay in the lee of the wind and waves and slowly observed the zebra mussels and the coral below. I went to the edges of the south and north creeks. I thought that the no-motor zones were as much for the good of the boaters as for the wildlife. If you had a heavy dinghy you could not pick up and drag, it would be easy to be caught in these shallow bars and creeks on a falling tide.

We planned to wait out the forecasted high winds the next day. I woke up and installed the new carburetor on the old Honda 2 HP. I had not ordered the paper gaskets that the Seloc manual said should be replaced every time the carb was removed. Thus, my installation was suspect in that regard, but at least the carb had a working drain screw. I put new gas in the old outboard. It ran for 11 minutes before dying. This was really disappointing. I guess the parts guy at the Honda dealer guessed wrong.

Looking for insight into the disappointment, I read the *Seloc Honda Outboards 2002-2008 Repair Manual* on page 3-14. It said,

> *"A wise man once said, '90% of all fuel system problems are actually ignition system problems. And another 5% are actually bad or contaminated fuel or problems with fuel delivery. It is very rare that the carb is a problem <u>unless</u> you've allowed the motor to be stored for long periods and run with bad gas."*

I added the emphasis to "unless." I did not believe the "unless" was true because the watery gas only was used briefly not stored in the carb and gas tank and not used. I had put in several new spark plugs that I had gapped in this engine. Thus, the only replaceable part of the ignition system was the coil itself. I would have to wait until we got to Miami to replace the ignition system. It turns out this was bad advice. I would discover about a month later that the problem was with the fuel filter.

With little else to do, I convinced Janna to take out the kayak and explore one of the creeks with me. I suggested that we paddle 250 feet east straight to the rocks against the wind and waves. Then, we would head south in the lee of the rocks until we entered the south creek. Janna did not follow my advice to be in the lee of the rocks and paddled straight to the south creek entrance. Sophie, who was with Janna, asked her mom to turn around by the time they reached the mouth of the south creek. I followed.

While I was making lunch, we heard on VHF channel 16, "Contango, your blue kayak is floating away." Janna and I struggled to load the new outboard on the rubber dinghy as the kayak floated from 100 feet to 500 feet away. By the time I loaded the 2.3 HP onto the trash--filled dinghy, a man from the boat who had called had retrieved it from his 15 foot dink that had a 50 HP outboard permanently attached to its back. We thanked him for his kayak rescue. I must have used a questionable knot when I tied the kayak to the boarding ladder. I should have used a cleat.

I was glad that I suppressed all urges to swim after it. I would rather lose a couple hundred dollars (the value of the kayak) than my life. The only thing downwind was Andros Island 45 miles away. Even if you were immediately deposited on the shores of Andros Island there is a good chance you would die in the wilderness before you found your first human being.

After lunch, I dropped off our mooring ball fee in the drop box on the beach just north east of us and saw a sign for a well. I hiked up 50 feet on rough sandstone and saw the well. The water looked unappetizing, but it was surprising that this island had any fresh water. I descended and relaunched the kayak off the small beach. There I paddled to the first creek that I had seen yesterday with the shallow bar entrance. I lacked motivation to further explore this creek. I wanted to find the "sailor's camp" marked on the park map. Evidently, this free spirit of the sixties had squatted on this island there. I thought finding the remnants of this hippy desert island camp, "Camp Driftwood" on the park map, would be cool. The map that I had seen was not really chart quality, and I did not even have that to guide me. I had the vague idea that the "sailor's camp" was accessed by a creek on the north side of the island. I thought that paddling to it would take you almost to the Atlantic, Exuma Sound, on the east side of the Cay.

I paddled past the north anchorage past many large boats looking for a creek. After an hour of this, I came upon a creek near the north tip of the Shroud Cay. The tide was going out, making the progress slow. I veered off some mangrove channels which at first were deep. However, I could feel the mangroves closing in, and I had no desire to do extensive portages through mangroves. My kayak is only 25 pounds, but walking on mangrove roots is not easy. I re-entered the main channel after sliding over some mangrove roots. I incorrectly remembered that the creek went more or less straight east. Thus, when it turned south, I doubted my navigation and landed the kayak, hiding it behind some brush, and climbed the large loose sandstones. I climbed this part of the hill without scrub to the Atlantic side. I looked along the beach and could see no sight of a cabin or other structure. I only saw angry breaking waves along the deserted beach.

I called Janna over the portable VHF, "Contango's kayak to Contango. Over." I repeated this several times. I raised Janna to tell her I was coming back after she said that she could not find the map either. Then, I spotted the first other boat that I had seen since entering the creek, and signed out. In fact, three inflatable dinghies with outboards converged going in opposite directions. I guess you could have motorized vehicles here. The floodgates of rubber dinghies with 25 horse power or greater outboards on the back had opened, and I was able to ask directions to the sailor's camp from four of them. However, only one professed to having seen the map that I had, and none said they knew where it was. At least a couple of retired couples acted like I was a pirate with paddles. They would have shot me dead in self-defense had they brought their guns with them. "Who was this degenerate using paddles in this no-motorized vehicle zone!" they must have thought.

I turned around and never found Camp Driftwood. As I paddled down the north anchorage. I noted that a 60 foot sport fishing boat anchored in the fish preserve was using a 28-foot sport fishing boat as its dinghy. I certainly had missed the memo saying bigger is better.

45. REVENGE OF THE IGUANAS

The next day we slipped off the mooring lines and headed north with a following breeze and sea. With the wind between 10-to-20 knots, we made 4.5-to-6.3 knots under sail. We started with the full main in lighter winds but reefed down to the second reef to reduce the weather helm.

Sophie wanted to make chocolate cookies. We used the chocolate cake mix to make four. Sophie insisted on having two-and-a-half, not three, not two, but two-and-a-half cookies. She only ate one-and-a-half, and her mom and I ate one each before we anchored between Allens and Leaf Cays.

It was a crowded anchorage because this was one of the closest anchorages in the Exumas to Nassau. Plus, everyone wanted to see the iguanas on the beach. Janna, Sophie, and I landed the rubber dinghy on the beach, which was full of at least two dozen iguanas. Many more were hiding in the rocks behind the beach and would emerge if they thought we had food. The guide recommended against this, and I remembered the aggressive sow on pig beach. Therefore, we brought none. Their sharp claws and long teeth made me wary of leaving our rubber dinghy unattended, and I stood point while Janna and Sophie walked cautiously around. If I had any doubt what could happen, I only had to look at the abandoned and deflated 12 foot rubber dinghy right next to us.

Linus Wilson

An unkempt man with a rat's nest of a gray beard introduced himself. "That is my cat over there," he said pointing to the 32-foot sailing catamaran. "My buddy is planning on beaching his trawler here on high tide." Clearly these men had been out in the sun too long. Why would anyone choose to beach a boat on one of the smallest and most visited beaches in the Bahamas was beyond my comprehension. The largest beach on Leaf Cay was 60 feet wide.

"I guess it is hard to find a place to haul out in the Bahamas," I offered.

"Haul out fees are too expensive in the U.S. and the Bahamas," he said. Pointing to the fast motor boat landing on the beach, he said, "They ship in tourists by the boatload." That was yet another reason why their plan to avoid Nassau haul out fees was mad. Spoiling their nature preserve and source of tourist dollars would surely catch the ire of the tourist boat operators and the Bahamian authorities.

By this time, Janna and Sophie had got tired of the iguanas. After depositing Janna and Sophie in Contango I took the look bucket to find our anchor. After much searching, I found it on its side with most of the chain buried. I saw many conch on the way and tried diving the bottom. By Contango's stern, the 15-to-20-foot depths were too deep for me. I could only get to the bottom by diving, but never could find my targets. I always held onto a long line, but the current seemed nonexistent. Diving meant my progress was more or less random and usually far from my conch targets. Next, I tried diving in the 6-to-8-foot depths where the anchor was. I dragged the dinghy painter. All the large ones were harvested, and the midsized, live ones, which I found, were not mature. I now saw our plow anchor face up and stem down. I knew that I did not have the stamina to swim down eight feet and stay submerged long enough to bury it. So I did not even try. Dragging the dinghy against the wind and current while swimming was exhausting.

By the time I boarded Contango, I was beat. However, it was clear that we were much closer to the rock shore of Allens Cay than when I started diving. The 150-foot anchor drag alarm had not gone off, but as Janna and I examined the zig zag of our track, it was clear we were dragging. The cruising guide warned of what a poor anchorage that this was because of the currents. We had Leaf Cay to our east and rocky Allens to our west. The east trade was blowing us onto the rocks on Allens Cay. We agreed to move, but this proceeded slowly because I had to unload the gear and outboard from the dinghy. I needed to put on dry clothes too.

An hour later, at 4 PM, I was hauling chain. I thought the east side of Highbourne Cay offered the safest anchorage. If we dragged to the west, there were no hazards save any boat that may anchor near us. The anchorages here were full of hazards. The motor to Highbourne took excruciatingly long because of a reef that blocked us from going due south. There was an unmarked gap in it, but we had no stomach for running it. The water west of Highbourne is very deep. I did not understand why so many boats snuggled on the north side of Highbourne Cay. We put out 130 feet of chain in 16 foot depths 250 feet east of the southernmost boat. Unfortunately, the chain snagged at 125 feet. I had to move the secondary chain and rode to free the lengths of chain between 125 and 135 feet. That meant being stretched across the v-berth with my hands manipulating chain and rode above my head. It was exhausting, and I was still weary from diving.

Our old mooring field neighbor in Staniel and Shroud Cays a new gray 50-foot Beneateau Sense tried to anchor just downwind of us and a trawler. This boat, which never said hello, always seemed to come into the moorings and anchorage after us. They backed down right on the trawler 120 feet behind us. This time the gray Beneateau moved. In Shroud Cay a couple days before, they had picked up a mooring close to an anchored boat and forced the anchored boat to move.

I'm not sure if we should be proud or ashamed that this boat seemed to be endorsing our overnight stops. I'm pretty sure the moorings at Shroud and Staniel were less comfortable than many anchorages near those places, but we certainly did not drag as we had

Linus Wilson

this afternoon by Leaf Cay. I am probably falling victim to the old malady of "the water is always more turquoise in the other anchorage."

Our laundry situation had turned dire necessitating at least one night at a marina in Nassau. Thus, I hoisted the rubber dinghy and lashed it on top of the Walker Bay 8 to make docking in Nassau the next day easier. This took longer than usual because the spinnaker halyard used to hoist it got caught in the radar reflector in front of the mast. If the anchor alarm went off in the night, I was too tired to hear it.

46. ATLANTIS!

I hauled and hauled up the 130 feet of chain the next morning, and we set a course for Nassau while I made many trips to the anchor locker access in the v-berth to move the chain pile away from the hawse pipe. It should be stressed that the last part of our transit up the Exumas was propelled by long-range weather forecasts of dying trade winds. These light winds and small seas created the prospect of an easy transit to at least to Bimini and possibly all the way to Miami. With only 5 knots from the southeast and one-foot waves, we motored up to Nassau with only the third reef in the main for stability. We agreed that I should helm into the next marina in Nassau.

Janna said she wanted to spend no more time in Palm Cay despite its "bargain" price of $1.75 per foot. The only marinas that I was willing to try was Atlantis with its outer slips going for $4 per foot or the Hurricane Hole. I called up Hurricane Hole, and they quoted me $4 per foot. I knew that Atlantis close to the shopping was a better deal at the same price. Atlantis is a huge casino, hotel, and waterpark that draws in foreign tourists by the thousands. Its towers are one of the most visible landmarks in the Nassau area. So I said to Hurricane Hole's operator, "Give me the best deal you can." They dropped the price to $3.50 per foot. I asked them to assign me a slip but they insisted that I wait until their dock attendant showed me where to go. They would not hold any slip for me, and I agreed to wait and see.

As we entered the east side of Nassau harbor the traffic from fast-moving boats picked up. We saw the cloisters anchorage to the north where I had stayed for a few hours previously looked full, but the south anchorage which I had fled in haste in January had some space. I called Hurricane Hole to say I was a minute away, and they said they would sent someone out to meet us but were not going to say what slip number we had.

After hovering at the entrance to the egg-shaped marina basin for several minutes, Janna, who was at the bow, did spot the red clad attendant, but I could not from the helm. A 60-foot sport fishing boat was jutting out from the first slip to our starboard on the west edge of the entrance. The point of the egg was where the attendant was motioning, but I did not like rounding the huge sport fishing boat, which was taking up much of the widest part of the turning basin. The Hurricane Hole was much more crowded and full of boats that did not fit in the slips than I remembered when I had dinner there in January.

By this time, the attendant was on the VHF and he repeated "Go in and turn right."

I responded, "My sailboat is very hard to maneuver. I would like a slip that is easy to get into." I said. There were plenty of open slips right by the entrance and there was no need to have us go into the coffin corner. If I was going to pay $100 or more a day for this place, I was not willing to dock in the most dangerous slip in the marina.

"Go in and turn right," he continued to bark over the VHF, but by this time I had had it with Hurricane Hole. I backed back into Nassau harbor and started hailing Atlantis marina. This option to not go into a marina or slip if I don't like the situation, is very valuable and has probably saved me from damaging Contango more than once.

The Atlantis slips were even on the chart. They lay on the west side of their channel with no boats on the other side. That seemed to make for a pretty easy docking. They were in the lee of a large hotel or condo complex, which would block any east wind and would make

Linus Wilson

made backing in easier. Atlantis had a slip available, and, after I circled for 10 minutes, they gave me the slip number. The wind was 5 knots from the north. As I moved north up the entrance channel to slip seven, I turned to port to back in. The wind blew our bow south more than I wanted to go while the dock attendant stood on the finger slip on the north end of the slip with the pilings to the south. Backing in, we would have a starboard-side tie. I tossed the attendant the starboard stern line. Janna handed him the starboard bow line. I relieved him of the stern line when I jumped on the finger pier with the engine in neutral. Then, I walked the stern back towards the sea wall.

What was amazing about Atlantis for me after two months in the Bahamas was that they had instilled American-style customer service into every employee. They were always friendly and smiling. With the exception of Shark in Cave Cay, I had come to expect customer service which ranges from surly to laid back. Another amazing thing was that dockage at Atlantis includes admission to their water park. I had already factored in the ease of shopping, but I had not counted on this perk. A similar water park in the U.S. would have cost as much as our dock fee. Moreover, Atlantis was better than any U.S. amusement park because there were no lines whatsoever. We stayed an extra night just to ride the slides, watery playgrounds, and artificial rivers. We relived our watery adventures in the dinghies and kayaks in the water park's tame fresh water environments.

At one point, I and the other middle-aged fathers floated on the inner tubes down the raging river. We were enjoying the peace of the manmade four-foot waves. It was not at all exciting compared to a dinghy ride from Stocking Island to George Town. The "raging river" ride was a transitory respite from our kids and responsibilities.

The other thing about Atlantis that amazed us after floating along with retirees mostly for six weeks was the children. There were American families with young children everywhere. We had almost forgotten that there was a world of families with young children out there when you left the anchorages and remote islands behind. We had been derived of consumerism for so long that we could not but marvel at all the shopping choices a few yards away. It was a culture shock in the extreme, but we loved it unashamedly. We gained weight packing in pizza, Dunkin Donuts, Ben and Jerry's ice cream, and Starbucks cappuccinos. We loved milling in crowds of Americans straight off the plane.

The most expensive slips at $7 per foot were used by mega charter yachts with large professional crews. Our favorite was the one with a helicopter on the top. Most had put up the sign "No Boarding—Private Yacht" to keep tourists not paying the $10,000 a day from tramping on their decks. We were a long hike from the outdoor mall where the tourists roamed and instead of a gang plank that your grandmother could scale, a boarder would have to jump two to three feet below the dock to get to our boat. Sophie colored a picture at dinner and at the top I wrote, "NO BOARDING— PRIVATE YACHT" which I taped to our companionway. It seemed to work.

47. THE NASSAU 10-K

The night before we left Atlantis, I fretted in the wee hours of the morning about the dangers of anchoring in Nassau harbor enumerated by the cruising guide. However, when I awoke, I saw how silly those sentiments were. The water was completely calm. We barely slipped off the dock lines by the 11 AM, checkout time. The exit was as easy as possible when I helmed. The 5-knot north wind was turning our bow south where we wanted to go and the slip next to us was vacant. Thus, we did not have to worry about another boat sticking out of its slip. Janna brought in starboard bow line which was doubled while I brought in the doubled starboard stern line which was also doubled. The timing was great and the wind was fair.

We initially planned on anchoring on the east side of the bridges, but when I zoomed into the Garmin, I saw why I had passed on this anchorage the first time around. The east anchorage was nearer

Linus Wilson

to the Pirate museum and downtown Nassau, which were on our itinerary. There were many tricky shallows to traverse before entering this anchorage so I decided not to risk it. Instead, I turned east and cleared the bridges, and saw the Cloisters anchorage was free. There was a sailing cat way on the east side of the anchorage; so we could drop the hook on the west side with plenty of room. We dropped in six foot depths with 60 feet of chain.

We untied the inflatable and loaded it up. Because Janna had left her towel in the showers, we dinghied back to Atlantis. Since we were so far west by this point we went to the western dinghy dock on the south, Nassau side, of the harbor. This one traded the suspicious looking men for a grumpy guard who tossed out orders left and right. After paying our $5 fee, we hike a mile-and-a-half west from the dinghy dock to the Pirate Museum, which was no cheesier than I imagined.

I had some fuel and oil filters to get for the diesel inboard. Google maps told me they were near the dinghy dock. We walked for two miles on this road, which had no parallel streets for over half a mile. We got to a churchyard where the sidewalk and the berm disappeared. Fast moving traffic made it impossible to walk against the traffic. There was no room for both a human and a compact car. We were running out of time as it was 4:30 PM, and the only Yanmar dealer in the Bahamas that I knew about closed at 5 PM. Backtracking would take at least a half hour and Sophie was near the limits of her endurance. I had never seen the four-year-old walk so much.

The stone wall looked low. So I jumped. I hoisted Sophie over, and Janna jumped over. We walked in the front lawn. Unfortunately, the front door did not open to the wider berm. Jumping over the higher wall was risky. It was securely locked and six feet high. The wall was four feet high, but jumping it in this traffic was madness. If I scaled it, I would jump over the wall into an onrushing car. The only option was to turn around or scale the side wall between the church yard and the grave yard next to it which was four feet high. The gravestones were not moving at 50 miles per hour. Thus, scaling the wall into the grave yard seemed safer than scaling the wall into the road.

Slow Boat to the Bahamas

We passed Sophie over, hoping that dead men told no tales. The wall to the street and the sidewalk was five-and-a-half feet high. The sidewalk returned at the east end of the graveyard that dead ended into another building built all the way to the sidewalk. We found a stone by the street wall and used that as a step. The wall was flat on top. I scaled it with the step. Janna passed Sophie, and then scaled it herself. We were free from the churchyard and grave yard, but still very late.

The street numbers followed no discernable pattern. The neighborhood took a turn for the worse. Janna started carrying Sophie. I called and the phone directions made no sense. I started running ahead to find the place, but I could not. By 4:55 PM I ran back to Janna and called off the hunt for the Yanmar dealer. I could see boat yards that I recognized on the east side of town, and I at least knew where I was.

We could use some fresh food. We could be stranded in Bimini for weeks waiting to cross the Gulf Stream, and shopping in Bimini seemed very unappealing compared to going to Solomon's Fresh Market tonight. In addition, we had found the only pharmacy that stocked scopolamine was in the same shopping center on the east side of the waterfront. Somehow we had run out despite our huge stock. We bought four scopolamine patches for a princely $43 each.

There was no way we could walk two-and-a-half miles back to the dinghy dock with the groceries. When we emerged from grocery shopping trying to dial cabs, a fifty year old man with bloodshot eyes offered his services. He was "off duty" and would drive us in his car. We negotiated a fare of $13 and loaded our groceries into his nearly totaled gray compact car. It had been rear ended. The trunk was tied shut. With every bump in the road, his muffler scraped. He chattered endlessly as I looked out the broken windows and wondered which alley he would turn down and rob us. He left the road and turned into an apartment complex. I was prepared to run. I could call for police while the ladies practiced their jujitsu. "This is a shortcut. It's my

Linus Wilson

brother-in-law's apartment complex. He is kind of high and mighty these days all messed up in politics," he went on. To my shock, it really was a shortcut, and we emerged at the marina where he helped us unload groceries. The dinghy ride back was dry, and we got to bed earlier than we ever had at Atlantis.

48. THE SARCOPHAGUS

We planned to make a three day saunter to the edge of the Gulf Stream. First, we would stop in either Frazer's Hog Cay or Chub Cay in the Berry Islands. Next, we would anchor on the great Bahamas bank. Finally, we would choose a crossing point in the Bimini chain at or south of Gun Cay Cut by North Cat Cay, where I had anchored on my way to Nassau. Hopefully, the calms and partially south winds would last for four days or more as forecast.

We pulled up anchor in Nassau at 7:30 AM. I could see our anchor as I got ready to take up the chain. In the calm, we were floating right over it and even in the "dirty" water of Nassau it was easy to see in the six-foot depths. Janna did not have to run the motor to pick up the chain. I could haul it in easily in the flat water.

As we motored out the west side of Nassau harbor by the cruise ships, the VHF channel 16 crackled. "Quantum of da Seas, Quantum of da Seas, dis is Enchantment of da Seas. Over," called an eastern European man's voice. After about five minutes of this Quantum of the Seas responded and said "wait a minute." Then an eastern European's woman's voice took over the VHF for Quantum of the Seas. At this point both Quantum of the Seas and Enchantment of the Seas, the 10-story-plus cruise ships were towering over us tied to the docks.

They switched to VHF channel 10. We could not miss this VHF radio version of *Love Boat*. "I vas tinking of coming by around noon. Do you have a BTC card yet?" said the man.

"No, I vas tinking about getting von today." She replied midway through their 10 minute chat.

"I vill meet you on zee dock by Quantum of da Seas. I kunnot beir to vait," he said.

"OK, zee you den. I villy miss you, und I kennot vait to see you" she replied. Thus, their date was arranged for all to hear.

Despite the light 5-to-10-knot south breeze the sails did most of the work for most of the trip to Frazer's Hog Cay. We could not spot any of the charted day marks for the entrance channel. Eventually, Janna spotted a green can buoy on our port. It was on the land propped next to a tree. That really was not helpful.

The guide said there would be 23 moorings at the Berry Islands Club. We spotted two. All other boats chose to anchor north of the club. The pendant was a tiny eyelet which could not be picked up except by jamming the boat hook's eye into the hole and hoping that the momentum did not break the boat hook in two. Further, complicating the procedure was that the float at the end of the loop was not buoyant enough to float the loop. Naturally, I was a bit hesitant to do this, and Janna, at the helm, made four excellent passes. Eventually, I did thread the needle, but the small amount of momentum bent the already bent boat hook farther. It went from a 2 degree bend to a 30 degree kink, but it did not break. I tied off the mooring lines and extracted the hook on the deck. I dived the mooring and I saw a huge concrete box which looked substantial enough for me. However, no other boater would endorse our decision to pick up the mooring. We were the only boat on those moorings.

I got out the dinghy and paid the club our $25. A couple of local fishermen were cleaning their conch. I said hello, but since they did not offer it for sale, and I did not get any. I still had some more in the freezer. No one was using the docks, and a sailboat was beached on the hill just north of the club ominously.

The bar man in the club took my money and informed me that the gas pumps were out of commission. They did let me get rid of my trash. I also got some free fresh water. Chub Cay's marina, a few miles west, had said they could sell me some diesel fuel. My calculations said that motoring all the way to Miami at 0.6 gallons per hour and averaging 5 miles per hour would leave us with only have 5 gallons when we got to Miami. Further, I suspected we could burn 0.7 gallons per hour, making our margin of safety very thin. A close to empty tank makes it more likely debris in the bottom of the tank will clog the fuel filters, which we changed in George Town. Thus, I thought it was essential to either refuel in Chub Cay, North Cat Cay, or Bimini before crossing the Gulf Stream.

When I slipped off the mooring lines, the calm water better revealed what our mooring was. It was a sarcophagus, a stone coffin, as are seen above ground at the grave yard at Canal Street in New Orleans. We owed our good night sleep to this coffin. We had slept like the dead.

49. TRIANGULATION

We anchored at Chub Cay six miles away. I had Janna come to the bow to see how the first 20 feet of chain just lay in a pile on the dead calm. I told her to watch the chain to see if it chose a direction based on the current or wind. Then, I showed Janna how to let it out and snub it with our shackle and looped dock line. She kept the motor running in neutral.

As I was getting the gear ready, I called one more time. Chub Cay's marina informed me that they had run out of diesel yesterday. The calm weather had brought out the sport fishing boats as well as the cruisers going west and east. We would have to press on and hope there was fuel in North Cat Cay.

Before leaving Nassau, I had posed a question to the Island Packet Facebook group. What was the best place to cross from the

Bahamas and enter Miami? They universally discouraged me from entering the ship channel of Government Cut. Instead, they said you should approach Miami from the southern tip of Key Biscayne south of the Cape Florida Light. The crossing location from the Bahamas was more contentious. Some advocated heading as far south at Brown's Cay. Hayden Cochran for example thought crossing at Gun Cay was the best bet. I was hesitant to do that because I thought my slow boat would be fighting the north flowing Gulf Stream too much from Gun Cay which is only about six miles south of the Gun Cay Cut. I did current triangle diagrams for three scenarios:

1) Depart over 20 miles south of Gun Cay Cut near South Riding Rock.
2) Depart about 10 miles south of Gun Cay Cut at Brown's Cay.
3) Depart at Gun Cay Cut.

The rationale for departing south of Gun Cay Cut was that it was a good ocean cut and the shortest distance to the Cape Florida light channel at 43 miles. The rationale for departing further south is that you would avoid turning into the Gulf Stream and cross it at 270 degrees or higher where the Gulf Stream is giving the boat an increase in speed not slowing it down. Ultimately, I brushed up on my triangle current diagrams from my coastal navigation certification and found that choice 3, the direct route, would minimize our boat's time in the Gulf Stream. The problem with departing the Great Bahama Bank further south was that the bank bowed east making the Gulf Stream wider and the crossing further the more south you went from Gun Cay Cut. I assumed the Gulf Stream moved 2.5 knots and started as soon as we left the bank. Further, I assumed that Contango made five knots over the water in these calculations. Choices 1, 2, and 3, were estimated to take 10.2, 10.1, and 9.2 hours in these scenarios.

Linus Wilson

Besides minimizing the time crossing the Gulf Stream there were other good reasons to favor a departure from the Gun Cay Cut just north of North Cat Cay. First, the other two departure points lacked good anchorages, and we would have motored south from North Cat Cay on the bank wasting daylight hours and the crew's stamina. In addition, I found that we could refuel at North Cat Cay so we would have to stop there anyway. Finally, Brown's Cay and South Riding Rock are very far from the beaten path where cruising boats go. We would have little support if we got into trouble. Our paper charts for these places were small scale, underscoring how remote they were.

The Northwest Channel is a choke point and we had several large sport fishing boats pass us then. However, after that the bank was largely deserted. The wind built to 10 knots at dusk. This made my plans for anchoring on the bank less appealing. It was one thing to anchor in a calm, but I worried we would not sleep much with the bigger seas in the unprotected expanse of water. I told Janna that North Cat Cay was one port in the Bahamas that I felt I could enter at night. It was not unfamiliar because I had anchored there before. I had seen its runway and marina with more lights than I had seen anywhere in the Bahamas save Nassau. Moreover, the entrance was wide. The only hazard was a charted sandbar to the south which was easily avoided. So we pressed on after dark.

Janna took a nap until 10:30 PM and emerged to be the first one to spot the lights of North Cat Cay. I was using my headlamp to do my current math, and that may have hampered my night vision. As we got close, I saw two boats at anchor near the shallows east of the airport where I had anchored in the east wind on my way to Nassau in January. I would find out in the morning there were three boats in that part of the anchorage. With southwest winds blowing and in the forecast, I thought west of the runway exclusion zone nearer to the north east side of the island was the better spot to drop the hook. We dropped the hook where the chart depth was 7.9 feet on the Garmin chart. The depth gauge showed 11 feet. I snubbed the chain, and went to bed at midnight.

50. BUSTED

I got fuel in the morning. There was a family of six who had just crossed the Gulf Stream in a 22-foot open fishing skiff. We were indeed experiencing weird weather conditions, and the calms were forecast to last for the next couple days. Janna and Sophie joined me in the afternoon for lunch at North Cat Cay. The docks were so high that I could not land anywhere but next to a ladder. However, the ladders were all next to occupied slips. I had to climb up the ladder and drag our dink to an unoccupied slip. I found a very well stocked American-style convenience store. It was better than any place I had seen on Bimini.

Janna and Sophie went shopping at a clothes store and gift shop. Janna wanted to buy gifts for her family that said the Bahamas on them. While Janna was checking out, Sophie tipped over a glass display, Janna caught it, but then, thinking it stabilized, let go. It shattered into hundreds of pieces in the manner of an auto windshield. The shop attendants were kind and did not charge us for breaking the glass.

We went on the path north past the cheery-looking, building marked "JAIL." I wanted to walk to the north point and observe the Gun Cay Cut, but a sign saying that the impeccably landscaped road was for members and residents only. So, we turned south. We found our first playground since Palm Cay in New Providence. Sophie played on the slides and swings. After a while, I got bored and went in search of a bathroom. I told Janna I would fill up the diesel jugs and meet her back at the dinghy. I soon was greeted by a security guard in a golf cart.

"Are you a member or a guest of a member?" he asked.

"No, we just got lunch here, and are anchored nearby," I replied.

"Why did you go past the members and guests sign, here?" he asked.

Evidently, I was too busy examining the jail to note the no trespassing signs. "I'm sorry. I did not see it. If I had seen that sign, I would have never gone down the road," I replied.

"Are you alone?" he asked.

Then, I snitched on my wife and daughter without a plea agreement. "No, my wife and my daughter are at the playground. I can call or text them to leave." Janna did not pick up. I warned her it was time to leave by text, but the security guard broke the news to her. He kicked Janna and Sophie off the otherwise deserted playground. Janna was none too happy about being kicked off one of the few playgrounds in the Bahamas. Perhaps it was for the best. Janna said to me later that she had seen condom near the play area. Yuk! That probably was not a jungle gym we wanted to frequent anyways.

"You need to leave," he said. I agreed to. I got the dinghy and started filling the diesel cans. I was happy to not be touring the jail that afternoon.

The focus on North Cat Cay is selling second, third, fourth, or fifth homes to rich Americans and Canadians. The marina is more a means to sell property than to get slip fees. Visiting boats are limited to one day clearing into the marina and then have to go elsewhere. As a result, the marina is almost completely empty. To me, more boats in the marina would make it easier to sell houses. They could always get rid of transient spaces when the place became more crowded. However, what do I know about real estate marketing?

51. BACK IN THE U.S.A.

The time to cross the Gulf Stream had come. Calms were supposed to prevail that day. Based on my readings of the forecasts, this seemed like the best crossing day among many great days to cross.

We got up in the dark. We started picking up chain at 6:45 AM. I had hoisted the rubber dinghy on top of the Walker Bay 8 rowing dinghy, making visibility poor. At the bow, I observed that the waters were churning but less than one foot high. The anchorage was calm.

We had a deal that I would helm through the cuts, and Janna and I switched as we rounded North Cat Cay's northernmost point. Janna was reading the water with the walkie-talkie, and I was just trying to see over the dinghies and keep my wits about me. The water was blue fringed with pink as the rising sun was behind us. I could discern little from this rose colored view of reality. I increased the throttle to 2,300 RPMs, and we were making 6 knots over the water, according to our paddle wheel gage. Our GPS speed dipped to 3.3 knots. Thus, the flood tide took away 2.7 knots. Sophie awoke just as we were entering the cut. As we cleared the land and the shallows to the port and starboard, our speed rose.

The Gulf Stream was glassy. It had a lazy two foot swell. My rusty foldup bike had been lashed to the deck, making the boat look like a junk yard for weeks. It had been unused since my first visit to Nassau two months earlier. I was tempted to throw it into the depths while off shore to disintegrate thousands of feet down, but I figured I could sell or give it away in Miami. Instead, I clipped in and took close up pictures of it for Craigslist from the starboard beam. I ended up leaving it unlocked at a bike rack at a marina in Florida. A buyer did come after a couple weeks. I told the buyer that he could have it for $40 if they mailed me a check. They mailed me a check for $50, and took it off my hands.

I saw two container ships pass north of Bimini. One stayed to the north and the other turned south and crossed well in front of our bow. At 10:00 AM, I did a slight and temporary course correction to avoid a Del Monte fruit container ship. My plan was to correct the steering by autopilot so that we stayed on the straight line between the entrance channel to the Cape Florida light and the Gun Cay Cut. We would only briefly steer south of 270 degrees. Thus, we only briefly

Linus Wilson

steered south of west. Our minimum speed under power the whole way was 4.7 miles per hour. It was an ideal crossing from my perspective. I wanted a crossing that would not scare Janna and a crossing that would not break anything on the boat. Nothing broke, and this Gulf Stream Crossing was not exciting.

We saw small fishing boats with lines out this sunny Saturday, March 21, 2015. There was one big unexpected swell as we entered the shallows by the entrance channel to Biscayne Bay. However, we could have just been blindsided by a fishing boat wake. Everything changed when we entered Biscayne Bay at 3:30 PM. Fast boats zipped this way and that. Bikini-clad women and bare-chested men were everywhere burning fuel as fast as their boat's pistons could fire. How Janna dealt with the boat traffic and wakes with such equanimity was beyond me. I was really glad that she was helming.

I had read Dinner Key Marina had mooring balls and was within walking distance of a Whole Foods grocery store. They assigned us a mooring ball, and we motored forward while I took down the last scrap of sail. The winds had picked up by the time we got there at around 6:00 PM, and were coming from the east at 10 knots. Dinner Key's mooring field was almost completely unprotected from the most common type of winds, east winds. The winds had picked up from the east in the late afternoon and there was a sloppy two foot chop in the very full mooring field. As we wound around the channel slowly, we spotted our ball. As with Frazer's Hog Cay, the eyes were tiny. However, unlike Frazer's Hog Cay, we did not have a calm and plenty of room to maneuver. Our ball was not on the end. It was in the middle of a very closely-packed, full row of sailboats. Janna could hardly control the boat in the windy and choppy channel at low speeds.

"Janna, I don't feel very confident about picking up this ball," I said over the walkie- talkie. "How do you feel? Over."

"I don't like it," she said. "You can try helming if you want. I think the boats are too close together," she said.

"I don't want to try. I want to get out of here. Over," I said.

Slow Boat to the Bahamas

"OK. Where are we going?" she replied.

"Motor down the channel to the east. We are going to try anchoring at Marine Stadium. Over," I said.

"What is that?"

Marine stadium is a nearly 360-degree protected anchorage, which was about three miles away. It was used for cigarette boat races, but it is currently more or less abandoned by Miami-Dade County. We arrived at the abandoned park around 7 PM with the fading light. We entered the southwest entrance just south of an island protecting the stadium's west side. Several small powerboats were beached and having an impromptu party. At least half the boats were deserted. Some had been deserted for a long time. We anchored near a large schooner, which had several tall young white men with dreadlocks on it. One of them yelled, "Is that an Island Packet 31? I love Island Packets! The 31 is my favorite!" That was both friendly and disconcerting in this weird anchorage.

The stadium was on the southeast side of the giant track-shaped piece of water. The stadium was covered in graffiti, and a large fence seemed to close off the bleacher area, which was large as a big high school's football stands. On the southwest, there was a boat launch for small power boaters who paid the storage facility to put their boat in a large shed when not in use. This launch was clearly marked as off limits to people who were not tenants of the giant boat shed, and none of the anchored boats seemed to use it. Interestingly, we saw many row boats on a rocky shore under some scrub trees. There were no dinghies with outboards except electric trolling motors. That rocky beach looked like an informal dinghy dock, which was not mentioned in the cruising guide. We had no idea how to get out of the huge fenced-in area, but the abandoned dinghies indicated that there was a way.

I had checked in to customs and immigration over the phone as we entered Biscayne Bay over four hours earlier. They said all the crew (expect our dog, Daly) had to show up at the nearest customs station to clear in. The nearest one they told us was near the cruise ship docks about two miles as the crow flies and 10 miles by road. If we got there before 10 PM, we could clear in that night. We loaded up the Walker Bay 8 rowing dinghy because I was afraid of exposing the Honda 2.3 HP outboard to theft on the rocky patch under the scrub trees. (I still always chained the outboard to the dinghy. Moreover I used a 12-foot long thin stainless steel and plastic covered rope with eyes for locking the rubber dinghy to any dock.) I never wanted to have the nicest dinghy on any dock or beach. This looked like a place someone might bring wire cutters to.

Janna rowed Sophie and I to the shore, and I chained her oars and her boat to a stout tree. Then we stumbled around in the mud and weeds with our headlamps until I spotted the exit in the southeast corner of the fence around the dinghy shore. It was a human sized cut in the 15-foot high chain link fence. By this time is was 9 PM, and we were running out of time if we wanted to clear. With unlimited, fast data in the U.S., all the features of the iPhones were available in a way that they were not with the expensive and slow data in the Bahamas. I summoned an Uber ride, but it was Saturday night in Miami, and there was 3 times surge pricing. This meant that fares were tripled on the way in, and 1.5 times surge pricing on the way back meant the fare back was 50 percent higher than normal. By the time we cleared at 9:55 PM and got home well after 10 PM, we had paid $100 in Uber fares. However, we now could roam the land of the free and the home of the brave!

52. TENNIS AND MOORING BALLS

Janna was worried that prolonged anchoring was not an attractive option because we had laundry to do every four days or so. The dirty clothes were piling up since Nassau, and we needed to find a solution. By passing on the Dinner Key mooring, we had passed up on our laundry facilities. While we could land here near a restaurant, coin laundry facilities were not nearby.

I found some more inexpensive mooring balls, $22 per night, in Key Biscayne at the Crandon Park Marina. Laundry was on site and there were cold-water-only showers too. Moreover, we would have dinghy dock rights instead of the squatters' rights in Marine Stadium.

Any tennis fan will recognize Key Biscayne and Crandon Park as the home of the Miami Tennis tournament. It is the fifth largest professional tennis tournament, just after the majors—the Australian Open, Wimbledon, the French Open, and the U.S. Open. It attracts all the best professional tennis players both men and women. My parents visit the tournament most years making the long drive from the west coast of Florida. My dad was at the time the men's high school tennis coach for Bayshore High School in Bradenton, Florida and had coached a few state runner-ups. Both my parents love to play and follow the pro tour. Thus, it would be great to have them visit us during the tennis tournament.

Unfortunately, the Crandon Park Marina refused to assign us a mooring ball if we did not dock at their fuel dock first and fill out the paperwork. The Gulf Shores, Alabama and Naples, Florida experiences had made me swear off docking Contango at fuel docks. I went round and round with them saying how we did not want to dock and pick up a mooring ball, but they would not bend. We had to pay them and fill out the paperwork before they would assign a mooring ball. Finally, I realized I could jog or walk to the marina. By road it was only two miles to the marina.

When I got back after requesting a ball on the outer edge of the mooring field, we motored out the five miles, dragging the Walker Bay 8. We went under the bridge to Virginia Key, where the marine stadium was—the Rickenbacker Causeway Bridge—and around the entrance channel to Crandon Park Marina on the northwest tip of Key Biscayne. The Rickenbacker Causeway Bridge was a nightmare of fast boats and stupid boat operators outdoing themselves trying to create a

Linus Wilson

collision in that narrow space. Most of these boats had no reason to use the highest span, but I'm sure none of them owned a chart or ever had a boating safety course. Biscayne Bay further convinced me to avoid the narrow stretch of the ICW north of Miami. I wanted to go back home via the more sailboat-friendly Florida Keys to the south.

Our ball was by the mangroves on the northwest side of the mooring field. Unfortunately, our pendant was either too small or snagged. It could not be picked up more than a foot above the water level, and our freeboard at the bow was three feet. This made looping a mooring line virtually impossible. You had to be at water level to loop the mooring line in the little eye that was used also in Frazer's Hog Cay and Dinner Key Marina. Finally, one of our mooring ball neighbors got in his dinghy and rowed over. He put the lines through the loop and handed them back up. The mooring field offered nearly 360-degree protection. We would not leave the mooring for three weeks from March 22, to April 12, 2015.

Even paying twice as much as the folks who signed long-term leases, we were getting a deal. One bedroom condos in Key Biscayne were going for $1 million. We were paying less than $700 per month. Very few boats in the field were live aboard. Most were day sailors who took their boats out on the weekend. It was too far to walk to the grocery store or other shops in Key Biscayne, but the marina did sell drinks, ice cream, and fishing supplies. The bus stopped at the marina every 30 minutes. The Uber ride back from the grocery store was only $6.

There are so many good places for a boat to stay in Miami inexpensively that I will not say we found the perfect spot. The shower just had a curtain and was not separated by gender. You had to hold down the button for the cold water. Lacking hot water in the spring in Miami is not usually a hardship. The marina had gas and diesel pumps. Diesel was $3 per gallon not the $5 per gallon that I had paid in the Exumas. Moreover, with the mooring, water was free and the washing machines were onsite unlike any mooring ball we visited in the Bahamas.

Slow Boat to the Bahamas

We saw the tennis on our own and with my parents, who spent a night at the boat. We wanted a rigid inflatable boat (RIB) with a hard bottom and a high bow that would be less wet. I sold the roll-up dinghy right after arriving in Miami, but had not yet received the replacement (RIB). When my parents visited and stayed overnight at our boat, Janna had to ferry my parents one at a time in our Walker Bay 8 because it did not have the capacity to carry three adults.

We spent a week around Easter visiting my parents' new house in Venice, Florida. Janna enjoyed the time off the boat, and Sophie had fun with the Easter egg hunts and playing with her grandparents. Janna's good looks were enough to get both of us into the weekly meeting of the Venice shuffleboard club. We got our clocks cleaned by some retirees who insisted on playing something like 20 games of shuffleboard. One of shuffleboard sharks carried a copy of the official shuffleboard rules at all times. At my parent's house, we also picked up our two month old mail. I got the Honda shop manual for the Honda 2 HP and 2.3 HP motors. I found this manual much easier to understand than the Seloc manual, and it would prove a life saver when we used the outboard in the Keys.

At Crandon Park Marina, the water was typically so calm and the distance to the dinghy dock was so short that most mooring ball tenants rowed their dinghies as did we. I learned to row more efficiently and loved the Walker Bay 8. I did not know you were supposed to move in the direction of the bow. Janna had to tell me to stop rowing the boat stern first and face the stern, not the bow, while rowing! There was only one squally afternoon, which would clock the highest wind speeds of the trip—40 knots—where the rowing was difficult. However, I found the Walker Bay 8 could make progress against the twenty-knot-plus-winds and the two-foot swells once I got far enough off the dock to stretch the oars.

We got some deferred maintenance done in Miami. Besides changing oil and belts, I had one big engine maintenance item. Janna was really worried after reading an article in *Good Old Boat* magazine because we were overdue on inspecting the air water exhaust elbow. I had held off on this prior to departure because I lacked time. Then, in the Bahamas, I was afraid of pulling a major piece of the engine without mechanics and Tow Boat U.S. around. I got a replacement air water exhaust elbow, manifold elbow, and joint from a Yanmar dealer in Miami. I had to buy a huge 24-inch wrench and use a vice at a Miami West Marine to turn the joint after removing it. The whole sooty process took two days and Janna requested that I had to use a drop cloth before messing with such dirty parts again. Much scrubbing and Formula 409 could not remove all the soot stains from the cockpit. It took several days to get the dark marks fully cleaned off my hands. I had put on all new parts because it was so hard to remove the sooty old ones. I kept the unclogged but dirty elbow as a spare.

We thought south Florida would be the ideal place to pick up a RIB. That did not mean it was easy. We needed an unusually small one—8-feet-6-inches or less, which could fit on our foredeck, and this complicated getting one. The first dealer refunded my money when she could not deliver the Mercury RIB when she promised. The second said they had sold me the $3,000 RIB, and then said they had sold it to another customer through some miscommunication with another salesman. They did have more expensive boat that they could sell me. I complained to the Florida Attorney General and Better Business Bureau about this classic bait and switch. Finally, a third dealer actually had a boat to sell. We bought a Highfield 260 ultralight aluminum-bottomed PVC RIB for $1,800. I picked it up in Homestead Florida south of Miami after renting a large SUV to transport it. We loved it. It was light, 64 pounds, and had a high bow. The only problem was that the Honda 2 HP and 2.3 HP clamps were not big enough for the stern mount. I had to sand down part of the plastic outer cover of the stern mount to get the outboard on.

I was missing some papers to complete my taxes, and flew back to New Orleans to get the documents that I needed. On the way, I wanted to register the dinghy with Louisiana. This involved first visiting the state tax office in Baton Rouge and getting a signature. Then, I had to visit the Lafayette Parish tax office in downtown

Lafayette about sixty miles away. Then, I had to drive to Baton Rouge another sixty miles away. Even though the office closed at 4:30 PM, you could not enter the office after 4 PM. I arrived after 4 PM. A member of the staff took pity on me and met me at the security counter. Surprised that I had succeeded in filling out the tax forms certifying I had not avoided sales taxes, I handed her a check, and she handed me the decals.

The new RIB is lashed to the foredeck in the picture. Its v-shaped hull made it easier to row and drier than the rollup inflatable dinghy that we sold.

53. ON TO MARATHON

We threw off the mooring lines for the first time in three weeks at 7:30 AM on April 12, 2015. If we were going to get home before hurricane season started and visit Key West before Janna left, it was time to get moving. I had just flown back from New Orleans the previous day. The plan was to head south to Marathon, anchoring the whole way. At Marathon we would refuel, do laundry, and reprovision. Then we would get a mooring ball in Key West and spend at least a week there. Key West, like Miami was one of the few places in Florida that my family had only visited briefly when I was a kid. I was eager to go back thirty years later and Janna wanted to see it for the first time.

Our diesel's engine hour gauge stopped turning and our RPM gauge ranged from 700 to 1,300 instead of the 1,000 to 2,300 as it usually did. These readings would not return back to normal until the next day. I made no attempt to fix the gages. We motor sailed in light east southeast winds close hauled heading south down Biscayne Bay to Pumpkin Key.

We anchored in eight feet of water close to Key Largo. I let out 60 feet of chain. I thought Key Largo would provide better protection from the east winds than tiny Pumpkin Key. However, a lot of boats would go between some residential canals to the south and Angelfish Creek the access point to the Hawk Channel and Atlantic Ocean to the north and Janna correctly predicted this lonely anchoring spot would get a lot of wakes from passing boaters.

After dark, the traffic dropped off, but Janna and I could not sleep in the v-berth because of the heat. Sophie did not mind. We could not open the v-berth hatch because of the dinghies on top. Janna and I moved to the starboard settee double bed where we could open some hatches. The Honda EU2000i companion generator only ran at full choke. Running inefficiently, the Honda generator could not start the air conditioner. Sweating under the 12-volt fans was the only option.

I had noticed the 2.3 HP was also dying after running for a little while in Miami. I rebuilt and cleaned the new carburetors of both the 2.3 HP and 2.0 HP Hondas using carburetor cleaner that I had purchased in an auto parts store in Miami. They both looked clean although their fuel filters could be replaced. I wanted to get them both working well by the time we were in Marathon and Key West when we would rely on the outboard to avoid marina slip fees.

Slow Boat to the Bahamas

We got a late start the next day from fooling around with the engine seawater intake strainer. Janna read a book about it and thought it should be checked, but it would not close properly when we found it was clear. It dripped seawater when the seacocks were open. If I tightened it anymore, I was afraid the bolts on the bronze strainer would break.

Moreover, I decided in the sometimes rough Hawk Channel that we should only drag the RIB. The Walker Bay had taken on three gallons of water in our 20-mile cruise of Biscayne Bay the previous day. So we hoisted and lashed the Walker Bay 8 on deck and moved the RIB from the deck to being dragged from the stern.

This all meant we were entering Angelfish Creek at flood of an outgoing tide at 10 AM versus slack water, at our planned departure time of 7:30 AM. The wind was against the current. The entrance to the creek was charted at four feet, and the exit at the Hawk Channel was only five feet. We were entering a shallow channel on a falling tide with the flood tide opposing the current. Those were not encouraging facts. We cleared the Biscayne Bay entrance OK, but faced one-to-two foot breakers at the last few markers. This was not the flat water of the creek, but it was not dangerous or uncomfortable. We were lucky that no other boats were coming because the channel narrowed to about 30 feet wide. Once in Hawk Channel, we took it easy and laid off the motor, sailing three-to-five knots until we anchored behind Rodriguez Key, which is on the south end of Key Largo.

Janna used the Walker Bay as a wind scoop, which cooled off the v-berth. She hoisted its bow with our spinnaker halyard and tied down its stern over the forward hatch. (We destroyed one wind scoop in less than a couple weeks in the trade winds of Stocking Island.) Janna hated the wind scoop anyways because it was so noisy. We had a second one, but we never got it out. The Walker Bay was quieter and more durable. Meanwhile the high sided RIB was totally dry from a day of dragging. It was a good decision to switch their positions that morning.

When we picked up anchor, Janna noticed that the autopilot was not keeping up, but as we increased speed from two to five knots, it seemed to do fine. The southeast wind that prevailed the previous three days continued. Fortunately, as the Florida Keys turned more westward and less southward, we went from being close hauled to having a beam reach on our south west course towards Marathon.

Janna argued that we should follow the policy advocated in sailing schools that goes "when in doubt let it out" as the wind moved more to our beam or stern. However, I thought we should keep the sails more close hauled because the variance of the wind angle matters here. In particular, we agreed that the poorly pointing Island Packet 31 cannot get closer than 60 degrees to the wind. Our autopilot steers a compass course, ignoring the apparent wind angle because we had never set it up for apparent wind angle steering. We typically do not tend the sheet constantly while cruising. When waves bounce us around, and we were set for a beam reach, then the sail would go from luffing to being too close in. I believed the luffing would slow us down more than having the sails too tightly in. If we are close hauled and the waves change our apparent wind angle say 25 degrees from a mean of 90, then our range of apparent wind angles will be 65 to 115 degrees off the wind. In that case, the sails never luff, and we are never severely depowered. "In our sailing courses we had a helmsman, not an autopilot and there was always a crew member tending the genoa sheets," I said. Janna let out the sails anyways as the wind moved further behind us. There was no good way to settle that debate in those conditions.

We anchored by Long Key. This Key has a bay of shallow charted water of six-to-four-foot depths in the center just south of the highway 1 bridge. To get protection from the east southeast wind, I wanted to be as far in as possible in the four foot depths near the south end of the bay. To get to the five foot depths it appeared we had to skirt the four foot depths. The five foot depths turned out to be 4.5 feet at datum. I helmed slowly in at three miles per hour or less. I chickened out 100 feet short of my goal. In neutral, I was not willing to rev the engine to gain steerage, only to run hard aground as I had at the shallow marina at the panhandle of Florida on the trip up. I put out 60 feet of chain in grassy five foot depths.

Our hopes of repeating the Caribbean showers of the last two anchorages were dashed when we observed half a dozen man-o-wars over the stern.

I hailed the sailing catamaran whose skipper gave us a thumbs up as he passed us earlier in the day. It was anchored on the northeast side of the bay exposed to the wind and swell. His antics reminded me of the people pointing out my flipped dinghy in the first trip to Nassau.

He came over. Apparently, earlier he was doing a victory dance that his 42 foot custom sailing catamaran had passed us. Since I could not remember when our 31 foot sailboat had not been passed, I found that explanation funny. He said his boat had a top speed of 16 knots. Ours rarely exceeded six knots.

He had been single-handing his boat to the Bahamas and was planning on going under the 65-foot vertical clearance Channel 5 bridge right next to our anchorage and anchoring in the Shark River in the Everglades. After that stop he would be a day's hop away from his home port of Sanibel Island, Florida. He had been retired for years after cashing out his stock options from working as a mid-level executive at a famous tech company almost two decades ago. I thought his route home was interesting, but I said that we wanted to see Key West and avoid the Everglades and its mosquitoes, which would be thick in mid-April.

That night our anchor dragged on the grassy bottom. Janna and I reset the alarm from 120 feet to 250 feet. We did not want to pick up the anchor and risk running aground in the darkness. We had room to drag a long way before we hit any charted hazards. The catamaran, the only other boat, was not nearby. We resolved to leave before high tide at 7:30 AM so we would avoid running aground on a falling tide.

We actually got off at 6:10 AM and had a great beam reach into Marathon. I tried entering Boot Key Harbor from a new direction— the south through Sister Creek. A fishing boat refused to stop casting in the channel as we passed and, as a result, we found a $25, huge Rapella fishing lure caught in the dinghy's seaweed tangle after docking. The Marathon City Marina was more accommodating in April than in January. They assigned us a mooring ball without requiring us to come into the office first and assured us that there were plenty of vacant balls. I had just come during the high season of January. South Florida was a pretty hot place to live in April especially if you have limited air conditioning.

While Janna and Sophie visited the Dolphin Research Center and paid an exorbitant sum to have a dolphin named Delta paint a t-shirt for Sophie, I ran errands with the rental car. I obtained a new sea strainer for the one that we had checked and then had started leaking slowly. While that new one fit, I would have to cut the hoses off to replace it since they were not coming off any other way. The different size of the strainer that West Marine regularly stocks in its stores meant a major reshuffling of hoses. The hoses ran through the bilge to the head and the engine. The same seacock was used to flush the toilet with saltwater and go to the engine's saltwater pump. It looked like a multi-day job.

When Janna came back, she voted for ordering a new gasket for our old strainer and sending it ahead to my parents' house. If the leak did not get worse, we could wait to change it then. As it turned out the new gaskets did not fit, but the leak did not get worse so I waited until the end of the trip to fix it. Months later, I found the correct (cork) gaskets in the West Marine catalog. After plunking down $30 to West Marine after the $20 that was wasted on the wrong gasket set, the leak was stopped. Another boater told me that he used Teflon plumbing tape for the same problem on that strainer, and it only cost him $0.25. I'm not convinced that our 100 times more expensive solution was 100 times better!

On our first full day in Marathon, I went to get our propane tank filled across the street from the City Marina at 10 AM. The

Slow Boat to the Bahamas

cashier said I should ask George around the back to fill it up. In the back, George was sitting talking to a sympathetic fifty-something cruiser about his tale of woe while drinking a 24-ounce Colt 45. He wore short cut-offs and no shirt. He was gaunt except for his distended beer belly and lacked front teeth.

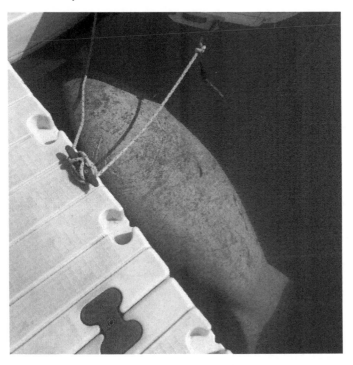

This baby manatee was hanging around the dingy docks at the Marathon City Marina.

"Hi, George, can I get my propane tank filled?" I asked.

I had said something wrong. "You people gadda stop asking for propane," he exclaimed in his Jamaican accent.

"There are a lot of boats across the street, and most of them use propane," I replied.

"They donna pay me enough to do dis! You gadda wait," he said.

"That's, OK," I replied. Hey I've owned boats for five years. I know about waiting. However, ten seconds later he was filling the container and ranting all the way. He then proceeded to give the cashier or owner a chewing out.

Marathon City Marina had a cool lounge with a small library, tables, and a couple of TV rooms tucked quietly away. It also had places to work on sails or other heavy duty projects. Many cruisers hung out there as did the kids. There was a six-year-old girl, who was interested in playing with Sophie, but her parents were often no-where to be seen. Janna was disturbed by the black-clad barefoot teenagers clustered around some video game console probably using the WIFI. "Where are their parents?" she asked.

"Teens typically don't like to be around their parents," was the best I could muster.

We saw a baby manatee hanging around the dinghy docks most of the second day. When I reached to pet it, another cruiser warned against touching it. I would harm its skin and be liable for a nasty fine from the Florida wildlife police. It looked slimy anyways.

We enjoyed the daily cruisers nets, but Marathon is a bit boring to spend a lot of time at, and we were ready to move after three days. The Honda 2.3 HP seemed to be doing well, getting us back and forth. However, on the last night, it would not start after a rain squall while we went out for dinner. We ended up rowing back and refusing tows. Our new RIB had better oar locks and was much easier to row than the old roll-up inflatable. However, it was much slower to row than the Walker Bay 8.

The Honda 2 HP motors were the favorite outboard of cruisers in Marathon, making up perhaps one-sixth of the outboards for the dinghies of the boats on a mooring ball. In George Town, Miami, and later Key West, I would observe the size of the outboard was related to the median distance to the dinghy dock. In our Key Biscayne mooring, the distance was short—less than 0.25 miles, and most rowed as we did while we were there. The distance was below half-a-mile for most people on the ball in Marathon, and the Honda 2 HP or other small outboards dominated. In Key West, the distance would be closer to 0.75 miles to the dinghy dock from our mooring ball, and a 10 HP was closer to the median. Finally, in Stocking Island and George Town the outboards were typically 20 HP for the mile or so ride to the dinghy dock to Exuma Markets in George Town.

54. END OF THE LINE

Janna took the helm on the way out. She went out the west entrance to Boot Key Harbor that I took in and out in January. We had a beam reach with south winds on our beam of 5 to 12 knots to Key West.

If I could not get the outboards working, we could not stay at the Garrison Bite mooring field in Key West. I was a little grumpy about having so much trouble with the outboards. All I saw were other boat owners who seemed to have few problems with their old outboards. In contrast, I had two new outboards—one from 2011, 4 years old, and one from 2015, brand new, which broke down. I did not think other owners carried the manuals and tools and spare parts that I did.

I tested to see if non-fuel problems were the cause of the 2 HP motor's lack of reliability. Using my new shop manual, I did two new tests. While I could not see a spark, I could feel the shock from the spark plug test, indicating the ignition system was good. This involved taking the spark plug out of the engine but keeping its cap on and pulling the starter cord while holding the gap near some steel nuts on the outboard. Because this creates a spark, it is better to do this with the engine drained of gasoline! Moreover, I used a compression gauge from an auto parts store to find that my outboard had perfect compression. The engine was fine. There was probably something wrong with the fuel system.

Linus Wilson

I found with the 2.3 HP, I had not tightened down the spark plug after gapping it. Once I had done that, it started up. At least that should work when we get to Key West! As for the older 2 HP Honda, I had ordered a new coil, gaskets for the carburetor, new fuel filters, and spare drain screws which should be at the Honda Dealer in Key West the next day, a Monday. The new carb gaskets and fuel filter should solve the 2 HP reliability problems. I had eliminated all other causes of its intermittent dying.

Our knot meter had been on the fritz all trip. In Marathon I had pulled it out letting water rush into the bilge and quickly put its plug in behind it, stopping the water. After cleaning it with Sophie's old toothbrush, (never use your own) I put it back in. We calibrated it on the way, and it was working again. The marine growth we took on in Miami was truly astounding. It was even worse in Miami than in the Bahamas. Our hull was a seaweed lawn. It needed to be mowed! We had to haul out first thing when we returned to New Orleans. In the brackish waters of Lake Pontchartrain, boats can go four years without any serious marine growth, but the Miami sailors have to haul out every year. I met one sailor in Key Biscayne that scrubbed his bottom every month with scuba gear.

The coast guard was warning of a sport fishing tournament that ended in Key West that day on VHF channel 16, and, as we approached the south side of the island and prepared to round its southwestern tip, there was a procession of boats rounding that corner at top speed and then stopping at some imaginary check point just west of Key West.

We saw the anchorages on our port at Tank and Wisteria Islands that are near the northwest corner of Key West as we headed north. Many boats had dragged onto the beach of Wisteria Island. Thus, that anchorage did not appear appealing. Fleming Key was connected to Key West by a low fixed bridge and seemed to have some old military installations on it.

We would see a large military presence on, Key West, the home of southernmost point of the continental U.S. and the closest port to

Cuba in the United States. As we sailed, the Obama Administration was loosening travel restrictions between the two countries. Since the 1960's the U.S. had an embargo against Cuba and its communist government. I hoped that the antiquated embargo would end and relations between the two countries would be normalized, but that may help explain the military presence on the island. Another explanation is that soldiers love the beach. If you were a General or Admiral, wouldn't you want to have a base in Key West! The bars on Key West's Duval Street are strategic locations that must be defended at all costs.

We rounded the channel north of Fleming Key and our speed was slowed to 2.5 knots because of the outgoing tide, running a three-knot current. We picked up a mooring ball about 0.8 miles from the dinghy dock at about 5:30 PM. In most weather conditions, it was a well-protected mooring field, with good protection from the west, east, and south.

55. AIR CONDITIONING AND OUTBOARDS

Our stay in Key West and that $18-per-night mooring ball would stretch from April 18, 2015, until May 6, 2015. This was probably a couple weeks longer than it would have been otherwise because we decided to have Janna and Sophie fly out of Key West so that she could be back for work on May 4, 2015. Thus, we were waiting to off-load crew. A week's stay would have kept us wanting more, but by the end we were all disillusioned with living off the grid in the South Florida heat.

Often people think they want to sell their house, live on a boat, and sail around the world by the tropical trade wind routes. However, when hurricane season approaches, living on a boat without an electrical hook up is hot. Hurricanes are formed in part by hot water. You guessed it. When the trade wind belt gets hot, the hurricanes form.

Linus Wilson

I completed the 2013 New York Marathon in a slow but steady 11-minute-per-mile pace. (That's faster than Contango's average speed on the trip!) However, before I went to New York, I ran half marathon training runs almost daily in the Louisiana sultry summer sun and heat. In high school, I did afternoon training runs for cross country in the Orlando, Florida, summers. There is no sea breeze in Lafayette or Orlando. I worked for many hours outside on the boat, and most of my cruises prior to 2015 took place in the summer in the deep U.S. south. I think I am better acclimated to the heat than most Americans, Canadians, or Europeans.

However, I wanted to swallow the anchor in June as much to get climate-controlled living as to avoid hurricanes. (Janna, too, was really happy to return to work in May.) A casual reader of Lin and Larry Pardey's *Seraphin* books will show that they did not cruise all the year. Large parts of the year they worked. Often they moved into temporary accommodations off their boat when the sailing season was over. Other strategies are to move to higher latitudes during hurricane seasons. However, this often means people repeat the same cruises every year (repeat visits to the Bahamas are an example.) Some cruisers do long ocean passages to leave the trade wind belts, and then undertake long ocean passages to return to them. However, the simplest thing is to get some land-based accommodation out of season and fly or drive there after putting your boat in a "safe" place. (Did I mention that cars and planes move much faster than sailboats!) Living on a boat is just tough in the low northern latitudes during early hurricane season June, July, and August if you don't have 24/7 air conditioning.

I faced three challenges to keep the boat air-conditioned. The easiest of the three was keeping my stocks of gasoline high. Refilling gas in a generator is a pain, and constantly going back to the pump is a drag, too. Luckily, our dinghy dock was right next to a fuel dock with gas. The second problem was the air conditioner intake and outtake lines were clogged early on. I have come to realize that we needed to close our air conditioner water cooling intake and outtake seacocks before going on a long sail because seaweed would clog them.

However, that meant that I could not use seawater in the galley sink to wash the dishes while underway because we used the same seacock for the salt water tap and the air conditioner intake. When we hauled out next, we had the yard install an external strainer that prevents large debris from getting in the cooling water intake line for the air conditioner. The third problem was that I needed to keep the Honda EU2000i running and running efficiently. A lot of watery gas plagued this generator, and I had to rebuild its carburetor to get it running at full throttle, which is necessary to run our 16,000 BTU Marine Air with a Smart Start installed. (The Honda generator could not start the air conditioner without the Smart Start because starting amps are much higher than the EU2000i's amp rating.) I replaced the inline fuel filter on our Honda EU2000i Companion with a small motorcycle fuel filter. This gave me easier access to the fuel filter and I also lacked Honda EU2000i inline fuel filter spares in Key West. I got a second EU2000i so I could keep at least one in service before leaving. I slept in air-conditioned comfort on the ball in my last days of Key West and at anchor when I moved north of Key West.

I was also always fighting a battle with the outboards. I found that the tiny white 2 HP fuel filter was black as charcoal in Key West. (I suspect spraying carburetor cleaner on this plastic part may have been misguided.) After I replaced it with parts obtained at the Key West Honda dealer, it ran great until the pull starter mechanism broke after losing a plastic piece. I ordered and received a new pull starter before Janna and Sophie left.

All the breakdowns of the 2.3 HP were related to water in the fuel system. By this time, I started pouring suspect gas in Hefty Slider bags. Those clear and easy-to-seal bags came in sizes of a quart some to 2.5 gallons. If I could see clear water pool in the bottom of the yellow gasoline, I had a fuel system problem. I used my carburetor spray and a tiny 12 volt compressor to clean the metal carburetor pieces with air. Eventually, I also used the bottled air that people clean out their computer keyboards with also. Replacing the filters, draining the tanks, and/or rebuilding the carburetor always fixed the problem, but I spent a lot of time fixing Hondas in Key West. The alternative was $2 to $4 per foot, per night transient, marina fees.

Many of the mooring ball tenants had outboard problems. So I was not alone.

I never brought the Hondas in for service and only ordered parts because I knew that the motors would not be fixed in any reasonable time horizon. The Key West Honda dealer had many outboards in the shop and many 2.3 HP and 2.0 HP Hondas that were partially repaired. If I could not repair at least one outboard within 24 hours of the second one breaking down, we were effectively stranded on the boat because a 0.8 mile row seemed too much to do several times a day. Janna tried to row the Walker Bay 8 to the dinghy dock with Sophie one day. It took her 40 minutes each way or about 1.2 knots per hour. Janna and I liked rowing but not that much.

In contrast, the tiny Honda 2.3 HP went 3.3 knots if we had some weight in the bow to increase its waterline length or 2.8 knots if I was alone and the bow rode high, decreasing the waterline length. The 2.3 HP could not make the RIB plane, which could have allowed it exceed hull speed. The theoretical hull speed is about 1.34 times the square root of its waterline length. Boats with a longer waterline can go faster. However, if a boat planes above the water with a powerful (and gas guzzling) engine it can exceed its theoretical hull speed. The Walker Bay 8 and the RIB had almost identical theoretical hull speeds. The Honda 2.3 HP was just much more powerful than Janna or I, using oars.

56. PIRATE TOWN

The rum runner and human trafficker by night and sport fisherman by day, Harry Morgan, the main character of what I believe is Ernest Hemingway's best novel *To Have and Have Not* paints a seedy picture of Key West. I too found an the undercurrent of criminality there. Gentrification has not completely taken over in Key West even

Slow Boat to the Bahamas

eighty years after Hemingway lived there. One of our mooring ball mates celebrated the end of his probation by the dinghy docks on our first day in Key West. Let's call him Hank. His lean, bulging biceps, with graphic tattoos, and shaved head cut a mean form, but he always was a friendly guy in the laundry or by the dock. Around me, he seemed to have mellowed in his middle age. He seemed like a good member of the neighborhood watch. He thought Janna, Sophie, and I were squatters and had the marina staff verify we were paying tenants.

The next day I used my $8-per-week bus pass to get the Honda parts. I was the first person on the long bus ride. The second two were a tall, 20-year-old man and his short, square girlfriend. He took an interest in my orange iPhone float case, which I must admit is pretty strange-looking. You could tell he was not all there. He was kind of jumpy. The fourth passenger was in his middle age and wore an "I'd rather be golfing" t-shirt. This man was apparently an acquaintance of the younger man. They started telling stories about the violent crimes that they had committed to land in jail. I pulled the cord. Ding. It was time to get off the bus. The *ex* cons stayed on.

That episode did not deter us from using the excellent Key West busses in the future. Key West had the best public transit of the trip. It could get you to any part of the island, and the city had a webpage that showed you the bus' progress. That webpage accurately predicted a bus' arrival time at your stop.

Early on, one of the ladies on a mooring by herself, told me that someone's outboard had been stolen. The dinghy dock was locked on the first night we arrived, but it never was after that. On the first night, a Sunday, I told the security guard that we came in after the marina office had closed, but we had spoken to the office. They said we could pay the next day. She was OK with that explanation, and I balanced on the railing, which led me to the dock side of the door which was not locked. That allowed us to dinghy back home for the night. The mooring ball facilities were not high security. The security guard coverage was spotty and several showers did not lock. The

Linus Wilson

laundry was always open, and Hank was justifiably nervous about new people not being tenants.

We went to the Conch Republic festival festivities. About thirty years prior, a mayor of Key West declared in jest that Key West was a separate nation, the Conch Republic. The motto on the t-shirts for tourists was "We seceded when others failed." This declaration of independence was in protest to a checkpoint on US Highway 1, which was frustrating locals and tourists alike in the 1980s.

The conch covered truck in Key West is not the only thing that looks silly. Sophie, me, and my big orange phone case in Key West.

For one Conch Republic event, Daly attended the dog-pirate parade, which had eight other pooch participants. I rushed home from our shopping excursion to get Daly. Because I was running late, and it was a calm day, I took a shortcut to the downtown area where the parade was being held. I drove the dinghy under the bridge between Key West and Fleming Key. There was a $5-per-day dinghy dock by the entertainment district. The strong current popped Daly and me out very quickly on this calm sunny day. However, on the way back, in addition to dealing with the boat wakes in the west channel, we were standing still underneath the Fleming Key Bridge. We finally emerged from the current, but it was very close. Janna and Sophie wisely decided to take the bus and meet Daly and me at the mooring field's dinghy dock, which was not affected by the current.

I had wanted to participate in the Duval Street Mile run/walk. However, after a day of walking around in the heat, I wanted rest and air conditioning and watched from the Margaritaville restaurant with a frozen drink. There we saw five very slow men running and another five strolling to finish. Even, with my middle-aged flab, I could have won or placed in that group. In short, not many people paid attention to this festival, which true Conchs, residents of Key West, regarded as just another festival to increase tourism out of season. Janna bought and hoisted a small Conch Republic flag to the spreaders, which stayed up for the entire trip home.

Key West is like a mini New Orleans. Key West's Duval Street is not the equivalent of the puke-soaked and constantly packed Bourbon Street. Instead, it is like a random street in New Orleans' French Quarter. Key West has better weather, but worse food than the Big Easy. It is a wonder that more conferences do not go to Key West. Key West does seem lacking in downtown hotel capacity necessary for bigger conference traffic. Janna did not trust the outboard on the morning of her flight. So she booked one of the cheapest hotel rooms. The place was nice and well done, but it was strip-mall-adjacent for $200 per night in the off season. In a place where trailer parks are not uncommon, one would think that someone would take advantage of the under-utilization of real estate and build expensive hotels.

57. ALONE

I was broken up to see Janna and Sophie leave on Saturday, May 2, 2015. At the time, I believed we had squandered a great weather window to head north by waiting for the flight in Key West. A low pressure area had descended and rising seas were forecast. By Monday, May 4, 2015, the seas between Marco Island, my next port, and Key West were forecast to be 7 to 10 feet. After I dropped them off with the rental, I drove to the Southernmost Point in the continental United States buoy where my Mom, sister, and I posed for a picture when I was ten-years-old, almost thirty years before. I'm actually older that day than my father was when he snapped that photo. I just cried. I was emotional about the temporary nature of childhood, Sophie's and mine. I got to know Sophie more in the three months on the boat than I had ever had when I was shuttling her from pre-school and day care on land. On this trip, Sophie didn't need a sippy cup and could climb a ladder with ease. She is no longer a baby or a toddler. Before I know it, her childhood will be over. I felt like I had come full circle. However, I was sad about facing a trip of 680 nautical miles alone to get home.

I epoxied in the holes that were made by the Maxwell HRC8 windlass. Previously, I had just put some teak over the holes. However, heading offshore, I wanted them more permanently sealed. After all the trouble in the Bahamas, the troubleshooting, and the expensive phone calls, their tech claimed it worked on their shop bench. They planned to ship the same unreliable unit back to me. I complained about the windlass' unreliability and their poor warranty on their Facebook page. The North American CEO intervened and gave me a full refund. On the trip down the GIWW in December and January, I could not use the chain because it was trapped by an old Maxwell 800 windlass. On the way up, I would be free of the windlasses and would use my anchor and chain extensively.

A 35-foot, semi-derelict trawler, which was towing a 22-foot sailboat, which had been dragging its anchor in the previous week's storms and was on the edge of the entrance channel to Garrison Bite.

Slow Boat to the Bahamas

The sailboat had a 40 HP outboard on the back with the cowling off. Its sails were poorly tied down and lacked a cover for the main. To my horror, after dropping off the rental and returning to Contango, the raft of those two boats were on an upwind mooring right next to me. With more bad weather forecasted, I was worried that the trawler would break its terribly tied mooring. Instead of a two strong nylon mooring lines 5/8 inch or thicker, it was using a single 3/8-inch halyard braid under a lot of strain. After several discussions with the marina, which was upset about two boats on one mooring, I was able to have them put on a second, stronger mooring line before the worst of the storms hit.

There was a low over the southern Bimini Islands over 100 miles east of us. NOAA kept on upgrading its chances of becoming a cyclonic storm with each passing day. It would turn into the pre-season named storm Ana. It was May, and I had to worry about hurricanes. It was time to go home.

The weather cleared by Wednesday, May 6. The storm that would be named Ana was moving north and was projected to continue doing so and stay in the Atlantic. I had decided that the channels between Fleming Key and Key West were too tricky and crowded to transit by night. I would leave Key West in the afternoon so that I would have daylight when leaving Key West. I wanted daylight also when I would pass by the last buoy seven miles northwest of Key West before entering the desolate Gulf of Mexico. However, I would leave late enough that I did not arrive in Marco Island before day break.

Daly had a terrible night and was in a lot of pain from his vaccination shots on Tuesday, May 5. However, by the morning and afternoon, he seemed back to his pillow-lounging self. His stiff leg moved well; whereas, before he could not stand. At least my first mate was healthy!

I picked up both mooring lines at 2:30 PM. At least three dozen jet skis zipped by as I motored around Fleming Key. The boat traffic had created four-foot breaking waves around Key West Bite.

Every powerboat skipper was dead set on burning fuel as fast as they could. However, as I turned northwest towards the Gulf of Mexico the traffic disappeared. The strong currents of the outgoing tide boosted my speed around Fleming Key by two knots. Unfortunately, I lost two knots motoring up the Northwest Channel. It appeared that the Gulf of Mexico drains into the Atlantic Ocean because the outgoing current flowed south during my entire transit of that channel.

At 5:13 PM, I passed the last buoy for the Northwest Channel and entered the Gulf of Mexico. I could set a course straight for Marco Island. The winds were 5-to-10 knots, and the waves were only one-to-two feet high. The ship traffic that I expected was the Key West Express ferry that calls at Marco Island. It was supposed to depart at 5 PM from the west side of Key West. I spotted the first of only two boats that I would see prior to sunset. A 50-foot trawler with no one on the helm was on a collision course. I altered course 20 degrees to get out of its way. Hopefully, someone got to the helm before it entered the Northwest channel and rammed into the shallows on its edge. The second boat passed at 6:05 PM. It was the ferry, which was moving about 30 knots. It quickly overtook Daly and I. The motorized catamaran was much bigger and faster than I expected, but I got well out of its way.

I saw nothing after that until 4:30 AM. I took 15-minute naps from 9:30 PM to 4:30 AM. After my last nap, I could see two red lights to starboard when I was 20 miles from Marco Island's Capri Pass Channel. Those lights were probably from shore, but I stayed up after that. It was not until 6 AM that I spotted a white light to port. It was a very bright night when the full moon emerged from the cloud cover.

The RIB lashed on top of the Walker Bay 8 was a real impediment to seeing anything in front of the bow. On watch and in the entrance channel, I had to stand in front of the Bimini on the cockpit seats to get a good view of what was ahead. By 9 AM, I was motoring up the Capri Pass into Marco Island. The entrance channel to Marco Island was tricky with two channels intersecting near the Coconut Island shallows. I stayed close to but south of the green and red mid-channel marker.

I had decided to anchor in Factory Bay, which had a few marinas nearby and a fuel dock. I thought refueling on diesel was a good idea with two more days between me and my next fuel stop of Venice, Florida. Unfortunately, I was confused by its markings initially. Factory Bay was south of the entrance channel. On the west side were green 1, 3, and 5 daymarks. On the east were 2, 4, and 6 red daymarks. In the middle was a charted sandbar awash. I could not understand why the green was to starboard and the red was to port when you turned south, the returning direction. Further, how did you avoid the sandbar if you went between green and red? Then, I realized the channel was on the sides of the bay. If you keep one set of buoys on one side and the shore on the other, you are in deep water. If you go between the red and green day marks you run aground. I'm glad my sleep-deprived brain figured that out prior to having to call Tow Boat US! Several boats were anchored east of the red buoys between those and the shore about where the cruising guide explained where one should anchor. I found enough room to anchor downwind of the boats without swinging too close to red day marks 2 and 4. It was time to nap.

58. MOTHER'S DAY

I got more fuel at the nearby marina which was being torn apart by upgrades. On the way back I said "Hello" to the seventy-year old skipper of an Island Packet 31, the same boat as Contango. He invited me to stay, but I was too depressed by his talk of his recent heart attack. It was clear that he was too old to manage the boat, and was probably just working on the bright work, the teak trim, to ready her for sale. That was too depressing for me to dwell on; so, I did not return after I filled up the diesel tank. Overnight, I had to refill the gas in the generator to keep the air conditioning working. However, when I went out, I was quickly attacked by mosquitoes attracted to the chart plotter next to the generator. Marco Island was too close to the swamp.

Linus Wilson

I'm glad that I did not try anchoring in the Everglades. I would have needed a blood transfusion.

I woke up too late, 7 AM, to make my intended anchorage Useppa Island and did not get off until 8:30 AM. That was OK. There were plenty of anchorages in the Pine Island Sound. The anchor was well dug in and had to be tripped from the mud to be pulled up. Tripping is powering past the anchor so that the chain trails behind the boat. I was thankful to be back in Gulf of Mexico mud.

Ana was upgraded to storm status, three weeks before the official start of hurricane season, and projected to hit North or South Carolina. I motored into 5-to-10 knot north winds with one reef in the main towards the Pine Island sound. I heard a report over VHF channel 16 of a man in a nine-foot Caribe RIB afloat 18 miles south of Cape Sable, which I had passed during the trip to Marco Island. I could only speculate that the man must have made the distress call. Was he forced to leave his bigger boat? Was it a hose leak or isolated squall that swamped his boat? I would never get answers. The broadcasts went on all morning.

The light winds were going to persist for some time. It looked like clear sailing for several days. After tonight, I planned to anchor at Venice and visit my parents for Mother's Day and do laundry. I'm such a good son!

After that, two day-hops would put me in Clearwater ready to cross to Carrabelle. I had toyed with the idea of long hops along the Big Bend of Florida. With the longer days these seemed possible. The problem was three days of 70-mile hops seemed hard to pull off. Adverse currents could put me into these ports after dark. My Dad had volunteered to crew from Clearwater to Carrabelle, but, with his schedule, it was not guaranteed that he would. I was also considering soloing the Carrabelle passage of 24-to-30 hours. There was almost no traffic on the way up, and I could probably do a lot of 15-minute naps. I resisted advertising for crew. I felt Dean with all his faults was a pretty good crew member. Anyone else that I got would likely be worse. Another problem with taking on crew is that you have to wait around for them and accommodate their travel schedules. I felt that Janna and I had missed an opportunity to move the boat north in good weather, while waiting for her plane in Key West. I did not want to repeat that mistake by taking on an unrelated crew member.

Janna offered to fly out to meet me for Memorial Day weekend, but having done some quick trip planning I told her, "I plan to be back at home before Memorial Day." The weather was great for moving up the coast. I thought there was an excellent chance that I would be in New Orleans in two weeks. Besides, I wanted nothing to do with boat trips and non-refundable plane tickets. My second worst time in the Bahamas, after my passport problems, was waiting for Janna to arrive in Nassau.

I texted my Dad to take off Wednesday, Thursday, and Friday of the next week. He said he needed several days advance notice, and the weather looked perfect to leave on Wednesday morning. He would probably have to stay on board to Panama City to rent a car one-way for the trip back. Thus, we could either sail straight for Panama City or use the GIWW once entering the East Pass near Carrabelle.

The winds turned from north to west and picked up to 10-to-15 knots at 2PM. I unfurled the genoa fully with the third reef and briefly turned off the motor. As I rounded the entrance channel to mile 0 of the Gulf Intracoastal Waterway (GIWW) I furled it up and motored. I anchored in ten feet of water between the two entrance channels into St. James City on Pine Island. I was banking on the winds to shift to the north, which it did, and this spot gave good north protection. Supposedly, there was a waterfront restaurant, but all I could see were houses. I put out 70-feet of chain. I ran the generator and air conditioning most of the night.

After pulling up anchor at 7:15 AM, I motored in a near calm until 9:45 AM. Just then a large trawler passed and a screeching noise went off. At first, I thought it came from the trawler, then I realized it was inside the boat. It was not the autopilot or an alarm clock. Ugh! It was the engine. Both the charging and overheating lights were on. I tried to turn off the engine by turning the key. The engine alarms still screamed, and it would not shut down. Next, I pulled the kill switch, but the engine still hummed. Finally, I realized I was in gear, and pulling the kill switch worked the second time.

I suspected the alternator belt right away. I had been tightening the belts until they were on their widest setting instead of replacing them. I turned west out of the channel in deep water while I had steerage and dropped the anchor. It was the alternator belt. I had a spare. The new belt was tight and hard to get on. Its tightness meant I could not use my small turnbuckle to adjust it. Instead, I had to use the oversized straight screw driver to move the alternator on its arm so it was sufficiently taut. I was careful to not lever near the soft aluminum of the alternator. I levered only against steel bolts.

By 10:50 AM, I was underway again. However, the delay meant that I had a good chance of entering Venice inlet after dark. I could not stay in the Intracoastal Waterway. The number of boats had been increasing exponentially on this sunny Saturday with light winds. Parades of trawlers, sailboats, and legions of small, fast skiffs were marching down the ICW. I had to get out. The main channel to the sea, the Boca Grande Channel, had about 50 fishing boats no longer than 20-feet clogging it. If I followed the Boca Grande Channel, it would take me three miles to the southwest which was in the wrong direction. I wanted to head north. The chart indicated that, if I hugged the coast of Gasparilla Island, I would have at least seven-foot depths. I figured the incoming tide which opposed me cutting the channel may also help unstick me if I ran aground. However, the chart warned in note E, "Hydrography and Shorelines are Constantly Changing." In other words, the chart depths are not worth the paper they are printed on. I was willing to take the chance. I never saw depths less than eight feet.

While the GIWW was packed, hardly any boats ventured into the Gulf of Mexico, and I had easy sailing with 10-to-15 knot west winds. I busied myself converting a portable bilge pump back to an electric dipstick oil pump.

The Venice Inlet had three-foot waves when the west wind opposed the outgoing tide. I watched a sailboat and trawler pass through ahead of me, and I passed through without difficulty. I had scouted an anchorage by the yacht club and a public boat ramp. Several small sailboats were anchored or moored there, but the chart only showed four-foot depths. However, the boat ramp had a long dock to land the dinghy. I just was not allowed to tie up my boat overnight.

My depth sounder showed 4.5 feet where I anchored. The tidal stage was +1.6. My Garmin depth sounder shows depths 0.8 feet lower than they are. That means at low water the actual depth was 4.5 + 0.8 − 1.6 = 3.7 feet. Overnight the depth sounder showed 3.2 feet and the boat seemed to not move. My Dad met Daly, my laundry, and me at the boat launch. My parents were busy with home repair projects that weekend as is their custom. I got diesel, gas, and groceries the next day on Sunday, Mother's Day.

Selling your wife's belongings on Mother's Day is not usually the actions of a good husband. Nevertheless, with Janna's permission, I sold the green kayak and its paddle for $110. I had advertised it for a couple of days on Craigslist and had buyers lined up in Venice. I wanted to have more room on deck so that I could put the Walker Bay 8 amidships instead of on the bow. When my Dad and I would cross the Gulf of Mexico to the panhandle, I wanted to be able to lash down the RIB on the bow. The view was too restricted when both the RIB and Walker Bay 8 were stacked on top of each other.

I was careful to get out early before the tide started falling on Monday. When the anchor was up at 7:50 AM with the help of the engine chasing the chain, the tidal stage was +1.1 feet. The depth sounder showed 4.5 feet. The water quality was so poor that I could not see the anchor or chain in four-to-five foot depths.

The inlet was calm at 15 minutes to high tide. On the motor up the Gulf of Mexico with southeast winds of less than five knots, I marked the chain lengths at five and ten fathoms (30 and 60) feet with tape. Without the windlass to jam, I could use tape instead of paint. All the paint applied at the beginning of the Exumas cruise had flaked off. The boat got a boost from the two-foot south swell. In the afternoon, there was enough wind to sail with 1st reefed main and 105 percent genoa when it exceeded 10 knots, but then the wind fell to under five knots. Thus, I had to furl in the flapping genoa.

When I headed into Boca Chiega Bay by St. Petersburg, I had no trouble entering the North Channel. I saw several sailboats anchored in the bite between the Pinellas Bayway and Isla del Sol but the 0.7 foot chart depth on the Garmin and no guidance on the anchorages back depths gave me pause despite the seven masts bobbing around in the mini bay. My Navionics chart gave it an anchor symbol, but I was not feeling adventurous after the shallow anchorage in Venice. Besides, I had many good options a little farther north.

Anchoring near the marinas by Pass-A-Grille Beach seemed too tight. Instead, I settled on a place just under the 65-foot vertical clearance fixed bridge in Big McPherson Bayou. There a large mini bay opens up over 500 feet across where three canals meet. The first time that I dropped, I was too close to the houses on the east side. I moved closer to the mangroves by the busy road on the east side and dropped 70 feet of chain in 12-foot depths. The air conditioner got the cabin temperature down from 88-to-73 degrees as I had the anchorage to myself.

59. AGROUND, WAKES, SQUALLS, AND A DRAGGING ANCHOR: ALL IN A DAY AT CLEARWATER BEACH

I took a lot of time securing the anchor when I pulled it up. I secured the pawl, secured the shackle on the loop end of the safety line to the anchor, and tied off the safety line on the bow cleat. I should have moved quicker and just secured the pawl.

By the time I got to the wheel, the Garmin showed that the depths had fallen from 12 to 7 feet as the 5-knot winds blew us towards the mangroves. I throttled up to try to turn into the wind, but I had run aground. The Garmin showed 4.4 feet, but the old Datamarine depth sounder, which was almost impossible to read from the wheel, showed 3.0 feet. Evidently, part of the boat was partially aground. Backing up did not work, regardless of how I turned the wheel. I found some movement in slow forward and counterintuitively turned toward the mangroves and finally onto my old track. I was out! I was careful to follow my old track out since I feared a submerged pile charted nearby that I had missed on my way in. So I hugged the modest houses with private docks by the entrance canal.

Neither the Navionics nor the Garmin charts indicated that I should have grounded. One of the channels did have four foot depths, according to Navionics. Perhaps I had turned into that channel when I got stuck.

When back in the Gulf of Mexico, I only put up the main with the 1st reef despite the 5-to-10 knots and two-foot waves from the southeast pushing me north. I busied myself putting together a watch schedule for tomorrow and Thursday. I also cleaned out the storage from the quarter berth and made a bed for my Dad. Once I anchored, I had to get diesel and gas and change the oil before my Dad arrived. Once he arrived, I needed to hoist the outboard and RIB onboard. In short, I had a lot to do if we were going to cross the Gulf of Mexico the next day.

When I came into Clearwater, I tried to take the most direct channel to the anchorage near the only fuel dock at Clearwater Beach Marina where Dean and I had stayed on trip down. Unfortunately, I failed to notice that the controlling depth for this more direct channel was 4.5 feet. It was clear by looking at it that there was a lot of shoaling. I turned between the 1 and 2 day marks and found that the Garmin depths went down from 4.5 feet to 3.2 feet. Miraculously, I did not run aground as I tried to back out and turn around in the channel. Slowly turning, I eventually got out of that channel and took the long way around with the deeper water. I was sure that I transited that channel with Dean. How had I avoided running aground? Perhaps there was more shoaling since New Years'.

I found that the anchorage was pretty crowded and a boat anchored just before I did. I tried dropping behind a 24-foot sailboat that seemed largely abandoned. The anchor did not dig in, and I was dragging backward into the channel at one knot. I had to run quickly to the helm just to put the boat in gear to avoid hitting the perpetually ignored "NO WAKE" buoy. I picked up the 15-feet of dragging chain when I had some room. Since this boat lacked an owner, I suspected there would be no squawking if I dropped upwind of it. There was at least 120-feet in front of it. I dropped 55-feet in a six-foot chart depth at tidal stage +1. In other words, I had plenty of scope.

I got the dinghy ready and changed the oil. My problems with the pump previously almost surely were due to the slipshod way I put the dipstick hose in. When I carefully marked the length of the dipstick and lowered the hose a couple of inches lower, it sucked out the oil in no time. I had been relying on Dean and Janna to pump with the poorly sealed vacuum pump and hand pumps, but now I could solo the job with the electric pump. It took one person to pump and one to hold the dipstick in the right place. Fortunately, now I could hold the dipstick in the right place while the electrical pump took care of the rest. I put 12 gallons of diesel from jerry jugs into the tank, filling it.

The constant wakes from the tourist boats in this "NO WAKE" zone and a wind shifts seemed to set off the anchor drag alarm. I had set it at 120 feet after letting out the chain or almost 90 feet from its center of turn. Thus, wind shifts could set it off if I set it at less than 180 feet. I reset it at 150 feet.

I dinghied ashore and filled up the diesel and gas jugs again and tried unsuccessfully to find an oil dump at the marina. It was getting so late that I expected my Dad to arrive at the marina at any time, and I held off dinghying out. I got some last minute provisions from Walgreens across the street. Then, I got a quick dinner at the Bait

Slow Boat to the Bahamas

House, which had a bar and restaurant in addition to bait. It was steps from the fuel dock.

My Dad arrived at around 6:30 PM as the eastern sky was turning black with an approaching squall. This was the worst sky I had seen all trip. Part of me thought perhaps we should wait, but the part that won out rushed us to the boat. That was the right move. As the cold gust came through we arrived at the boarding ladder. Contango was slowly dragging onto the 24-foot sailboat. It was only 40-feet away. The anchor alarm was going crazy. I had Dad come up and handed up all the diesel, gas, luggage, and other gear to him. I was just about to bring the outboard up, but we were ten feet from the 24-foot boat by this point.

I climbed aboard. I fast counted to 30 to let the glow plugs do their work and started the engines. Then I started motoring away with 55-feet of anchor and chain down. I promised myself that I would never drag a dinghy with the outboard on it, but I was afraid of worse things than damaging the new outboard at this point.

"Take the wheel, try to steer into the wind and stay away from the land, the sailboat, and the channel, while I pull up the chain," I said to Dad as I rushed to the bow. However, since he had been a crew member for one minute, he made a hash of this, and the wind just started blowing us back to the 24-foot sailboat. I had to run back, give the engine some gas to make the turn into the wind, and started zig zagging away from that boat, while avoiding the shallows and the nearby channel. I put on the autopilot in slow gear, ran up, hauled, ran back, and steered away from the hazard. Repeating this process a few times, I was able to get the chain up. I then motored to my backup anchorage by downtown Clearwater to the east, with the anchor still dangling and the outboard on the dinghy.

The dinghy did not flip. The downtown anchorage south of the municipal marina provided protection from the squalls coming in from the east. Moreover, it was large and deserted with lots of room to drag. I got soaked, but I put out 70-feet of chain at 7 PM, just a little south of the anchor symbol on the Navionics chart because a crab pot marked that spot. Despite the rain and cold front, I ran the air conditioner and generator because the cabin was stuffy. The outboard and dinghy were brought on deck, and the boat did not drag again that night.

60. ADRIFT WITH AN EMPTY WATER TANK

I awoke with Dad at 5:45 AM, and we were off by 6:45 AM. Everything was wet from the night's showers. There were southeast winds of five knots or less. Because winds and seas were going to build late on the second day. The 40-hour direct trip to Panama City seemed like a bad idea. Plus, it would test our endurance. Instead, we would go for the East Pass just south of Carrabelle (a 24-to-30-hour trip) and spend the night in Apalachicola, given we could arrive there before daylight. Then, we would use the GIWW canals to arrive in Panama City where Dad could rent a car to go back home.

About two hours out, I noticed that the water pressure was low. I turned off the pressure pump and saw that the fresh water hose had popped off at a junction in the engine compartment. We had lost our 70 gallon main tank of fresh water. Perhaps I could not hear the pump running over the generator. Janna is always the one who hears the water pressure pump running first. It was too bad I did not hear it running earlier.

I told Dad about it, but it did not seem like a good idea to turn around. We would lose the whole day refilling the water. Two hours back, two-to-three hours to fill, and two hours to get back where we were. That could have us entering the East Pass at dark. We had several water bottles in the fridge for drinking, the 14-gallon auxiliary tank, and three gallons in the jerry jug. I texted Janna about our misfortune and plans to head on before cell phone service disappeared just before 9 AM.

I needed to shut down the engine to reattach the hose and switch the water tanks. Dad was skeptical about our water filter, and he was planning on using bottled water exclusively for drinking anyways. After lunch with the tank empty, I thought this would be a great opportunity to clear aluminum chloride crystals from the bottom of the 70-gallon tank. I took off the hose and poked my pencil in the junction, and, to my amazement, water streamed out. We had plenty of water in the 70-gallon tank. I had turned off the fresh water pump in time!

Water will only go into the bilge from the parted hose at the junction in the engine compartment if the pump is on. It can't gravity drain from that spot. I shut down the engine to make the repair. I pushed the hose into the barb and tightened the clamp down.

Since I did not know how much was in the 70-gallon tank, I turned the y-valve in the engine compartment that switches the tank from the main 70-gallon tank to 14-gallon bladder auxiliary tank. The gentle swell when moving became a big side-to-side roll with the engine off. I warmed the glow plugs and pressed the start switch. It did not start. I pressed the start switch again. It did not start. I found the sweet spot, and it rumbled back to life. We were headed northwest again.

A lethargy in the late afternoon overtook Dad and me, and we were napping in our two-hour daytime off watch periods. The water pressure was poor, and I fiddled with the tank under the v-berth to find a kink that may have been blocking that water bladder. I had to remove a kink in the freshwater line for this tank in the Bahamas. I found no blockage, but the water pressure was better after my investigations.

After dinner I noticed that batteries one and two were not being charged by the alternator. There was no engine warning, but their charge was closer to 12V than the 13V-plus it should be with the engine running. I looked in the hatch and the wire from the alternator to the starter had fallen out of its crimp fitting and shrink wrap cover.

I must have had popped it out when I reattached the hose. I shut down the engine and pushed it back in its plastic shrink wrap and ostensibly its crimp fitting. However, the engine was not charging when I restarted the engine.

I shut down the engine again. I took off the air filter to have easier access. Next, I unscrewed the bolt holding the crimp fitting. Then, I took off the rubber shrink wrap insulation. I put the wire back in the connector and redid the crimp. I started to bolt down that and all the other connections. However, the engine started firing up even before I could put on the air filter. I had not pressed the start button. I pulled the kill switch all the way out. All this did was have the engine try to start and die quickly instead of starting up and staying running.

I know that one way to prime the fuel line is to start but not turn over the engine. This runs the electric fuel pump. However, if you do these quick starts with the water intake seacock open, water can be sucked into the engine, and it won't work again. I quickly jumped into the cabin and closed the seawater pump seacock while the engine kept firing. "Pretty soon we'll drain the batteries completely," I said in desperation and out of answers.

"You could disconnect the batteries," my Dad offered. That was it! I turned the battery switch to zero, and the engine stopped trying to start. I had a spare starter on the boat that I ordered after I had heard that the starter often fails and ends cruises, but I did not think I had a starter issue. What I had done differently was to take off the shrink wrap insulation.

I got out some electrical tape and after removing the bolt to get to the crimp fitting for the alternator wire, I wrapped the electrical tape around this metal fitting. I reattached all the connections and reattached the air filter for the engine. Then, I turned on both batteries one and two to the on position. The engine did not start. That was a great sign! Next, I opened the seawater pump seacock. I was worried about running the engine on a low tank because this makes the filters more prone to sediment clogs from the bottom of the tank. Thus, we put in nine gallons of diesel into the tank before attempting to restart the engine. When I warmed the glow plugs and pressed the starter, the diesel engine fired into life. The batteries showed 13V+. Thus, the alternator also seemed to be working.

I saw a lightning flash in a cloud off to the east (starboard) at 8:30 PM. I had already reefed down the main from the first reef to the second reef. I went down to the third reef. The variable winds earlier in the day made the genoa flap too much, and I kept it furled up overnight.

Most of our discussion about being on watch had centered on identifying lights at night. I had tried to explain how we wanted to adjust the autopilot so the GPS heading equaled the bearing to our next waypoint at the East Pass. However, Dad was always confused by the concept of the autopilot being the course we steer and the GPS being the course we were actually going. This was made harder by the fact that the GPS degree course fluctuated. Thus, the helm had to decide what was the average GPS course. Then, that person needed to keep adjusting the autopilot so that the average GPS course equaled our GPS bearing of about 324 degrees, or northwest.

Every time I would come on watch, I would see that my Dad had not made any adjustments to the autopilot. As a result, we were being pushed east of our most direct course for most of his watches. Around midnight he spotted the port side of two boats (red lights). He woke me up, and we saw one passing us port to port heading south. The other passed us well ahead of our bow heading west. We never altered course.

At 10:30 AM on Thursday, May 14, 2015, we were parallel with the outer channel marker red number 2 for the East Pass. The southeast wind was in the same direction as the incoming tide, and we had only two-foot waves and got a boost from the current. A shrimper with his wings out was taking up most of the channel near marker number 7 in the East Pass channel. Seeing deep water no less than 11 feet deep, I steered Contango out of the channel angling to the GIWW heading west.

Linus Wilson

The Intracoastal Waterway was pretty deserted. We saw a trawler, a sport fishing boat, and small oyster or fishing boats. The 90-degree heat was pretty oppressive with little wind. Dad let me know that he wanted to go into a marina, but I was non-committal. I had not paid for a marina's transient slip since Atlantis on March 17, almost two months earlier, and I was not eager to give up my streak just yet. Before that our last marina slip was Emerald Bay on Great Exuma on February 24. He said he wanted a shore-side shower. Pride, dislike for marinas, fear of docking, and cheapness made me hesitant to visit another. Still, I looked for a marina with laundry and fuel in Apalachicola. Eventually, I would have to stop at a marina for laundry, and refilling the water tanks would also be easier in a slip. I put out and flaked the stern and bow lines before entering the channel. I picked out the marinas with laundry and waited to see what the anchorage looked like.

I noted that Apalachicola had a boat launch and a dinghy dock so anchoring would include more shore access than just from fuel docks. However, a sailboat with a dinghy had already filled the one boat anchorage by 2 PM. I thought the anchorage was only big enough for one. So I called my first choice marina. Scipio Creek Marina had a free spot on their sea wall next to another sailboat. They verified that they had laundry machines, gas, and diesel. I misread the chart and went north of the buoy "A" painted red and green when I should have gone south of it. Luckily, we never hit bottom.

It was slack water so current was not an issue, and the docking was easy. We backed into the end of the fuel dock, and I tied off the port stern line on a cleat. The south east wind was gently blowing us on the dock to the west. With the boat in neutral, I untied the port stern line from the dock cleat and walked the boat back away from the fuel pumps towards the other sailboat. Dad took his shower. I plugged in and got an "HPF" error from the air conditioner. I found lots of seaweed in the strainer and the intake line leading to the strainer. After removing the seaweed and sealing up the hose, the air conditioner worked well. I filled the jerry cans with 12 gallons of diesel before they closed at 4:30 PM, and filled the 70-gallon water tank to overflowing. I did my laundry, got a shower in the ant-filled men's room, and we went out to eat in the quaint town. Daly and Dad got some well-deserved shore time.

61. SWAMPS AND BIG WAVES

In the morning, the wind had picked up to 10-to-15 knots from the south. This posed a problem since Contango had its bow facing north. I thought better of just throwing off the lines and attempting to turn around against the wind in this narrow creek. I decided to use a long line on the starboard bow to flip Contango around as Dad and I had done when I had visited the marina in Venice on my way down in January. I let Dad sit at the helm with the engine in neutral. I untied the working port stern line and walked it forward. Contango's stayed close to the wall and its bowsprit was sticking out beyond the fuel dock in front of our berth and into the boat basin.

Then, the hard part began. I was not letting out enough slack on the stern line to flip the bow with the starboard bow line. I did not want to let the stern leave the dock. However, I needed to give the stern line enough slack to do that. After 20 minutes of working against myself, I gave the stern line a lot of slack and the bow came around. With the bow facing south, I had Dad push the bow off the dock with the boat hook while I was at the helm. It just started raining as we motored south down the creek.

It was not clear to me if the dock in the middle of the town was a public dock like what exists in Mandeville and Madisonville Louisiana, which are towns on Lake Pontchartrain. There was a fishing boat tied up there at 7:20 AM as if it had stayed the night. The anchorage had three boats, and the two new ones were only 10 feet apart as if they had dragged in the night. It was a good call to get the marina berth.

I put up some sail, the second reef to get an extra push from the south wind as we motored through the narrow canals of the

Intracoastal Waterway. This stretch was very swampy with many cypress trees. We only saw a 27-foot sailboat right before we entered Lake Wimico.

This was no place to transit at night, and I was glad for the daytime and good visibility. A floating log awaited us mid-channel in Lake Wimico, but I easily steered around it. In Searcy Creek, the chart plotter put us 120 feet into the shore when we were mid-channel. I'm glad I was not steering by chart plotter.

I still don't have a good answer for why I abandoned the GIWW and turned towards Port St. Joe. The best I can say is that I remembered my good sail from Panama City to Port St. Joe in December. During that sail, the winds were from the north, and I had experienced little swell. Further, I had done so much sailing outside the GIWW along Florida's west coast with little wave problems that I had grown complacent. However, the winds typically had an east component on my sail up the coast over the last few days and land to my east prevented waves from building.

I had decided against sailing directly into Panama City to avoid the forecast for 3-to-5 foot swell that day. That south swell had hundreds mile of fetch from the south. Once we left the protection of the St. Joseph Peninsula, we got walloped.

We were sailing almost dead downwind near hull speed at six knots. To avoid accidental gybes as we bounced in the waves, I sailed 30 degrees off the wind. I am also puzzled why I did not put up a preventer and sail closer to the wind, but I never did. I did keep the main pretty sheeted in and warned Dad to stay below the boom, which was easy since we sat under the Bimini, which was always under the boom. My Dad was concerned about the conditions. However, after everything was set, and it was clear that we had a few more hours to contend with these waves that were as big as five feet, I took a short nap on the low side of the settees. The v-berth was a wreck by this time. I could not write or do much else without getting sea sick. We both opted to not put on the Scopalamine patch because the conditions were not quite bad enough to have us getting seasick. In addition, we did not want the dry throat side effect or to waste an expensive patch. Closing my eyes was the best way to avoid motion sickness save putting on another patch. This had the effect of putting my Dad at ease that the conditions were really not that bad just a little uncomfortable. He was clipped in with his life jacket on.

As we approached the entrance channel to Panama City, the waves got smaller, but stood up more because of the outgoing tide opposing the wind. Just as we entered the breakwater, we got hit by a six-foot wave on the beam that rolled us 25 degrees side-to-side. Where that came from I did not know. I had cut most of the entrance channel to avoid being beam-on to the swell, but this one hit us right there.

62. SLOWER THAN A SENIOR CITIZEN IN A ROW BOAT

The entrance to the Grand Lagoon where I intended to anchor opened up on the west side of the entrance channel to Panama City and St. Andrew Bay. It was marked by a single red buoy that had us hug the sandy southern shore. I should have anchored in the southeast side by the state park, but I saw the piers and wrongly assumed they would be busy. They were not. Instead, I anchored on the northeast side. We were just east of buoy number 4. There, a constant stream of motor boats and tourist barges would roll us. In the morning, sport fishing boats lined up for a tournament starting around 8 AM.

We were set just before 5 PM, but it was too late to get Dad to his rental car that night. His reservation for the one-way rental was for the next day Saturday, May 16, at 9 AM. We dinghied the mile to the 24-hour fuel dock in the morning. I got diesel, gas, and water as Dad waited for the rental car place to open, and we said our goodbyes. He had been a big help and a good sport in good times and bad. I would miss him.

Linus Wilson

The southeast wind at 15 knots, made it hard to chase the chain relative to the near calms that I had been experiencing. I had to run to the stern to motor forward. I stopped feeding the chain into the hawse pipe because this took too long. Instead, I would engage the pawl as the wind started blowing the boat back. Then, I could feed the chain on deck at my leisure into the hawse pipe before I went back to the bow to motor into the wind. With just under 30 feet chain to pull up, I went to shut off the anchor alarm. Before I could, it went off. Then, I ran to the bow, and I found all the chain slack. I hauled it up on deck quickly and engaged the pawl. After that, I ran back and started motoring away.

With more strong south winds and big seas forecast, sailing outside the Intracoastal Waterway in a stretch with no barrier islands seemed stupid. This decision was confirmed when I looked south to the exit channel observed the waves, and observed all the boats turning around after motoring out to the Gulf of Mexico. After I turned west along the GIWW and the West Bay portion of St. Andrews Bay, I saw barely any boat traffic. I don't think it was just the stiff winds on this Saturday that made the GIWW so deserted. The Florida panhandle just has a lot less traffic than the East and West coasts of Florida. For me, that meant the Intracoastal Waterway along the panhandle was a nicer place to cruise.

In the narrow ditch section between St. Andrews Bay and Choctawhatchee Bay, I came across a fit, shirtless sixty-year-old man in a long rowing scull. For several miles, I had just been within sight of him and not gaining on him. At one point, he stopped. I thought he was meeting his buddy who was wading out. However, I realized that they did not know each other. The chubby wader was just fishing. The senior citizen was waiting for my slow boat. He wanted a race. Contango had some token sail and engines at full throttle. He was pulling at the oars. We were unfairly and unevenly matched. He beat me handily over the next half hour. I only overtook him when I entered the wide waters of Choctawhatchee Bay, and he turned around.

On the trip up, the question of where to stop in Choctawhatchee Bay had me tying up at a too shallow marina on the north side. Now, I wanted to sail the big muddy bay to Destin. However, I knew that I did not have enough daylight for that. Anchoring near the entrance to the southeast seemed like a good option, but I wanted more miles under my keel. I wanted to leave Florida as quickly as possible.

The shallow waters of this much smaller version of Lake Pontchartrain extend out too far to merely anchor on the south side of the Bay. What seemed like good anchorages were littered with partially submerged piles, which were not charted except to have a warning for the entire subsection of the Bay. For example, Hogtown Bayou would have provided good southeast protection as long as I did not sink the boat running into an uncharted awash piling! I was not really willing to play that game of Russian roulette.

Instead, I put up a lot of sail and drove the boat hard towards St. Joe's Bayou further west, which seemed a great anchorage both on the chart and in the cruising guide. With 8-to-12 foot depths in the middle I could leave the GIWW buoys far away and focus on sailing as long as I aimed for the upper spans of the two bridges that ran north and south. I fixed myself a spaghetti dinner to calm my nerves and stop worrying about running the boat on a beam reach at hull speed. Very few boats took advantage of these ideal sailing conditions. Moreover, I did not want to eat late and wake up late the next day.

I came upon the St. Joe Bayou entrance channel just as the sun disappeared from view. However, there was still plenty of light. The entrance channel proved to be simple and most of the water was much deeper than the charted six-foot channel depths. Most of the water in the channel was ten feet, but I took a sounding of seven feet when my boat strayed a little west of the channel. Only two boats were anchored in the Bayou on the northwest side, the least-protected side of an anchorage that could easily hold ten boats. I dropped the hook on the southeast side in ten feet of water and let out 65-feet of chain. I was over 250-feet from the nearest hazard. The Louisiana State

University (LSU) flag flapped at the dock of one of the large houses. I thought that was a good sign that I was getting close to home.

My 150-foot drag alarm went off at 7:30 AM. There were no hazards. So I expanded it from 150 feet to 180 feet. Filling up the diesel tank gave me a later start, and I was off just before 9 AM. The boat launch behind me would make a great dinghy dock, but I could not see any businesses nearby. Baby dolphins breached in the anchorage. I admired the big pines that had kept the 15-knot winds under 5-knots, and there were only wavelets in Joe's Bayou all night. I had an easy time picking up anchor when I was ready to leave this lovely spot.

63. DISTRESS CALL IN PENSACOLA BEACH

I left the muddy waters of Choctawhatchee Bay behind and entered the sand dunes of the Santa Rosa Sound. I decided against braving the three-to-four foot waves outside the Intracoastal Waterway. Besides the tricky and shallow sea entrance to Destin, I also would be pressed to make the Pensacola or Orange Beach, Alabama entrance channels before dark. I remembered that the Santa Rosa Sound was largely deserted. Thus, I was not pressed to avoid the traffic. I stayed in the Intracoastal Waterway and pressed on to Ft. Walton Beach.

The Brooks Fixed Bridge at Ft. Walton Beach had a 48-foot vertical clearance, and I was coming across at high tide. With the three foot VHF antennae Contango's bridge clearance was 46.5 feet. A two-foot wave could snap our antennae. Since Janna and I had to replace this prior to my departing New Orleans in December, I did not want to snap it. I waited as three powerboats rushed the upper span at full speed from the east with a big wake. Then, they each idled at trolling motor speeds as they eyed the sailboat that they would have slammed to the side of the bridge with their wake. I am sure they would have never slowed down if I had not slowed down and hovered near the east entrance to the upper span. After the parade ended, I went through.

The VHF antennae wiggled, but it did not break off, and the weather channel seemed to work fine.

There were many kayakers exploring the tiny islands and sandbars in the Narrows section. There was a 24-foot powerboat with its anchor embedded on the beach of the military base on the south side of the Santa Rosa sound. I had thrown out my back trying to pull up an anchor next to that beach before Christmas to avoid such a grounding there. However, this powerboat skipper seemed to have beached his or her craft voluntarily.

The other short bridge, the Navarre Bridge loomed. As I passed under its 50-foot vertical clearance, an alarm went off. I checked the engine. It seemed fine. I hoped it was an alarm clock. Oh no! It was coming from the VHF. "Had I damaged the antennae and this alarm was warning me?" I thought. No, actually, I found that someone had hit their VHF distress button. That broadcasted their unique MMSI number to all other VHF radios in the vicinity. Because their VHF was synched with their GPS, I was getting their coordinates. (I had never done that GPS sync with our VHF.) Eventually, I would get three distress alarms on both the cockpit VHF and the cabin VHF, which are hooked up to eight foot and 46.5 foot VHF antennas, respectively.

I spent the next two hours reporting the distress call to the Coast Guard and trying to disable these alarms. With the alarm going off, it was impossible to speak to the Coast Guard over the VHF. Instead, I called 911 and had them relay me to the Coast Guard, which took the coordinates, MMSI, my antennae heights, the time I heard it, and my location. I would see a small Coast Guard boat speeding by about 30 minutes after the first distress signal. It was considerably harder to both find and interpret the VHF manuals in the boat and online and to silence the alarms.

The distress VHF's coordinates put it at or next to the Pensacola Beach Yacht Club. That makes me think it was an accidental or prank call. Further, since only a distress button was pushed, but no voice call was made I doubt anyone needed rescuing. Instead, the boat was probably safely tied up to the dock. All these alarms distracted me from sailing, and I motored with little sail up in the Santa Rosa Sound, squandering a great breeze.

I got preoccupied with the idea of stopping to fill up the jerry cans by anchoring close to a fuel dock. I called several marinas. There was one open in Little Sabine Bay in Pensacola Beach. On the chart, this place looked like a good place to anchor and dinghy out to the fuel dock. So I entered. What I found was mayhem. There were 40 inexperienced paddle boarders flopping around in the deep channel as I and other more maneuverable craft slowly motored by. Little Sabine Bay would have made a great anchorage, but it was littered with no anchoring signs outside the channel that ran along its sides. Unfortunately, not one of the pre-teens, teens, and adults swimming next to or standing precariously on their boards though that they should move to the no motorized vehicle zone to avoid the multi-ton vehicles travelling between the yacht club, marina, and fuel dock. I turned right to avoid the biggest scrum of kids floating next to their paddle boards. Unfortunately, at 1.9 knots, I lose control very fast, and a 40-year-old woman in a paddle board kept paddling further into the middle of the channel. This was pinning me between her and the shore. Finally, I had yell, "Don't go that way."

She jumped off her board and swam it back away from the shore towards the no motorized vehicle zone. "Thank you," I said. I was happy to not have to choose between hitting a docked boat or her.

"This board is really hard to steer," she said from the water.

"Welcome to the world of boating!" I thought but did not say.

With all the good anchorages saved for ungrateful paddle board skippers, I found no place to drop the hook. I believe that the "NO MOTORIZED VEHICLES" signs in Little Sabine Bay were just a back door anchoring restriction. The anchorage for one boat near the yacht club had three big boats anchored on top of each other and within swinging distances of the slips. I did not have my lines out and the fuel dock was full. So docking there with Contango seemed a bad move. I was frustrated with the whole time consuming enterprise. So I left. I could wait until my next marina stop in Mississippi to refuel. I would run out of clean laundry long before I would run out of diesel. I probably had enough diesel to motor the whole way to New Orleans.

That detour ensured that I would spend one more night in Florida. An outgoing tide sped me along until I crossed the entrance to Pensacola Bay. However, as I entered the Big Lagoon's sandy entrance channel, Contango's speed dipped below four knots. With the south wind, all of Perdido Key, which formed the south side of the Big Lagoon area, was a great anchorage. In the fading light, I dropped the hook well south of the channel between buoys 13 and 15 just before Perdido Key widens. I put out 75-feet of chain in 12-feet of water. A lot of sailboats favored the southeast side of Big Lagoon, but I saw no reason to snuggle and moved four miles to the west.

64. GOODBYE FLORIDA

Some motoring was required to bring up the chain and trip the anchor. If I had wanted to refuel, I could have anchored by buoys 29 and 31 in the seven-foot depths. Unfortunately, the fuel dock there had limited opening hours, and I would get a late start (after 9 AM) if I had waited for it to open. That anchorage would have given me good north and west protection with the pine trees and some south protection. More importantly, it is within dinghy distance of the Oyster Bar to the south and its fuel dock and the public boat ramp if you want to tie up and walk to Publix on the north side. However, this stretch can get a lot of wakes on a busy day.

I decided to stay in the canals where Contango almost foundered when its propeller got wrapped in December. It made no sense to brave the three-foot waves and lee shore of the Gulf Shores, Alabama coastline by entering the Gulf of Mexico at Perdido Pass. That route would also put me in the ship canal of Mobile for a long time too. I could have a good flat water sail once I exited the GIWW canal into Bon Secure Bay. I passed by the spot where I had tied up in distress in January. This day in May, barges were moored to that shore.

In Bon Secure Bay, I had a nice beam reach and put out most of the sail on the genoa and the main to get the most out of the eight-knot southeast breeze. I left the channel to let two eastbound tug-and-barges pass under the Dauphin Island Bridge ahead of me. The first one, instead of following the channel south, went northeast right in front of me. This confused me. I did not know if they were making a wide turn. I wanted to know if I should turn north or south to avoid them. I just wanted to get out of the way.

"This is the sailing vessel Contango hailing the eastbound tug that just passed under the Dauphin Island Bridge. Over," I said on channel 16.

"Are you the sailboat," the tug responded.

"Yes, I'm the sailboat pointed right at you. Are you going to turn? Over," I said.

"No sir, I've already made my turn. I'm headed 55 degrees. You should pass right behind me."

That is what I did, passing to the south of the tug. "Thank you. Contango, out."

I was toying with the idea of the Bayou Aloe anchorage at Dauphin Island since it had good south protection. This anchorage was mentioned in both Clairborne Young's dated cruising guide and the frequently updated *Waterway Guide*. However, as I entered its channel, and I studied the charts closely, my chart plotter said the depth in "the anchorage" was 2.5 feet. Navionics said there were only four-foot depths in "the anchorage." Both readings seemed too shallow, and I turned around.

I had called Janna the previous night to get directions for the Laffite Bay anchorage. I had left my favorite large scale and bulky charts at home after Christmas. These paper charts covered our cruising grounds in Alabama, Mississippi, and Louisiana. I had forgotten the sailing directions to the shallow, privately, and poorly marked channel with a depth of four feet at mean low tide if you hit it perfectly. I wanted to line up the boat just west of red buoy 2 on the Bayou Aloe entrance channel, pointing 165 degrees and holding that course until I am 20-feet from the dock on the northeast side of Laffite Bay. The boat needed to stay west of the markers. That course should put the orange traffic barrel covered in pelican poop on a piling just a few feet from the boat's port as it passes. Further, I wanted to line up so that the bow would be going straight for the northwest tip of Laffite Bay.

In this "channel" the Garmin read depths of 3.9-to-5.0 feet at tidal stage +0.6. Since the Garmin read 0.8 feet lower than actual depths, that means that the low tide depths are as low as $3.9 + 0.8 - 0.6 = 4.1$ feet I dropped the hook at first too close to the narrow entrance as I usually do. I reset the alarm and pulled up the chain and moved further south 100 feet or so. The second time I dropped 55 feet of chain in seven-foot depths at 4:10 PM. I ended up running the air conditioner and generator on two gallons of fuel for about nine hours, to beat the heat. There was only about five knots of wind when the houses in the bay were not blocking it.

Since I planned to go into a marina in Mississippi the next day, I hoisted the RIB onto the foredeck and lashed it down before bed. My anchor alarm of 120 feet went off at 2 AM after a wind shift. Seeing no immediate hazards, I increased it to 150 feet, and it did not go off again. Because the alarm is 30 feet from where the anchor drops, even setting it and dropping it immediately may mean that you will need more than two times scope to prevent the alarm going off in a wind shift.

I pulled up gray mud. On the way out, I lined up with the buoy 2 and barrel marker in a straight line to starboard on a course of 345 degrees. On a higher tidal stage, +1.15, the Garmin sounder read 4.7 feet 20 feet abeam of the orange barrel marker. I sounded the lowest point, 4.5 feet, north of the barrel near the northeastern edge of where the chart's tongue of five-foot depths projects out from the two-foot shallows. After controlling for my sounder's -0.8 calibration error and tidal stage, that means the low point is 4.15 feet, which is just deep enough for Contango's shallow four-foot draft.

The winds were less than five knots and shifty in the morning. I motored and did not put up anything more than the double-reefed main. The wind picked up in the afternoon from the south southwest, and I unfurled the genoa after passing south of Biloxi and sailed close hauled. From Mobile Bay to New Orleans, the tugs and commercial fishing boats outnumber pleasure boats by about 10-to-1 on the wide open GIWW.

I came into the large modern Gulfport Small Craft Harbor. No expense was spared in rebuilding this facility after Hurricane Katrina destroyed most of Gulfport's waterfront in 2005. The marina is better than ever with mobile pumpouts, beautiful showers and laundry, a full service fuel dock, wide slips, and big turning basins. The facility and fuel dock are open 24 hours. Unfortunately, most of the boats have not returned and, unlike the marinas in Biloxi which are nearly full, Gulfport Small Craft Harbor had a vacancy rate over 50 percent.

The well-marked entrance can be tricky because a few small container ships use the docks right next to it. In addition, there is maze of buoys pointing towards Ship Island several miles to the southwest, which can confuse the uninitiated. However, I had docked in Gulfport many times, and I knew where to go.

As I passed by the fuel dock, the attendant yelled good naturedly, "Are you Linus Wilson? I'll meet you down at dock 3." However, a sport fishing boat came up to the fuel dock just then, and he said, "I have to take care of this first." That was typical I thought. I would have no one to catch a stern line.

The slip opened to the south with the dock on the north and the finger slip to the east. It looked like I had lined up really well to back in to the outermost west piling. I wanted to tap it so I could wrap a line. Unfortunately, I came in too fast and bounced off. After that, my bow was blown east by the southwest wind and faced the seawall about six slips away which connected to pier 3. Contango got pinned by the southwest wind to the outer pilings of the slips east of my own. The sport fishing boat in the slip just to the east of Contango's slip luckily did not stick out. With the engine in neutral, I was able to use its bow lines to walk Contango to the easternmost piling of the slip I had been assigned. Once I wrapped a line around the first piling I was able to fend the boat into its slip and ultimately walk it back from its port stern line on the finger slip. Still the damage to the rub rail from Staniel Cay Yacht Club caught on the piling and complicated the process of pushing back the boat into the slip.

Daly had started barking after I had tied everything up and was eating my pizza dinner in the shore-powered air conditioning. The dock attendant had come by. He actually was a sailboat owner. He just bought a Bristol 32-foot sailboat for $7,000. It seemed that he had gotten a great deal, but he was very nervous about sailing, having no experience or training in sailing. I told him, "Sailing is easy. Diesel engine repair is the hard part." He looked at me skeptically.

65. LOUISIANA WATERS

With clean clothes and full diesel tanks, I left at 7:10 AM on May 20, 2015. Conditions were as ideal as possible to leave the slip. A gentle east wind blew the bow west in the desired direction of turn as I took off the doubled starboard bow line on the southwestern piling last. I gave the boat a little push off that piling once I brought in the last line so the boat would not snag on the piling. Then, I went back and put it into gear and motored off.

In nearly six months, we had only faced light sprinkles while underway. However, rain threatened as I passed north of Cat Island. I nearly ran into a wreck, which was not on my Garmin chart plotter. It was on my more recently updated Navionics app. I noticed its masts sticking out of the water. There was a red buoy placed next to it, but I thought that was an Intracoastal Waterway marker until I was close enough to see the mast. The waters south of Pass Christian, Mississippi are littered with these wrecks. The dock attendant last night said he sailed out of Pass Christian. I hope he is careful to avoid the wrecks or his Bristol 32 will add to the hazards.

I had to dodge some of the two dozen shrimpers that were fishing around the invisible but charted Half Moon Island. I and many other boats had to wait for the maintenance truck on the railroad tracks to leave the Rigolets CSX railroad bridge. The bridge tender would not respond to my first twenty hails on three different VHF channels, including many on the preferred bridge channel of VHF 13. The incoming tide gave Contango a boost of one to two knots.

Near calm conditions dominated most of the day, and I only put up the third reef since getting much out of the sails was unlikely. Further, I was readying the boat to be put back into day sailing not cruising mode in New Orleans. However, in the Rigolets, an improving breeze convinced me to raise the main up to the first reef. However, I quickly dropped back down to the third reef as squalls threatened.

As I got closer to Slidell, Louisiana, I observed new McMansion developments were right on the water. None of these expensive homes had stilts. The lessons of Hurricane Katrina seemed to have been forgotten only a decade after the eye of the storm had devastated Slidell.

I had to dodge camouflage-colored brown and green crab pots as I approached the Highway 90 bridge in the Middle Ground of Lake Pontchartrain. Most crabbers are smart enough to not put their pots in the channel. Most are also savvy enough to paint them brightly. They don't want their pots' floats damaged by boat propellers almost as much as boaters don't want to have their propellers wrapped.

Unfortunately, I stopped getting chart depths as I entered Lake Pontchartrain because the Garmin decided it will not give depths for "lakes" in its latest charts. (Lake Pontchartrain is technically a salt water estuary.) The sounders still worked, and Navionics on my phone still gave chart depths.

I did not have to wait for the highway 11 bridge opening and finally no swing bridges or obstacles kept me from plotting a course straight to my destination in the West End of New Orleans, 18 miles away. I passed no boats until I got within a mile of my destination as is usually the case on the wide open waters of the large lake that is as much as 50 miles east to west and 30 miles across north to south. Glassy calm and haze dominated for most of the last leg of the trip, but as I approached the Southern Yacht Club at the entrance to the West End the wind picked up to 12-knots as squalls loomed.

I waved at passing sailboats, who were going out for the Wednesday night races. The crews looked at me like I was crazy. Unlike cruisers who wave at passing boats, day sailors, and racers rarely do. The cruise was almost over.

The amazing thing about the West End of New Orleans is the ratio of sailboats to powerboats. It is at least four sailboats for every one powerboat. In marinas in south Florida and the Bahamas, the ratio of powerboats to sailboats was more like one sailboat for every four powerboats. That is a testament to what a great body of water Lake Pontchartrain is for sailing and the great sailing communities that form along its shores.

I was worried about the wind, but I forgot how calm the inner harbor of Orleans Marina was. Boat houses around the harbor block the wind. I had arranged to haul out at Sintes Boat Works where I had taken possession of Contango nearly two years before. There was an upside-down lawn growing on our boat's hull. It was 5:30 PM after they had closed for the day. So no one was there to help me. The docks around the yard were packed with boats rafted together. I tied up Contango to the end of the dock pulling the starboard bow and stern lines tight so the beam of the boat with fenders hugged the three foot section of the dock.

Linus Wilson

Then, it really rained. It poured like it had never done on the whole cruise. You have to pay for fresh water in the Bahamas in part because those islands have very little rainfall. As a result in the Bahamas, the sun shines almost every day. However, in Louisiana fresh water is everywhere and a lot of it falls from the sky. I was home.

We flew the asymmetrical spinnaker for the first time on a day sail after returning to New Orleans.

About ten days later Janna, Sophie, Daly, and I picked up Contango with a newly cleaned and painted hull. It was a knot faster with its clean bottom. After we got back to our old slip, I carefully shoved the Walker Bay 8 over the lifelines onto our finger slip and washed it out with the hose. A lot of sand from Volleyball Beach from Stocking Island in the Exumas washed into the muddy waters of Lake Pontchartrain.

We went out for a day sail the next day. Janna and I deployed a sail that we had never hoisted before. As I pulled up the dousing sock, it revealed the billowing asymmetrical spinnaker with purple, yellow,

Slow Boat to the Bahamas

and green stripes, the colors of Mardi Gras. Despite winds of only four knots, we accelerated to a speed of three knots. Going to the Bahamas never required a passage longer than Contango's range under power. However, not every trip can be accomplished on a tank of diesel. Perhaps, someday we will need the light air sail to cross a bigger stretch of ocean.

The End

AFTERWORD AND ACKNOWLEDGEMENTS

If you want to sail to foreign islands, this is the story for you. This is the story about the exotic foreign islands more U.S. and Canadian boats visit than any other—the Bahamas. Most other narratives talk about places most sailors rarely visit. In this book, I talk about how my wife, my four year old daughter, my four pound dog, and I kept the boat moving and working when bad stuff happened. Most sailing books won't tell you what cruising is like, because the author has forgotten due to poor records and the passage of time (a.k.a. Alzheimer's). I kept detailed records of our adventures (many), failures (a lot), and successes (one or two).

The most common sailing memoir talks about the author's circumnavigation of the globe in a small sailboat. Joshua Slocum's excellent *Sailing Alone Around the World* is the first and probably the best example of the sub-genre. While dreams of circumnavigations sell many sail boats, a small fraction of boat buyers even embark on a two month coastal cruise. Very few sailors will hug the low latitudes of the trade winds in their own sailboat for over 30,000 nautical miles at a jogging pace around the world. My guess is that Jesus walked on water, because the sailboat was too slow.

The most popular first big foreign cruise to "the islands" for American and Canadian sailors from the Atlantic, Gulf of Mexico, or Great Lakes shore lines is the Bahamas. At less than 50 miles from Miami, the Bahamas are tantalizingly close. Fewer than 400,000 people populate this nation of 700 islands with almost half the population residing on the island of New Providence where the capital of Nassau is located. That means most of this country is an unspoiled sub-tropical wilderness. You can even bring your dog. Just remember to bring your passport.

While one is lucky to find water clear enough to see the bottom at six feet in Florida, the Bahamas' turquoise waters allow snorkelers on the surface to see the bottom at 30 or more feet down. That means you can navigate by water color. If the water color is blue, go through. If it is brown, you'll run aground. If it is yellow, do evasive maneuvers. Yellow means some boat dumped their poop tank.

Slow Boat to the Bahamas

It is a rare tourist that complains, "It was no fun at the beach because it never rained." In the cruising season of December to April, the average monthly rainfall is less than three inches per month. Thus, most days in the Bahamas are sunny when one visits outside of hurricane season. In our six month cruise, it only sprinkled a couple of times when we were underway.

The Caribbean Island of Trinidad I believe is a good proxy for the number of sailors who visit the eastern Caribbean's windward and leeward islands in their own boat. It lies outside the hurricane zone and has a large marine services industry. Thus, it is a popular place to store a boat over the North Atlantic hurricane season for cruisers of the Lesser Antilles. According to Jimmy Cornell, 1367 foreign boats visited Trinidad in 2010. Bermuda is a mid-Atlantic stopover for sailors headed to or from the Eastern Caribbean. It only had 905 foreign yachts visit that year. In contrast, in the same year, the Bahamas had 18,467 foreign yachts visit.[2] Thus, the Bahamas is likely 10 times more visited by foreign boats than the eastern Caribbean. That means a narrative about the Bahamas, which is often skipped by circumnavigators is much more relevant to potential cruising sailors than a memoir of the trade wind passages.

For every one sailor that reaches the Bahamas, there is likely another 10 that have dreamed of it. Since so many of the cruising boats in the Bahamas are retirement-age couples, it is conceivable that many skippers and their spouses dreamed about the Bahamas cruise for over 20 years. Thus, for every one of the 18,000 boats that visit in a given year, 20 that will go are still dreaming about it; and there are 200 sailors who will never go in their own boat, but are also dreaming of that cruise. That puts the potential market for this book at about 4 million sailors contemplating a similar trip. (Would you have believed me if the back of the envelope estimate was 4 billion?) The Bahamas are not only visited by sailors, but also many powerboat enthusiasts. Our trip mirrors the portion of the Great Loop Cruise around the

---

[2] Jimmy Cornell, November 22, 2012, *Cornell's Survey of Global Cruising Yacht Movements*, accessed online at http://cornellsailing.com/de/2012/11/cornells-survey-of-global-cruising-yacht-movements/ and http://cornellsailing.com/de/2012/11/cornells-survey-of-global-cruising-yacht-movements/2/ on June 22, 2015.

eastern United States and great lakes from New Orleans or Mobile to Miami and the Bahamas. For that reason, this coastal narrative is relevant to those interested in either power and sail boat cruises.

A cruising boat is its sailors' home. Cruisers primarily come from the richer developed nations. Running water is universal. Every home has a refrigerator. The mass migration in the United States to the Sun Belt of the southern United States from the east and Midwest was encouraged in part by near universal air conditioning. It is unlikely that you will want to live on a pre-1900 technology boat if you go for a long cruise. If you don't drive a horse and buggy to work and live in a cave, you probably will not want a boat without electricity or running water.

Only running water was widely available when Joshua Slocum wrote his classic narrative. Lin and Larry Pardey wrote the *Seraphin* series of four memoirs about their circumnavigation in an engineless 24 foot cutter with no electricity. Herb McCormick in his biography of the pair *As Long As It Is Fun* points out that without an engine they had no way to charge batteries and thus electrical gear just would not work. In 1963, the largest bank of solar panels in the world was rated at 242 watts.[3] (Our 31 foot sailboat Contango had 260 watts of solar capacity!) Solar charging was just not available for boats built in the 1960s like Seraphin.

Cruising sailors today live in the information age. In the richer developed nations, most people in the workforce are employed in climate-controlled offices in front of a computers. Modern sailors rely on information and communications from the internet for so many things in their shore-based lives that it is too tedious to list. Ignoring up-to-date data about weather, the depth of the water, or one's location via GPS is bad seamanship as well as contrary to the instincts of most modern sailors. Modern sailors can ask other sailors to troubleshoot engine problems or give advice on Facebook. Modern sailors watch YouTube videos on tough installations. A sailor with a broken system may find her dock deserted and her favorite expert may be unavailable, but she can get almost immediate feedback if she crowdsources her problems on social media. Narratives that are over 20 years old will

---

[3] U.S. Department of Energy, "The History of Solar", accessed online on June 20, 2015, at https://www1.eere.energy.gov/solar/pdfs/solar_timeline.pdf.

likely ignore an important aspect of what cruising would be like if you went "out there."

While Lin and Larry Pardey were great ocean voyagers, most sailors do zero ocean crossings in a boat under 60 feet in a lifetime. Instead, most modern sailors hug the coasts. As you will see, coastal voyages even with an engine contain plenty of adventure. The hazards are more numerous in coastal voyage than in ocean passages—groundings, other boats, unpredictable natives, and hard stuff that can break your boat. Most ocean passages are conducted outside of shipping lanes in deep water. Extreme weather and waves are risks in coastal passages as well as ocean voyages. Floating debris is more common along the coasts than in the oceans. Breaking waves are more common near shore. Most coastal sailors would endanger themselves, their crew, and other people on the water if they attempted to forgo an engine. (One of the three times when my engine failed in the six month cruise, the Coast Guard came out because a third party called the Coast Guard, fearing the potential for loss of life.)

Nevertheless, Lin and Larry Pardey rightly point out that complicated plumbing, electronics, and engines mean that modern boats are prone to have multiple systems that break down. That means their crew must be able to get these systems fixed. Early on I learned that, even in a port in the United States, having other people fix, replace, or repair these systems was slow going and ruinously expensive. In the remote islands of the Bahamas, the Caribbean, or the South Pacific it will often be impossible to find skilled tradesmen and parts to fix these systems. Even if you have an unlimited budget, finding and waiting for people to come and fix things will slow your cruise. One woman living on a boat said, "I know a mechanic who is always available, and he never charges me; but I do share a bunk with him."

As a Ph.D. economist and a finance professor at a business school, this necessary self-sufficiency goes against the basic tenets of my discipline. In 1776, Adam Smith, the first economist, in *A Wealth of Nations* showed how society gains from specialization. On our six month cruise, I only paid for a diver, and I only agreed to do so under duress. Besides that, I never paid for a second hour of labor. Janna, my wife, and I fixed all of the many gear and engine failures ourselves. Our toy poodle and four-year-old daughter, Sophie, never helped.

Moreover, all our systems were operational when the boat returned to its home port of New Orleans in May 2015. This narrative deals with our management of those gear failures because that is such an essential part of a successful cruise.

In the popular business book, *Rich Dad Poor Dad* by Robert Kiyosaki, Mr. Kiyosaki argues that the "poor dad" a Ph.D. believes that specialization is the key to success. (I definitely fit the description of "poor dad"!) In our increasingly complex and interconnected economy, specialists with in demand skills such as computer science, engineering, finance, and medicine do command a large premium over the average worker. Nevertheless, the greatest of society's gains go to people who are more jack of all trades who put together large successful organizations. Entrepreneurs are the "rich dads" in Kiyosaki's way of thinking. The very rich with say $100 million or more in wealth are almost exclusively entrepreneurs. They own and run a large businesses. Perhaps we should see cruising sailors more as entrepreneurs than specialists.

Successful entrepreneurs are not self-sufficient. They are connected to the economy around them. They rely on their customers, suppliers, and employees. Likewise, successful cruising sailors can never be and would never want to be truly self-sufficient. They rely on their cruising grounds for food, water, fuel, and trash disposal. They rely on chandleries and part suppliers that source from all over the world. Without deep global economic connections, the pass time of cruising would not be possible.

Slocum writes in 1900 of how he was attacked by the Yahgan Indians of Patagonia who had little connection to the outside world. Lieutenant William Bligh and 18 other loyal men were cast adrift in a 21-foot sailing launch by mutineers on HMS Bounty. Bligh writes in the *Mutiny on the Bounty* how his crew member was killed by natives in Tofua in 1789 when they tried to trade for water and food. That is because there were economic connections that were primitive by today's standards. As a result, the crew of Bligh's 21-foot open boat nearly starved to death and died of thirst trying to reach an outpost over 3,000 nautical miles away where trade relations were better established. Today the island residents in places like the Bahamas will happily trade your dollars for goods and services. That is a good thing.

In addition, I think this memoir is unusual in that it concerns sailing with a child in the womb to age four. Most cruisers are couples without children or couples whose children are grown. If potential younger cruisers are going to listen to Lin and Larry Pardey's advice about "going now," that often means going with kids. Thus, I believe this story is of interest to younger sailors who are wondering how having kids on board changes the equation. My research indicates that only six percent of the boats that went to the 2015 George Town Cruiser's Regatta in the Bahamas had kids on board. Solo sailors were more common than kids' boats at 8 percent of participants.

Unfortunately, most memoires are begun many years after events have taken place. By that time memories are fuzzy. Essential sailing details are forgotten and only the vague details of events can be reconstructed. Most circumnavigations by cruisers, not racers, typically take anywhere from two to twelve years. At the end of the cruise, key details are often very distant. Moreover, a cruise of more than a year can only be written about in cursory terms for space considerations.

I have resisted the memoir cliché of dredging up all the overused quotes of famous people or famous books about sailing or boats in this manuscript. Nevertheless, Mark Twain, America's greatest travel writer if not America's greatest writer of all time, wrote some advice to budding memoirists, which I have never seen quoted. Writing in 1869 in *Innocents Abroad*, Mark Twain told a young fellow passenger, "'Yes, a journal that is incomplete isn't of much use, but a journal properly kept is worth a thousand dollars—when you've got it done.'" Mark Twain kept his journal though out his cruise, but his fellow passengers stopped after a few days. Mark Twain's journal became *Innocents Abroad*. The stories of his fellow passengers are lost to us.

I tried to follow Mr. Twain's advice even if his mentee on that cruise did not. I filled over seven sailing logbooks of 82 pages each with my observations over nearly six months of the sailing between New Orleans to George Town, Exuma in the Bahamas and back. I estimate that those log books contained 120,000 words. On average, I spent an hour or more drafting a daily log entry. (I was tempted to write log entries about keeping a log!) While I did not transcribe the paper logs word for word into this draft, I would have never been able to recall our adventures in detail without them. I'm still waiting for the $1,000.

I want to thank the people who made these adventures possible. My wife Janna Wilson, M.D. is the brains of the organization, a great partner, a great sailor, and easy on the eyes. My daughter Sophie amazes me every day. My father-in-law, Tom Flint, spent hundreds of hours fixing our boats and taught me that it can be fun. My parents Larry and Linda Wilson hosted us on the big trip, collected our mail, and provided emotional support. My Dad, Larry, a high school English teacher, helped proofread the text and crewed on adventures chronicled here and others that he wants to forget. Our toy poodle, Daly, is the family member with the second most days at sea. I will support him if he wants to sit the captains' exam.

Linus Wilson

July 2015

APPENDIX I: CRUISING EXPENSES

Prior to leaving we spent about $21,000 for repairs and upgrades in addition to the $41,500 purchase price of Contango. Some of the bigger expenses were for the initial haul out, sanding, and bottom paint; new seacocks, which were professionally installed; new roller furler; new autopilot; new chart plotter; new air conditioning compressor, ventilation, and Smart Start; and a Honda EU2000i companion generator. We paid for some engine maintenance and the installation of a temperature gauge early on. Besides that, all the labor for the above the waterline work was performed at a rate of $0 per hour by my father-in-law Tom or me. Since this was our second big sailboat, expenses were surely less in part because I was more experienced with boat work. We also had gear from our previous boat that we removed before listing it. For example, we already had an outboard and dinghy before we bought Contango.

I added up the trip expenses since departing in December. We spent about $10,000 in boat repairs, parts, import duties for parts, and upgrades. That includes the new Honda 2.3 HP outboard (our second), the new Highfield Ultralight RIB, and a new Honda EU2000i generator (our second). We decided we wanted a better dinghy, and needed duplicate Hondas if one broke down. With the exception of paying a diver for an hour, I never spent a penny on hiring labor to work on the boat or the motors during the big trip. Our expenses would have been much higher if I had because such labor usually goes for $70 to $120 per hour. Marina and mooring fees were over $5,000 and groceries were a little less than $5,000 as the third biggest expense. Diesel costs probably came to about $1,200 over the cruise. Gas expenses were much less, perhaps $200.

I see the transient slip fees at marinas in the Bahamas as the biggest waste of money. We have to eat no matter what. All the maintenance and upgrades serve to maintain the boat or improve the experience of living on the boat. The outboards, RIB, Walker Bay 8, and even the generators helped us to forgo costly transient slip fees. Only visits used to avoid bad weather that may have led to badly dragging anchors have a decent justification. Otherwise, once you leave the transient slip, the benefits from that expense disappear.

In south Florida and the Bahamas, those fees probably averaged $2.75 per foot in 2015. Thus, over 180 days a 31-foot boat could burn through over $15,000 before tax. That is money wasted in my opinion. Further, every time you dock in a strange marina you run the risk of damaging your boat or worse, a more expensive boat. At the Staniel Cay Yacht Club, which is actually a marina despite its name, we sustained damage that was not repaired by the end of the trip. The damage was sustained while we were tied up to the dock in mild weather. In addition, when you are tied up at a marina, you are more likely to eat out than on a mooring ball or at anchor. All in all, the shadow cost of marina visits is much higher than transient slip fees. I consider most of the money that I spent on marinas slips in the Bahamas as money wasted.

Linus Wilson

Marina slips are a bad deal for cruising, but are a much better deal for one's home port. Long term slip fees are typically a third to one fourth of the transient slip fees. Moreover, you have the advantage of pre-tied lines on the dock and pilings when entering your home slip. Familiarity with the marina makes the docking less stressful and more predictable.

APPENDIX II: PORTS OF CALL

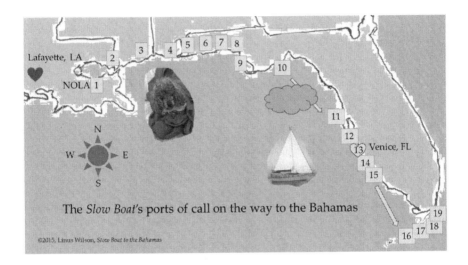

The *Slow Boat's* ports of call on the way to the Bahamas

©2015, Linus Wilson, *Slow Boat to the Bahamas*

Port No.	Departure Date	Start	Nautical Miles
1	December 9, 2014	New Orleans, LA	26
2	December 10, 2014	Double Bayou Lagoon, LA	50
3	December 13, 2014	Biloxi, MS	45
4	December 14, 2014	Dauphin Island, AL	35
5	December 15, 2014	Ingram Bayou, AL	43
6	December 16, 2014	Santa Rosa Sound, FL	35
7	December 17, 2014	Lagrange Bayou, FL	40
8	December 21, 2014	Panama City, FL	36
9	December 22, 2014	Port St. Joe, FL	52
10	December 30, 2015	Carrabelle, FL	153
11	January 2, 2015	Clearwater Beach, FL	53
12	January 3, 2015	Sarasota, FL	14
13	January 4, 2015	Venice Inlet, FL	37
14	January 5, 2015	Useppa Island, FL	54
15	January 5, 2015	Naples, FL	95
16	January 9, 2015	Marathon, FL	31
17	January 10, 2015	Indian Key, FL	25
18	January 13, 2015	Key Largo, FL	26
19	January 14, 2015	Old Rhodes Key, FL	60

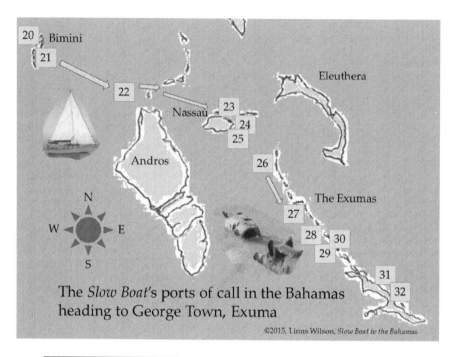

The *Slow Boat*'s ports of call in the Bahamas heading to George Town, Exuma

©2015, Linus Wilson, *Slow Boat to the Bahamas*

Port No.	Departure Date	Start	Nautical Miles
20	January 20, 2015	Bimini, BS	11
21	January 21, 2015	North Cat Cay, BS	56
22	January 22, 2015	N. of Andros Island, BS	61
23	January 29, 2015	Paradise Island, BS	2
24	January 30, 2015	Athol Island, BS	6
25	February 5, 2015	New Providence, BS	31
26	February 8, 2015	Highbourne Cay, BS	33
27	February 11, 2015	Warderick Wells, BS	23
28	February 17, 2015	Staniel Cay, BS	26
29	February 22, 2015	Cave Cay, BS	5
30	February 23, 2015	Little Farmer's Cay, BS	31
31	February 24, 2015	Emerald Cay, Exuma, BS	12
32	February 25, 2015	George Town, Exuma, BS	1

Slow Boat to the Bahamas

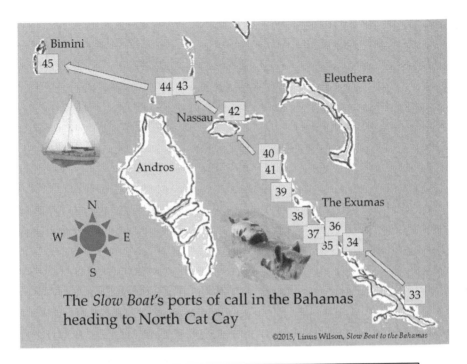

The *Slow Boat*'s ports of call in the Bahamas heading to North Cat Cay

©2015, Linus Wilson, *Slow Boat to the Bahamas*

Port No.	Departure Date	Start	Nautical Miles
33	March 7, 2015	Stocking Island, BS	36
34	March 8, 2015	Rudder Cut Cay, BS	18
35	March 9, 2015	Black Point Settlement, BS	10
36	March 11, 2015	Staniel Cay, BS	2
37	March 11, 2015	Big Major's Spot, BS	18
38	March 12, 2015	Warderick Wells, BS	18
39	March 14, 2015	Shroud Cay, BS	17
40	March 14, 2015	Allen's Cay, BS	4
41	March 15, 2015	Highbourne Cay, BS	37
42	March 18, 2015	Paradise Island, BS	37
43	March 19, 2015	Frazer's Hog Cay, BS	
44	March 19, 2015	Chub Cay, BS	9
45	March 21, 2015	North Cat Cay, BS	

Linus Wilson

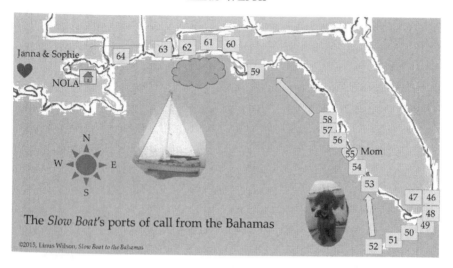

The *Slow Boat*'s ports of call from the Bahamas

©2015, Linus Wilson, *Slow Boat to the Bahamas*

Port No.	Departure Date	Start	Nautical Miles
47	April 12, 2015	Key Biscayne, FL	26
48	April 13, 2015	Pumpkin Key, FL	24
49	April 14, 2015	Rodriguez Key, FL	26
50	April 15, 2015	Long Key, FL	27
51	April 18, 2015	Marathon, FL	48
52	May 6, 2015	Key West, FL	95
53	May 8, 2015	Marco Island, FL	41
54	May 9, 2015	Pine Island, FL	47
55	May 11, 2015	Venice, FL	46
56	May 12, 2015	St. Petersburg, FL	28
57	May 13, 2015	Clearwater Beach, FL	1
58	May 13, 2015	Clearwater, FL	168
59	May 15, 2015	Apalachicola, FL	55
60	May 16, 2015	Panama City Beach, FL	52
61	May 17, 2015	Destin, FL	54
62	May 18, 2015	Perdido Key, FL	44
63	May 19, 2015	Dauphin Island, AL	52
64	May 20, 2015	Gulfport, MS	64

2442

ABOUT THE AUTHOR

Linus and Sophie Wilson on SV Contango in New Providence, Bahamas

Linus Wilson earned a doctorate in financial economics from Oxford University in England. He learned nothing there that prepared him for sailing from New Orleans to the Bahamas in a small sailboat. He is an associate professor of finance at the University of Louisiana, and is the author of over thirty peer-reviewed technical articles. His analyses have been featured by the *New York Times*, *Wall Street Journal*, and the *Financial Times*. He is married with one child, Sophie above. This is his first book. In 2010, he sailed for the first time, and his sailboat landed in the Bahamas in 2015. He started studying comedy in 2015 and plans to tell his first joke in 2020. He also likes to jog because it is a quicker way to travel than sailing.

38414767R00195

Made in the USA
Middletown, DE
18 December 2016